"Dr. Don Little has written a practical b... [barcode obscures text] Muslim backgrounds (BMBs). Little w₁ .... research as well as many years spent actually discipling BMBs. Much of his research and conclusions are drawn from his in-depth interviews with seventy-five seasoned disciplers of BMBs. Little spends significant time exploring the unique problems one experiences in discipling BMBs and offers helpful guidelines in dealing with such situations. Multiple books have been written concerning power encounter, signs, wonders and exorcism, but Little is unique in relating these subjects to discipling BMBs. His insights are valuable. I highly recommend this excellent addition to literature that seeks to show disciplers how to become more effective in their pursuit of discipling believers."

Phil Parshall, SIM, author, *The Cross and the Crescent*

"Seventy-five disciplers were interviewed for this book. These mentors have walked the road of discipleship with more than three thousand Muslim-background Arabs. This is substantial data. Yet contemporary information and strategy are only part of the research. Whole chapters bubble with Paul's and Luke's understandings of discipleship. Other chapters trace discipleship through church history and throughout the Western and Muslim worlds today. Although no fan of the 'insider movement,' the author champions humble adaptation and relevant contextual communication. In particular, he wrestles with issues like the construction of identity, persecution, demonic realities, handling money and roles for expatriates. Workers in the Muslim world will find this book a stimulating dialogue partner and will learn a lot."

Miriam Adeney, associate professor of global and urban ministries, Seattle Pacific University, author, *Kingdom Without Borders*

"As the number of Muslims becoming Christians worldwide is growing, we need to assure that they do not haste into a kind of Western religion, but are wisely discipled as followers of Christ to be mature and credible testimonies within their own Muslim cultures. Never before have the problems and chances been discussed as broadly as in Little's book . . . knowledge that easily might influence the future of the relation of the two largest world religions."

Thomas Schirrmacher, executive chair, Theological Commission, World Evangelical Alliance (Bonn)

"Don Little, from tons of 'hands on' experience and wide interviewing among workers with Muslims in many countries, in *Effective Discipling in Muslim Communities* has provided us with a severely needed, though demanding practical guide that is destined to upgrade the discipling of Muslims toward becoming reproducers and a joy to God's heart."

Greg Livingstone, founder, Frontiers

"This book comes at a critical time. More Muslims are coming to faith in Christ in the beginning of this century than in all the other centuries combined since the rise of Islam; yet there has been significant controversy over how they should be evangelized and discipled. Don Little has been one of the leaders who seeks to foster understanding amongst evangelicals on these practices in a spirit of truth and grace. The present study, which draws broadly on Scripture, history and his experience, makes a significant contribution to the conversation. It thereby is a model for others to join that conversation from their different perspectives but with the same concern for truth and grace."

J. Dudley Woodberry, dean emeritus and senior professor of Islamic studies, School of Intercultural Studies, Fuller Theological Seminary

"A well-written, comprehensive and scholarly work. It is very much worth reading. I will recommend it to my students."

Nabeel T. Jabbour, author of *The Crescent Through the Eyes of the Cross*

Effective
Discipling

—— *in* ——

Muslim
Communities

SCRIPTURE, HISTORY AND
SEASONED PRACTICES

DON LITTLE

IVP Academic

An imprint of InterVarsity Press
Downers Grove, Illinois

InterVarsity Press
P.O. Box 1400, Downers Grove, IL 60515-1426
ivpress.com
email@ivpress.com

InterVarsity Press® is the book-publishing division of InterVarsity Christian Fellowship/USA®, a movement of students and faculty active on campus at hundreds of universities, colleges and schools of nursing in the United States of America, and a member movement of the International Fellowship of Evangelical Students. For information about local and regional activities, visit intervarsity.org.

Scripture quotations, unless otherwise noted, are from The Holy Bible, English Standard Version, copyright © 2001 by Crossway Bibles, a division of Good News Publishers. Used by permission. All rights reserved.

While any stories in this book are true, some names and identifying information may have been changed to protect the privacy of individuals.

Cover design: David Fassett
Interior design: Beth McGill
Images: round table with chairs: © pixalot/iStockphoto
Islamic mosaic: © komargallery/iStockphoto

ISBN 978-0-8308-2470-0 (print)
ISBN 978-0-8308-9852-7 (digital)

Printed in the United States of America ∞

 As a member of the Green Press Initiative, InterVarsity Press is committed to protecting the environment and to the responsible use of natural resources. To learn more, visit greenpressinitiative.org.

Library of Congress Cataloging-in-Publication Data

Little, Don, 1957-
  Effective discipling in Muslim communities : scripture, history, and seasoned practices / Don Little.
    pages cm
  Includes bibliographical references and index.
  ISBN 978-0-8308-2470-0 (pbk. : alk. paper)
  1. Discipling (Christianity) 2. Christian converts from Islam. I. Title.
  BV4520.L49 2015
  253.0917'67--dc23

                                                                    2015014880

P 23 22 21 20 19 18 17 16 15 14 13 12 11 10 9 8 7 6 5 4 3 2 1

Y 34 33 32 31 30 29 28 27 26 25 24 23 22 21 20 19 18 17 16 15

This book is dedicated to you,

my brothers and sisters in Christ from Muslim backgrounds,

who are living in faithfulness to your Lord in the midst

of your families and communities.

Your living faith in Christ and faithfulness to him

inspire me to continue to walk in obedience to God's call

to devote my life in service that Muslims might know the joy of

living in obedience to their rightful Lord, and that those Muslims

who choose to follow Christ will be able to persevere through

to maturity and ever increasing fruitfulness through

deepening communion with Christ.

It is my longing and earnest prayer that

this book on discipleship will encourage you and strengthen

your faith and the faith of your children in Christ for many faith and

biological generations. My yearning is that our God will receive

ever-increasing praise and glory as he graces your lives and

your churches with joy and fruitfulness inside your

Muslim families and communities.

CONTENTS

Acknowledgments   9

Introduction: The Quest for Deeper Understanding of Discipleship
and the Need for Seasoned Discipling Practices   13

PART ONE: BIBLICAL, HISTORICAL AND MISSIOLOGICAL
FOUNDATIONS FOR DISCIPLING BELIEVERS FROM MUSLIM
BACKGROUNDS   23

   1. Genuine Conversion to Christ Forms the Basis
      for Lifelong Discipleship   25

   2. Paul's Understanding of Discipleship
      and Spiritual Growth   39

   3. Discipleship from Christ to the Early Church
      in Luke-Acts   57

   4. Contemporary Western Evangelical Approaches
      to Discipleship   73

   5. Historical Understandings of Spiritual Formation
      in the Church   95

   6. Contextualization and Discipleship Within
      Muslim Communities   111

   7. The Goals, Processes, Roles and Stages in
      Discipling BMBs   127

   8. The Living Pyramid of Relational Communal
      Discipling of BMBs   151

PART TWO: SEASONED PRACTICES IN DISCIPLING
BELIEVERS FROM MUSLIM BACKGROUNDS   167

   9. The Biggest Obstacles to Effective BMB Discipleship   169

  10. Negotiating a New Identity in Christ Within
      Muslim Communities   189

11. Discipling BMBs in and Through Persecution   209

12. Discipling in the Face of Demonic
    Oppression and Attack   225

13. Understanding and Handling Money Well
    in Discipling BMBs   245

14. Discipling Believing Families in Muslim Communities   263

15. Suitable Roles for Expatriate Disciplers   281

Conclusion: Helping Believers and Churches Thrive in
Muslim Communities   301

Appendix A: The Demographics and Design of the Research
Conducted in the Arab World in 2007 on BMB Discipleship   313

Appendix B: Questions Asked During the Interviews   319

Appendix C: Supplementary Tables Giving Further Information   321

Appendix D: Navigating Between Two Identities   325

Appendix E: What About Witnessing Among the Sioux?   327

Works Cited   329

Author Index   344

Subject Index   345

Scripture Index   348

ACKNOWLEDGMENTS

FOR THEIR SIGNIFICANT CONTRIBUTION to this study of discipleship of believers from Muslim backgrounds (BMBs), I want to thank my family, our supporters, our mission family, those with whom I have shared this material over the past seven years in seminars around the world, the research project mentors and those who took the time to read and comment on the book manuscript.

My family have been very supportive of me through the entire process. My three children encouraged and cheered on their student-dad and sacrificed much time with him. Jeanie allowed our bedroom to double as my study for six years. A special word of thanks to my sister-in-law, Miriam Little, who assisted me by creating a custom-designed database into which I entered the interview data, which enabled me to do careful analysis of the hours of notes from the interviews.

God has given us an amazingly faithful and generous group of supporting churches, families and individuals who continue to support and pray for us as I have devoted large chunks of time to study, research and more recently to the writing of this book. Without their ongoing faithful support I would not have had the time or resources to devote to this project.

My entire mission family has also stood behind me in this research, and again in the book writing phase. The board of our mission in Canada supported me to begin work on the doctoral program in 2001, while I was serving as National Director. David Lundy, our International Director at the time, granted me an eight-month sabbatical in 2007 before I began my current role as Islamic missiologist, so that I could conduct my field research and write intensively. My trips to conduct interviews in the Arab world were greatly facilitated through the willing help of colleagues across the mission.

A special word of thanks to everyone whom I interviewed in 2007, serving in more than a dozen countries. Thank you for sharing freely and often opening your heart to me as I probed and learned from your experience as disciplers. I trust that you will find this book of value.

Since our mission's merger with a larger mission in 2010, every leader in the new mission family familiar with this book writing project has encouraged me to press on and complete it in order to server the broader community of those loving Muslims globally. During several two to three-month periods over the past few years, my mission supervisors have granted me freedom to write for several days a week.

Since 2008 I have been sharing various parts of the outcomes of my study with workers in more than ten countries in the Muslim world. Many of those who have sat through hours of seminars drawn from this project have encouraged me to get it into written form so as to serve more of those serving among Muslims. Their encouragement is a big part of the reason why I have persevered with the task of rewriting and considerably expanding my original thesis to create this book. Much of the content of the book took shape as I engaged with the feedback and questions that were asked as I shared this material. You significantly shaped this book. Special mention must be made of L. D. Waterman, who urged me to write the book and read the entire manuscript and offered insightful and invaluable critiques throughout.

Further, I give a special word of thanks to my two research project mentors, the late Abe Wiebe and Mike Kuhn, and to my Gordon-Conwell Theological Seminary thesis supervisor, Timothy Tennent, who all provided me with very helpful input and critique. Thanks also to the many friends and colleagues in other missions who have helped hone the research and analysis. Four others have also gone through the entire manuscript and offered invaluable critique that has improved the book immensely, though the many shortcomings that remain are fully my own responsibility.

Thanks to all who made this project possible, and thanks above all to God, whose grace never ceases to amaze.

Introduction

THE QUEST FOR DEEPER UNDERSTANDING OF DISCIPLESHIP AND THE NEED FOR SEASONED DISCIPLING PRACTICES

Beloved, I pray that all may go well with you and that you may be in good health, as it goes well with your soul. For I rejoiced greatly when the brothers came and testified to your truth, as indeed you are walking in the truth. I have no greater joy than to hear that my children are walking in the truth.

3 JOHN 1:2-4[1]

Some Christian workers would say that if the task of bringing people to an initial commitment is hard, the process of enabling them to grow and develop as believers who are integrated into some kind of Christian fellowship is often even harder. . . . Could it be . . . [that] there needs to be a more rigorous and honest study of the reasons why many do not continue in their Christian faith? Many of the reasons are no doubt obvious. . . . But if we can admit that it may sometimes be our failings that make them go back, we might have to rethink much of our practice and our proclamation.

DAVID SMITH,
FROM THE STRAIGHT PATH TO THE NARROW WAY

---

[1]All English quotations of the Scriptures are taken from *The Holy Bible, English Standard Version* (2001) unless otherwise indicated in context.

WHEN I ARRIVED IN NORTH AFRICA, twenty-three-year-old Mustafa[2] was one of the more enthusiastic new believers among the young men being discipled by my colleagues. Mustafa and I became friends and in my second year he worked with me to start a small cell church in a nearby city. He helped me with my Arabic and served as a cultural informant while I taught him how to lead Bible studies and care for Muslim seekers. At the end of that year, when I left on a study leave, Mustafa took charge of the tiny cell group of four new believers. It was satisfying to be able to work with Mustafa, and I left encouraged seeing that helping a young believer to disciple other new believers worked.

But when I reunited with Mustafa on our return to his city following a two-year absence, I discovered that he had changed. He was struggling with his faith because of a number of bad experiences with both expatriate workers and local believers. Three years later he had left town to take a good job, left his new faith, returned to attending prayers in the mosque, married a Muslim girl and cut off all ties with the house church in which he had once been an enthusiastic member. About seven years after first coming to faith in Christ, he was settled back into his Muslim community and into life as a Muslim after his years living as a believer in Christ.[3]

This account of failed discipling of Mustafa illustrates that we who are laboring to plant churches in the Muslim world must learn to dis-

<hr>

[2]All personal names of BMBs used throughout the book are pseudonyms used to protect these people from exposure and possible harm. Furthermore, I do my best to disguise their location. However, every person mentioned in the text is a real person, and I have done my best to represent the person and his or her story as accurately as possible.

[3]One positive update on this story is that Mustafa's younger brother came to faith a few years after Mustafa and is today one of the most gifted young leaders in the church in his country. Moreover, it seems that his perseverance in staying connected with his no-longer-believing older brother is showing fruit in that Mustafa's Muslim wife is asking increasingly serious and probing questions of her sister-in-law about her faith.

ciple more effectively. Far too many of those who are coming to faith in Christ out of Islam today will fall away from Christ unless workers and believers seeking to disciple them learn to disciple well. My years spent discipling believers in North Africa was an intensely stretching, profoundly satisfying and sometimes joyful challenge. The successes in discipling, as well as the many failures, left me with a deep desire to thoroughly and experientially investigate discipleship in Muslim contexts in order to help us all to disciple more effectively. In the years since my departure from North Africa, as I have talked with people who are discipling believers from Muslim backgrounds (BMBs)[4] around the Muslim world, many have repeatedly affirmed a need for research of BMB discipling. This book shares the understanding gained from biblical, theological, missiological and historical study of discipling, both among Christians generally and more specifically among Christians who were formerly Muslims. This book also shares a great deal of seasoned wisdom gained from interviews with experienced disciplers ministering across the Arab world.[5] It is my hope that the biblical, theological and practical insights and seasoned practices shared in these pages will help us all be more consistently fruitful in discipling believers from Muslim backgrounds in communities throughout the Muslim world.

EFFECTIVE DISCIPLING IS VITAL IN HELPING BELIEVERS IN MUSLIM COMMUNITIES THRIVE

God is at work in the Muslim world in unprecedented ways. He is in-

---

[4]The phrase "believer from a Muslim background," reduced to the acronym BMB, puts the emphasis on the current identity of believers, whereas the more commonly used MBB (Muslim background believer) emphasizes their former identity as Muslims. Many disciples of Christ, who were formerly Muslims, tell me that they prefer the term BMB because it subtly emphasizes their new identity as believers. This book uses the acronym BMB whenever appropriate. Using the acronym BMB is in no way intended as a label that diminishes the new identity of these brothers and sisters in Christ. It is used only to avoid distracting and unhelpful wordiness. When quoting authors who use the more commonly used acronym MBB, their usage is retained.

[5]This study was originally undertaken as part of doctoral studies in missions and cross-cultural communication at Gordon-Conwell Theological Seminary (Little 2009). This book is grounded in that research but represents a considerable expansion in scope over the work undertaken for the thesis.

creasingly calling men and women into loving witness among Muslims, and he is bringing growing numbers of Muslims to faith in Christ, even in the Arab world, which many consider to be the heartland of Islam. The more one becomes familiar with the remarkable story of God's work in his church through the centuries, the more one is encouraged by the tremendous growth of the church in the Global South in the last few decades. We are indeed privileged to live and serve in a generation that is seeing unprecedented growth of the church in many parts of the world—more than 60 percent of the world's Christians are now outside of the Western world. God is doing unprecedented and astonishing new things in our generation.

In 1977, during an overland trip to India, I had the privilege of driving through the Muslim-majority nations of Bosnia, Turkey, Iran, Afghanistan and Pakistan. This journey, which was undertaken in response to God's call to the Muslim world, took place when the evangelical world was once again awakening to the challenge and the opportunity of the Muslim world. Great heroes of ministry to Muslims in earlier generations such as Raymond Lull, Henry Martyn, Lilias Trotter and that great apostle to Islam, Samuel Zwemer (Wilson 1952), had been largely forgotten, as had the great nineteenth-century and early-twentieth-century legacies of extensive Protestant mission work in Asia, the Middle East (Vander Werff 1977), Africa and North Africa (Marsh 1980; Steele 1981).

At the time of my journey to India there were only a few hundred believers in Turkey and Iran, only a handful of believers and no known house churches in Afghanistan and very little outreach to the Muslim majority in Pakistan. The next year, in the fall of 1978, the North American Conference on Muslim Evangelization was held at Glen Eyrie, Colorado Springs (see McCurry 1979 for the papers from the conference). The focus of that conference was on imagining new ways of doing ministry, in particular of forming Muslim-friendly indigenous churches of Muslim converts, so that there would finally be breakthroughs in ministry to Muslims. In God's sovereign mercy, that conference marked the beginning of a resurgence of interest in the Muslim world among increasing numbers of evangelical churches in North America and the English-speaking world.[6]

Nearly thirty years later, in March 2007, a conference with about five hundred participants was held in Asia, bringing together representatives from dozens of mission agencies working among Muslims. The aims of the conference included getting a clearer picture of the progress in ministry to Muslims and assessing which practices in evangelism, discipleship and church planting were consistently bearing the most fruit. Those of us gathered for that week represented thousands of workers living among and loving Muslims in people groups across the Muslim world. The book that came out of the conference, *From Seed to Fruit: Global Trends, Fruitful Practices and Emerging Issues Among Muslims* (Woodberry 2008), comments on the encouraging fact that in the years since the conference in Glen Eyrie in 1978, God has blessed the growing number of ministries among Muslims. Churches are being planted, and increasingly, especially since the beginning of the third millennium in A.D. 2000, we can even speak of growing numbers of movements to Christ among Muslims.[7]

Significant progress is being made among Muslims; however, in other ways it seems we have barely scratched the surface. In 2006 David Greenlee published a seminal collection of research into how and why Muslims are coming to faith in so many Muslim contexts around the world entitled *From the Straight Path to the Narrow Way* (Greenlee et al. 2006). This movement forward in ministry to Muslims is heartening. At the same time, most of those working with new believers coming out of Islam soon discover how difficult it is for these

---

[6]In reading J. Christy Wilson's 1952 biography of Samuel Zwemer recently, it became clear that the needs of the Muslim world were very much a concern of large parts of the evangelical and Protestant world until well after the first world war. In fact, it may well be that there was more mission work among Muslims being undertaken by Christians in the West before the second world war than there is now, on at least a per capita basis. That great apostle to Islam, Samuel Zwemer, succeeded in an unprecedented way in raising awareness and action on behalf of Muslims as he traveled around the globe, wrote dozens of books and launched what quickly became, and remains to this day, the pre-eminent academic journal of the study of Islam: *The Muslim World*.

[7]Garrison's *A Wind in the House of Islam* (2014) describes characteristics of dozens of movements to Christ among Muslims that are occurring today as the wind of the Spirit blows in every region of the Muslim world.

believers to stay in their new faith and to grow into maturity as Christians. One senior colleague with more than twenty-five years of experience discipling converts out of Islam in North Africa told me that
more than three-quarters of the believers eventually either faded out
of Christian fellowship or returned to Islam. In his discussion of church
planting movements among Muslims instigated through the Camel
Method, Kevin Greeson makes this disturbing, and confirming, observation: "Throughout the history of missionary outreach to Muslims,
reconversion has been a consistent problem, with as many as 90 percent
returning to Islam" (Greeson 2007, 168). In the conclusion of *From the
Straight Path to the Narrow Way*, David Smith stresses the need for
more work on discipleship: "Some Christian workers would say that if
the task of bringing people to an initial commitment is hard, the
process of enabling them to grow and develop as believers who are
integrated into some kind of Christian fellowship is often even harder"
(Smith 2006, 290). Smith then goes on to explain the challenge we face
in discipling in Islamic contexts.

> The research carried out by Patrick Sookhdeo of the Barnabas Trust some
> years ago suggested that the proportion of new believers who return to
> Islam is remarkably high. Could it be, therefore, that alongside the analysis
> of the testimonies of those who have come to faith there needs to be a
> more rigorous and honest study of the reasons why many do not continue
> in their Christian faith? Many of the reasons are no doubt obvious. . . . But
> if we can admit that it may sometimes be *our* failings that make them go
> back, we might have to rethink much of our practice and our procla-
> mation. (290-91)

When one surveys the rapidly increasing number of books on ministry to Muslims, one uncovers surprisingly little written on the subject
of discipling believers from Muslim backgrounds, even though it is
widely recognized that effective discipleship is a crucial element in the
establishment of BMB churches. Muslim society far too often makes it
socially and spiritually repressive for those who are called to be disciples
of Christ in their communities. Discipleship for BMBs is an especially

challenging task, especially when they continue to live in the communities of their birth.[8]

THE VALUE OF RESEARCH INTO BMB DISCIPLESHIP

Having worked in international transdenominational mission communities for more than thirty years, I have observed that the way we approach discipling Muslims who come to faith in Christ often naturally reflects the way we ourselves were discipled or the way in which our local church or ministry group in our home country discipled. Many workers among Muslims come to the task of discipling BMBs with little training and with almost no previous experience as disciplers. Moreover, those who have some previous experience discipling often have not discipled cross-culturally, nor have they thought much about what discipleship is and how it is best carried out in Muslim contexts. We tend to disciple by instinct. Fortunately, the Holy Spirit is often at work shaping our instincts so that there can be lasting fruit. Though church planters in certain denominational mission agencies tend to have clearer ideas about how their church teaches them to disciple, I have not observed that they are any more effective than those of us working in interdenominational groups. The key factor seemed to be whether or not we learn from our failures and work together to do a better job than we did in the beginning.

At the same time, I believe that all of us, whether believers from Muslim backgrounds or disciplers of believers from Muslim backgrounds, can benefit from prayerful reflection and research into the nature of spiritual growth and discipleship that reflects on the special challenges and opportunities of Muslim contexts. If BMBs living in such contexts are to stand strong and reach out in love to their families and

---

[8]When I mention the huge number of believers from Muslim backgrounds who fail to continue in their faith, sometimes people suggest that the dropout rate for new believers in the West is similarly high. If this is indeed true, then such a tragic scenario should cause much heart searching and reflection on the part of Christians and church leaders in the West, but I have no way of knowing whether dropout rates are as high in the West as they are in the Muslim world. The all too frequent failure of discipleship in the Muslim world is the thing that drove me to study BMB discipleship. The possibility of similar failure occurring elsewhere underlines the pressing need to understand the reasons for this failure everywhere and seek to address them. It also suggests that the present study may be of value in helping tackle convert attrition elsewhere.

communities, then clear, biblically grounded, historically informed and culturally appropriate approaches to discipleship must be a central feature of ongoing church and ministry life.

WHERE DISCIPLESHIP FITS IN A BELIEVER'S JOURNEY TO FAITH IN CHRIST

Some argue, with considerable plausibility, that discipleship begins long before the point of conversion. In many situations, the actual decision to follow Christ comes after Muslims spend considerable time experiencing Christian community and fellowship, involvement in church services or Bible studies and learning much about the content of the faith. Furthermore, as will be discussed below, in collective cultures people often need to join a community in order to explore what commitment to Christ means, and often their decision to follow Christ occurs only after they have been part of the community and discipled into the meaning of Christian commitment. Though I wholeheartedly agree that this is often the way things work, and I use preconversion welcome into community as a primary strategy in evangelism with Muslims, I still am not comfortable with calling this vital initiation process discipleship. There is clearly an important spiritual change that takes place at the point of conversion, and even when the precise point of conversion may not be ·clearly known to the convert or to the evangelist, discipling people toward fullness in Christ really takes off once they have encountered Christ and chosen to follow him.

One incident in my ministry illustrates the distinction between being a seeker nurtured toward conversion and being discipled following conversion. In my first church planting effort in North Africa, a new believer invited his not-yet-believing friend to join our weekly study and worship meetings. This young man attended for several weeks and though he said almost nothing the whole time, he was listening and observing. Then one evening he declared to the group that, because of the experience of love and acceptance and genuine seeking after truth that he encountered in our little group, he had decided that he wanted to follow Christ. The next week, when we began to study the Gospel of John, he eagerly embraced the divinity of Christ presented in John because he had decided to follow Christ the week before. That point of decision to follow Christ was a crucial turning point for him. From then on, this brother was being discipled; before that point of decision, he was being nurtured and welcomed as a seeker.

Some Scripture passages that point to the tremendous spiritual change that takes place at the point of conversion include John 1:12-13, John 3:3-8, 1 Corinthians 2:14-16, Ephesians 2:1-10, Colossians 1:21-23, 1 Thessalonians 1:9-10 and 1 Peter 1:3-9. In the Gospels, as will be explored in detail in chapter three, the call to follow Christ is very clear—either you follow him or you do not. Discipleship is following him, and I do not think it is accurate or helpful to say that we help people in their discipleship to Jesus until they have chosen to accept Jesus' call to become his disciples. Though this question *may* be viewed as mostly a matter of semantics, it is important to make clear that "discipling," as the term is used in this book, refers primarily to the ministry of helping those who have left behind the straight path taught by Muhammad and have made, through conversion, a conscious choice to embark on a path of lifelong discipleship to Christ. The need for solid conversion setting the stage for effective discipleship is so important that I devote the first chapter of the book to understanding conversion in the New Testament and in practice in Muslim communities.

Biblical, Historical and Missiological Foundations for Discipling Believers from Muslim Backgrounds

Jesus stressed the importance of building on a solid foundation. When one first begins to help disciple BMBs, the help one seeks is often practical—advice on how to handle the often bewildering situations encountered. You may have picked up this book seeking the kind of practical advice on what to do in various situations that is given in part two. However, experience suggests that the longer one disciples and continues to encounter heartbreaking failure, one begins to reflect more deeply in order to better understand what is happening and what ought to be happening. In part one, then, before moving to the practical challenges covered in part two, we attempt to chart vital scriptural and historical bearings through a study of discipleship in the New Testament, followed by an exploration of how discipleship has been understood and worked out in several major historical and contemporary Christian traditions. This is done to help us have a starting point from which to better deal with what is happening in the diverse discipling contexts we encounter around the Muslim world. The theoretical foundation laid in chapters one through seven concludes in chapter eight with the introduction of a discipleship model that draws together many of the central elements in spiritual transformation explored in the first seven chapters.

1

Genuine Conversion to Christ Forms the Basis for Lifelong Discipleship

*And Peter said to them, "Repent and be baptized every one of you
in the name of Jesus Christ for the forgiveness of your sins,
and you will receive the gift of the Holy Spirit."*

Acts 2:38

*Baptism is the Christ-ordained means by which the faith
of the church is embodied in the life of its members.*

Gordon T. Smith,
Transforming Conversion

Conversion Is the Beginning of a Life of Discipleship

With more than seven years of experience ministering in North Africa and with solid ability in the local Arabic dialect, Steven considered himself a gifted evangelist, but he was increasingly frustrated that he was having trouble planting a church. Steven told me that he had led dozens of young men and some young women to faith but had seen nearly all of them fall away soon after their conversion (usually within a few weeks or months and most within less than a year). Now he and some co-workers were meeting with a group of about a dozen young believers on a weekly basis, and he was continuing his regular evangelism in the streets and cafés. He was hopeful that this group of believers would solidify and last as a house church before his planned departure from the country eight months later. His confidence in the ability of North African believers to remain in the faith was quite low. He was almost desperate for some new approach to discipling that would help him turn this persistently high discipling failure rate around.

Cheri's experience of evangelism and discipling in North Africa was quite different from Steven's. One of the questions I asked those I interviewed was something like: "How many of those who you have been discipling have fallen away?" Cheri's thoughtfully slow response surprised me: "None that I can think of." Over the previous decade God had used her to help lead perhaps fifteen to twenty women to faith in Christ, and she could not think of a single one who was not continuing as a faithful disciple of Christ. As I probed and sought to understand reasons for this unusual faithfulness following conversion, I discovered that it was closely linked to the way she approached evangelism. As she met and befriended women and shared the gospel with them, she would take months, sometimes years, in regular discussion and Bible study with them before they finally chose to follow Christ. She was insistent that they understood the gospel fully, and that they knew and understood what it would mean to be a disciple of Christ following their conversion *before* she invited them to become a disciple of Christ. At times, some of the women would express a desire to follow Christ after only several weeks of hearing about Jesus, but Cheri would not lead them in prayers of repentance and faith in Christ until she was fully assured that they knew, understood and were willing to embrace all that conversion to Christ might entail for them, including possibly severe persecution, being divorced by their husbands, losing their jobs, and so on. As a direct result of her approach to evangelism, all of the women whom she had the privilege of discipling became solid believers who were contributing members of local house churches and whose faith survived Cheri's recent expulsion from North Africa.

These contrasting experiences of fruitfulness in discipling underline how important it is that we understand the nature and meaning of conversion. Though I did not get a full account of Steven's approach to evangelism, he did tell me that sometimes he was able to lead a Muslim to faith in Christ during their first conversation. He had developed an evangelistic technique in which he was able to divert typical Muslim objections and turn the conversation to the person's need to confess his or her sins and embrace Christ right away. He was convinced that once people had believed in Christ, the Holy Spirit would enter in and help the new believers to understand more and more of the meaning of their new faith *after* they had confessed faith in Christ. His goal was to bring them to the point of praying to receive Christ for salvation as quickly as he could.

Though Steven's case is, I suspect, rather extreme, the contrast between Steven's and Cheri's approaches to evangelism underlines how important it is that we have a clear and biblical understanding of the nature of conversion. How much do people need to understand before they can meaningfully put their trust in Christ? How much does our own conversion experience color the way we expect Muslims to come to faith in Christ? What influence does the way someone comes to faith in Christ have on his or her subsequent life of discipleship? How much does an accurate understanding of the gospel and salvation prior to believing influence the discipleship experience following conversion? As the cases of Steven and Cheri illustrate, the extent of preconversion understanding of the gospel is very closely connected to the postconversion success in discipling and the likelihood of BMBs being able to persevere long term and thrive as disciples of Christ integrated into local bodies of believers.

This book is not about conversion, and space does not permit a long exploration of the biblical and theological meaning and experience of conversion, nor do we have time for a discussion of what conversion means experientially for Muslims who come to Christ.[1] However, it is

---

[1]For those who wish to pursue such a line of inquiry, an excellent place to start in exploring the way that Muslims come to faith is Reinhold Strähler's *Coming to Faith in Christ: Understanding Conversion* (2010). In this short book Strähler publishes the results of research into Muslim conversions in several African countries and explores the diverse influences at work leading Muslims to faith in Christ.

important to take time now, at the outset of the book, to think about the nature of conversion and the influence that one's conversion experience has on one's subsequent life as a believer. A good place to begin is to stress that conversion ought to be viewed as the beginning of a life of discipleship, and if a conversion experience has not launched a new believer into such ongoing discipleship to Jesus, then it is appropriate to ask if the conversion itself was genuine. In his compelling book on conversion, Gordon Smith stresses the close connection between conversion and the rest of one's life as a Christian: "Conversion is the genesis, the point of departure for the rest of our Christian life. . . . The whole of our Christian experience is the working out of the full meaning and implication of our conversion" (Smith 2010, 1). Going a step further, Dallas Willard argues that there is a direct correlation between the gospel one believes and the likelihood of a convert becoming a lifelong disciple of Christ following conversion to that gospel:

> Let us begin by noting that if we do not preach *the gospel of the kingdom of God* as Jesus did but preach some other gospel . . . we cannot truly progress in the formation of character into Christlikeness. That is because *the message preached will have no essential connection with constant spiritual growth*. We need to announce (preach), teach, and manifest the good news that Jesus Himself announced. That good news is of *the availability of life now in the kingdom of God by placing our confidence in Jesus as the Lord of all* (see Matthew 4:17, 23; 9:35; Mark 1:15; Luke 4:43; Romans 10:9-10; 14:17). (Willard 2010, 31, italics in the original)

Clearly, both the nature of the gospel message that people, including Muslims, believe, and the way that people come to believe in the message and entrust themselves to Christ's life, will have significant influence on what the believers become and do following conversion.

So, what is conversion, and are there any aspects of conversion that are vital, or even essential? Are there forms of conversion that by their very nature, as Willard suggests, will lead to stunted growth and failed discipleship? Are there forms of conversion that will, conversely, consistently yield a life of strong discipleship and growth toward maturity in

Christ? Might it not be appropriate to consider when the conversion experience of a BMB establishes a genuine and solid enough foundation on which to build lifelong discipleship? Taking time to reflect on the nature of conversion in the New Testament will provide some guidance in finding answers to these vital questions about the relationship of conversion to discipleship.

REPENTANCE, BAPTISM AND CONVERSION IN THE NEW TESTAMENT

As I have been sharing the outcomes of my research into discipling BMBs with workers around the world, I have often been asked about the role that baptism plays in discipling. Though I have long believed that baptism is an important part of obedience to Christ, I did not, unfortunately, include the topic of baptism in the interview research into discipling that undergirds this book. However, I have since come to understand a little more of the significance of baptism in the New Testament experience and teaching on conversion. In seeking to get a deeper understanding of conversion, one is hard pressed to do better than to turn to Gordon Smith's *Transforming Conversion* (2010), cited above. Much of what follows in this section relies heavily on Smith's study of the nature of conversion and the role that repentance and baptism play in authentic Christian conversion. Though Smith is not dealing with Muslim contexts in his book, he writes out of a wide experience of global Christianity and is very much aware of the challenges inherent in applying his insights to Muslim contexts.

The Philippian jailor asked Paul and Silas the classic question "What must I do to be saved?" (Acts 16:30). Many and varied answers to that question have been debated among evangelists, preachers, missionaries and theologians ever since. Peter helpfully answered the question he was asked on the day of Pentecost, "What shall we do?" by saying, "Repent and be baptized every one of you in the name of Jesus Christ for the forgiveness of your sins, and you will receive the gift of the Holy Spirit" (Acts 2:38). Taking time to reflect on Peter's answer here provides an excellent place to begin to understand the nature of Christian conversion in the Bible. This is the first appearance of this question in the New Testament subsequent to the death and resurrection of Christ, and it is quite plausible to argue that Luke is here setting out the theologically normative answer to the question for the church to whom he is writing a generation after Christ's resurrection. Throughout Acts there are numerous conversion narratives that describe what happens in conversion, but it is here in Acts 2:38 that an explanation is given as to what needs to happen for someone to be saved. Smith points out that this pivotal text has two distinct dimensions of human response: a call to repentance, which is an interior and individual response; and the call to be baptized, which is an external and social or corporate response to the preaching of the gospel. Smith explores how this pivotal text shapes our understanding of conversion in the New Testament: "The two-fold movement of repentance and baptism incorporates a dynamic interplay between the individual and the community. . . . Though there is more to conversion than repentance and baptism, this text profiles these two actions—or perhaps better put, this dual action—as pivotal to the conversion experience" (Smith 2010, 114).

Smith suggests that the twofold response to the gospel, repentance and baptism, can well be viewed as "the hub or locus of a Christian conversion" (119). He devotes a full chapter to each element. He first explains what repentance means (chap. 7) and then explores why it is essential that baptism accompany repentance (chap. 8), and that both be seen as core elements of authentic Christian conversion. It is helpful to reiterate a few of his points to clarify the relationship that conversion has to the life of discipleship within the church of Christ, as seen in the New Testament and as applied to Muslim contexts.

Genuine repentance is a foundational part of conversion. Smith begins his chapter on repentance with this strong statement: "Repentance is so much at the heart of the matter that in many respects it is virtually synonymous with conversion. One could almost say that to convert is to repent. . . . Repentance is the pivot on which the experience of conversion rests. . . . *The heart and soul of conversion is repentance*" (Smith 2010, 127, emphasis added). According to Smith, repentance is "the particular and biblical response to God's revelation to the heart and mind" (138). In the Old Testament, "repentance is fundamentally covenantal, *relational*; it is a turning to God" (130). The New Testament begins with John's calling the people of God to repentance, and Jesus himself also preaches repentance (Mt 4:17; Mk 1:15; Lk 5:32; 13:3; 15:7). Jesus comes calling Israel to repent in a way that fits with the entire Old Testament prophetic tradition (130-31). Two things are particularly pertinent in the biblical witness about repentance: confession and repentance are integral to the normal patterns of community life and worship in God's people and "the content of this repentance is a personal and corporate alignment with the reign of God in the world, through Christ" (132).[2]

To be a disciple is to be baptized. In the New Testament, baptism is clearly integral to the entire conversion experience and is closely tied to repentance. Baptism is the ordained means whereby we are united with Christ, and it is a conscious and deliberate identification with the death of Christ on the cross whereby following our resurrection with Christ in baptism, we are now identified with Christ and his reign as members of the kingdom of God. It is valuable to spell out what Smith believes to be the three primary dimensions of the meaning of baptism in the New Testament (141-48).

First, in baptism a believer appropriates the forgiveness of sins, so that as forgiven sinners we can now live in the light, renouncing our sins and walking in the light. Second, Christ's eschatological promise that we would be filled with the Holy Spirit is initially fulfilled in our water baptism. In baptism one is initiated into the life of the Spirit, without whom it would be impossible to live the new life in Christ. Water baptism is the believer's action, whereas Spirit baptism is Christ's action as we undergo water baptism.[3] Third, in our baptism we are incorporated into

---

[2]In chapter 10 there is a thorough discussion of the sensitive issues surrounding to whom, when and how new believers may confess their faith in Christ to others and thus publically identify with Christ. What is being stressed here is confession of sin toward God and, following conversion and entry into a local body of Christ, ongoing confession of one's sins both to God and to those whom we have wronged.

[3]To be clear, I do not believe that this baptism of the Spirit that occurs (ideally) along with water

the Christian community. There are no private baptisms, because baptism is mediated by the church and is the conscious and deliberate act by which the new believer is incorporated into the church. Contra the teaching of the Roman Catholic church, it is not the church that brings us into the salvation of Christ, but Christ who gives meaning to our membership in the church.

Thus, I would affirm that, based on a careful reading of the New Testament, baptism ought to be central to our conversion experience and ought to be the critical benchmark of our lives. Our baptism calls us back to our identity in Christ as members of a forgiven people who are together called to lives of righteousness, of ongoing repentance and continually renewed experience of forgiveness. As we think further about the nature of discipling in Muslim contexts in the remainder of this book, let us remember that in the New Testament a solid beginning in a believer's life of discipleship to Christ is inseparably linked to repentance and baptism.

CONVERSION AND BAPTISM IN MUSLIM CONTEXTS

The conversion experience of BMBs is as varied as the individuals involved. Among the men whom I helped disciple, one devout and faithful Muslim man, who had been prepared to follow Christ through five years of dreams and visions of Jesus, came to faith in Christ immediately after having understood the call of Christ in the gospel. Another believed following a long, slow search and an extended period in a one-on-one Bible study. Others came to faith through the influence of their believing friends.

Complexities and variations in Muslim conversions. Recent years have seen the publication of a number of excellent articles and books examining the phenomenon of Muslims turning to Christ.[4] Muslims are

---

baptism implies that that there is no longer any need for repeated and ongoing fillings of the Spirit. Once we have been joined to the Spirit in baptism, we will need to have repeated renewals in the power and filling of that same Spirit.

[4]Missiological researcher David Greenlee has convened two international consultations on conversion. Papers from the first were published as *From Straight Path to the Narrow Way: Journeys of Faith* (Greenlee et al. 2006), and papers from the second, in 2010, were published in 2013 as *Longing for Community: Church, Ummah or Somewhere in Between* (Greenlee 2013). Also, Greenlee's doctoral work studied the phenomenon of Muslim conversions to Christ (Greenlee 2007).

coming to Christ in a wide variety of ways, and there are significant discipleship implications inherent in the different means that God uses to draw them to Christ. Woodberry uses the analogy of the five fingers of the hand of God working in the glove of circumstances in drawing Muslims to faith: the resurgence of political Islam or Islamism; natural and human-caused catastrophes; the migration of Muslims out of their homelands; the Muslim desire for blessing or power (*baraka*); and ethnic and cultural resurgence (Woodberry 2006, 11-13). Woodberry also notes a number of things that appear to often influence Muslims and draw them toward Christ. He put these influences into two main groups: Muslim experience of encountering Christians, prayer answered by Jesus, dissatisfaction with Muslims or Islam and dreams and visions of Jesus; and finding that their spiritual needs were better answered by faith in Christ. In ranked order those needs are inner peace, forgiveness, assurance of salvation, the love of God, spiritual guidance through the Bible, spiritual fellowship, freedom from fear and loneliness and deliverance from demonization (14-17). Similarly, Gaudeul found five types of influences drawing Muslims to Christ: encountering the person of Christ, a thirst for truth, seeking a community of believers, seeking forgiveness and redemption and seeking a personal encounter with God through prayer (2006, 82-89).

Given the spiritual reality explored above, that the nature of one's conversion to Christ has enormous influence on the path of discipleship as a Christian, it is vital to stress that the discipling of BMBs must take into account the unique conversion experiences of the BMBs one is helping disciple. The issues that need special emphasis when discipling BMBs, especially in the early stages, must be closely adapted to the characteristics of the BMB's conversion experience.

Baptism in Muslim contexts. The question of baptism in Muslim contexts is challenging, and it is not easy to make wise and biblical choices

---

Gaudeul's *Called from Islam to Christ: Why Muslims Become Christians* is a helpful and comprehensive study by a Roman Catholic (1999). Dudley Woodberry has written several articles reporting on surveys of Muslim conversions (see, for example, Woodberry 2006; Woodberry, Shubin and Marks 2007). Refer also to the study of Muslim conversions in sub-Saharan Africa (Strähler 2010).

regarding whether, when and how to baptize new believers. It is telling that in the published report (Woodberry 2008, 97-171) of the consultation on fruitful practices in Muslim evangelism, discipleship and church planting held in March 2007, with five hundred practitioners from around the world, baptism was given only one short paragraph (138). It would appear that for those gathered, baptism had ceased to play any significant role in their understanding of evangelism, discipleship and even church planting, or at least its role is being overlooked.

It does not take long for a person beginning to live in a Muslim country to begin to understand why baptizing new believers can be such a challenge. More than thirty years ago Phil Parshall noted a nearly universal caricature of Christian baptism in the eyes of Muslims around the world. Parshall describes how a just-baptized believer is typically perceived by his Muslim community:

> Abdul Muhammad has openly declared himself a traitor to Islamic social structures, political and legal systems, economic patterns; and, worst of all, the religion of his fathers has been profaned and desecrated. He has now become a worshipper of three gods, a follower of a corrupted religious book, an eater of pork, a drinker of wine, and a member of an alien society of warmongers and adulterers. (Parshall 1980, 190)

In his discussion of baptism, Parshall noted that there was unanimous agreement—among the eleven workers with experience in fourteen Muslim countries that he surveyed—that handling baptism effectively is one of the biggest challenges in evangelism among Muslims (190). After discussing various ideas for substituting different, more culturally nuanced rites of passage for baptism, Parshall concludes that the rite of baptism needs to be preserved (194-97) but that the practice of baptism can be adapted to suit the realities of Muslim contexts. He notes that two departures from the apparent New Testament pattern of immediate public baptism following repentance and faith seemed to be appropriately and commonly practiced in Muslim contexts: a considered delay in baptism until there is a sizeable group of new believers ready who can be baptized together, and thus able to withstand the resulting rejection and persecution; and having the baptism in secret with a small group of local believers, sometimes in a distant location. This parallels the consensus of the previously mentioned five hundred missionaries who gathered in 2007 that baptism should be administered by other believers after time was given for quality discipling and that it should take place in the presence of other believers in an appropriate secure location (Woodberry 2008, 138).

What then can we bring from our examination of the nature of conversion, repentance and baptism in the New Testament and apply in Muslim contexts? Let me suggest several important principles. First, let us continually allow the powerful experience of conversion in the New Testament to influence our expectations and our practice of evangelism and discipleship in Muslim contexts. It is normative, in the sense of it being the normal New Testament expectation, that conversions of Muslims to Christ should involve a heartfelt repentance from sin and a turning to God and joining into Christ's body, the church, through baptism.

Second, given the fact that Muslims come to faith with a wide assortment of unbiblical understandings that must be sorted out, let us do what we can to ensure that there is thorough instruction in the Bible and in the biblical worldview before and after the point where a Muslim repents of his or her sin and joins with Christ in his body through baptism. Because most of the examples of conversion recorded in the New Testament involved either Jews or Gentile God-fearers embracing Christ, most already had the worldview background to ground their faith in Christ that Muslims do not typically have before they believe. Thus, it is reasonable to expect that BMBs will normally need a longer time of teaching and discipling before they will be ready for baptism.

Third, let us reflect and learn from the example of the ancient church in North Africa. It did not take long, in the centuries following the New Testament era, for extensive discipleship programs to develop that candidates for baptism had to undergo prior to baptism. Such extensive baptismal preparation programs suggest that conversion was viewed more as a journey than an event. Though I am not suggesting that we copy their system, it is instructive to examine the program North African

Saint Augustine implemented in his church. The program involved confessing believers participating in a two-year program of weekly teaching in groups, as well as personal mentoring under the guidance of an assigned sponsor, or discipler. Following this two-year instructional period, if individuals exhibited adequate quality of life and readiness to commit to the faith, then they went through a further season of formal testing and prayer, and instruction in the creeds, for forty days (often during Lent) that led up to the baptism itself (often on Easter morning). The baptism ceremony involved renunciations of the devil and the pleasures of the world, a pledge of allegiance to Christ and an affirmation of belief in the triune God, a triple immersion, and the anointing of oil and a rite whereby the convert was immersed in the life of the Spirit. The baptism was followed by the convert's first participation in the celebration of the Eucharist (Smith 2010, 53-55).

However much we may or may not want to emulate Saint Augustine's approach, it seems quite clear that if Muslims who came to faith in Christ were prepared for their baptism in such a thorough way, I suspect that there would be far fewer converts falling away following their baptism. Baptism would thus become a pivotal anchor point in their lives as they publically or discreetly joined a local church, the body of Christ, the person in whom they had come to put their entire trust and to whom they pledged to devote their lives. I suspect that, for many of us, the idea of spending months and even years giving careful and thorough instruction to prepare people for their baptism seems counterintuitive to our strong desire to see as many people converted and as many churches established as quickly as possible. However, I suspect that one of the commonly repeated counterintuitives for launching church planting movements applies here: "go slow in order to go fast."[5]

With such thorough preparation for a life of discipleship as part of the

---

[5]In one CPM approach that I am aware of, Muslims are taught to read and obey the Bible for months and months before they are asked to be baptized and join the emerging church. Perhaps one of the reasons for the apparent success of these CPMs, which report having seen thousands of Muslims become disciples of Christ in hundreds of informal house churches, is that they provide an effective way for new believers to have a thorough grounding in the entire biblical story as part of their process of coming to believe in and trust in Christ prior to baptism.

local church, one would expect a far higher success rate in BMBs becoming vital contributing members of the churches, living as disciples and seeking to do the work of the kingdom of God. As we better understand the nature of conversion and the central role that repentance and baptism play in the entire process, we will do well to strengthen our commitment to helping BMBs be thoroughly prepared for entering into their lives as disciples of Christ through baptism into the body of Christ existing within their Muslim communities. Let us not let the Muslim misunderstanding of baptism hinder us from understanding and practicing baptism in ways that more closely reflect New Testament teaching and example,[6] and the best of Christian experience through the centuries.

---

[6]For further fresh insight into New Testament understanding of baptism and implications for church planting among Muslims, I commend Steinhaus's "Reforming Baptism: A Call to Return to the Normal New Testament Way of Committing to Jesus" (2014).

2

Paul's Understanding of Discipleship and Spiritual Growth

*For you were called to freedom, brothers. Only do not use your
freedom as an opportunity for the flesh, but through love serve
one another. For the whole law is fulfilled in one word:
"You shall love your neighbor as yourself."*

Galatians 5:13-14

*The Mosaic covenant and its prescriptions are no longer
in force for believers now that Jesus Christ has come. . . . The law of
Christ now functions as the norm for believers, and Christ's self-sacrifice
functions as the paradigm of this law. . . . The law of Christ may be
described as the law of love. . . . Keeping the law of Christ is
possible only because the new age has been inaugurated
in Christ and because the Spirit has been
poured out into the lives of believers.*

Thomas Schreiner,
New Testament Theology

Thirty-four-year-old Nasif had been a believer for a
couple of years, was about ten years older than most of the other
men in the house church and was unhappy that he was still unmarried.

He was very serious, quiet and sober, and he mostly kept to himself. He was seldom joyous, and he struggled with being critical of all the other believers. He was unable to open up and share his thoughts and feelings in group settings. As he grew to trust me, he shared something of his difficult childhood, of having been seriously neglected by a distant and authoritative father who had married several wives, one of whom was his mother. It looked as if Nasif's path to maturity in Christ was going to be slow, long and hard.

So I was quite surprised when suddenly it seemed as if his whole personality had been transformed. He was now often joyful, could not stop smiling and was happy to share his thoughts with the other men in the group. What had happened to change Nasif in such profoundly positive ways in such a short period of time? A small ministry team from a Middle Eastern country had visited and had some special meetings with many of the believers we knew. Some of them prayed that Nasif would be filled with the Spirit. Nasif had begun to experience, in deep new ways, the reality of living by the power of the Spirit of God living in him. He told me that the way he viewed other people was totally different. Having experienced God's love in powerful new ways, he now looked at everyone he saw around him as being loved by God and that made him feel loving toward them—even complete strangers. The encouraging story of Nasif's experience of deeper transformation being greatly helped through a powerful encounter with the Holy Spirit aptly illustrates one of the apostle Paul's central emphases that spiritual transformation occurs as we live our lives in the power of the Holy Spirit.

REFLECTION ON DISCIPLESHIP PROCESSES EVIDENT IN THE NEW TESTAMENT

Before examining the apostle Paul's understanding of spiritual transformation, I need to explain how I am approaching the New Testament and why I am making an attempt to strengthen our understanding of discipleship in the Scriptures. For those of us who have known the Scriptures for years it is often difficult to see clearly what the Scriptures are saying because our perceptions are shaped by our longstanding personal, often culturally conditioned, ways of interpreting what we read.[1] In this study of discipling, I found it difficult to gain fresh insights into discipling in the New Testament because I already knew what was taught. After all, I have been reading the Bible my entire life and have been a believer in Christ for more than fifty years.

Most of us involved in discipling BMBs set about our task with confidence that we understand the nature of discipling—the challenge is simply to do a better job.[2] Most of those whom I interviewed had no hesitation in immediately giving their definition of discipleship. Similarly, in examining approaches to discipleship as understood and practiced across diverse Christian traditions throughout church history (chaps. 4 and 5) I was struck by the easy confidence with which contemporary evangelical writers typically approached the task of discipling convinced that they already understand what discipleship was all about. This self-assurance makes it much more difficult for us to view the New Testament materials afresh. Yet, in this chapter and the next, I endeavor to examine discipleship as it was understood and practiced in the New Testament in order to shape a solid biblical foundation for discipling BMBs.[3]

The order in which the books of the New Testament are placed (first the Gospels and Acts, then the Epistles) can significantly influence our implicit understanding of the gospel and the Christian life. Because Jesus' teaching and his life, death, resurrection and ascension were the foundation on which the church was built, we rightly view the ministry of Jesus and his teaching in the Gospels as the source of the earliest Chris-

[1]*Misreading Scripture with Western Eyes* (Richards and O'Brien 2012) offers significant help with this challenge.

[2]As explained earlier, the acronym BMB is a convenient shorthand referring to believers in Christ whose religious heritage was, in some way, Islam. Using BMB is in no way intended as a label diminishing the new identity of these brothers and sisters in Christ. It is merely a convenient way to avoid unhelpful wordiness.

[3]Though this study examines only New Testament documents, I believe that the Old Testament is indispensable for correctly interpreting the New Testament. Likewise, in discipling BMBs, it is important to help new believers become familiar with key Old Testament stories and passages in order to give them solid basis for interpreting the New Testament in light of the Jewish Old Testament worldview and prophetic expectations. That said, it is still from the New Testament that we get our understanding of New Covenant spirituality, and it is primarily from Jesus in the Gospels that we learn about discipleship per se.

tians' growth to maturity. When we examine the order in which the New
Testament documents were written, we realize that it was the teaching of
the apostles that interpreted the oral traditions of the life and teachings
of Jesus until the Gospels were written. The accounts of Jesus' life and
teaching that we have in the four canonical Gospels were written down
only after most of the epistles had been penned. This adds a different
dimension to our reading of the Epistles.

In my effort to listen to the New Testament authors afresh, I found
that examining the New Testament teaching on spiritual growth in the
order in which it was written yielded fresh insights. It gives more weight
to Paul's understanding of spiritual growth. It also gives us helpful
context as we seek to better understand and interpret the meaning of
discipleship that is taught by Jesus as he is presented to us by the apostles
in the Gospels following several decades of church life after Pentecost.
One thing that we see is that the first generation of Gentile Christians'
experience of the spiritual life was probably based as much on the apostolic message of repentance and forgiveness of sins through trusting in
Christ, and on the apostolic understanding of the post-resurrection Jesus,
as it was on the emphasis on the incoming reign of the pre-crucifixion
King Jesus that is often stressed in the Gospels.

One of the first intriguing observations is that the vocabulary of discipleship, though perhaps not the idea, is primarily in the Gospels and
Acts—the books written in the latter half of the first century. The word
disciple does not appear in the New Testament documents until we get
to the Gospels and Acts.[4] To help tease out some helpful nuances (and
I am not claiming much more than nuancing) in the New Testament
teaching on discipleship, we will begin our look at the teaching on spiritual growth and maturity presented in the New Testament by reflection
on the earliest documents, before the word *disciple* and the concept of
discipleship was commonly used in writing. We will deal with just two
of Paul's letters—Galatians and Philippians—as representative of early
and late post-resurrection New Testament understanding of spiritual

---

[4]In Greek the word μαθητής (*mathētēs*), which we translate as "disciple" in English, appears 264
times, but never in any book other than the Gospels and Acts (Muller 1975, 1:486).

growth, before we examine, in the next chapter, the concept of discipleship that is central to many of the later New Testament documents (the Gospels and Acts) that were written near the end of the New Testament era.

Our study of the teaching on discipleship found in the Gospels, in the next chapter, will examine the Gospel of Luke. Though other Gospels have varied emphases and insights into discipleship, a careful examination of Luke provides enough representative insight into the nature of discipleship as it is presented in the Gospels as a whole. We will also look at Acts because it covers the time of transition from Christ's ministry to the ministry of the apostles and the early church, and thus we will have come full circle back to our chronological starting point.

The understanding of the composition order of the New Testament is not something new.[5] However, it is helpful to recall this historical process as we study the New Testament perspectives on discipleship, because the teaching found in Paul's epistles is the earliest written expression that we have of what it means to live as believers within Christ's covenant community. Examining Paul's writings first, before Luke-Acts, will help us be more sensitive to how the early believers came to learn what it meant to live in Christ before they had access to the more extensive written information about Jesus and his teaching on discipleship recorded later.

PAUL IN GALATIANS: MANIFESTO FOR LIVING BY THE SPIRIT INSTEAD OF UNDER LAW

Galatians, Paul's earliest epistle, is the first written record we have of Paul helping believers grow in faith. It is believed to be Paul's first letter, written in A.D. 48 or 49.[6] For the purposes of our discussion now, we will

---

[5]Most accounts of this process paint a similar picture. See, for example, Wenham and Walton (2001); Marshall, Travis and Paul (2002); DeSilva (2004); Barnett (1999).

[6]See, for example, Witherington (1998b, 8-20); Barnett (1999, 277); DeSilva (2004, 487); Marshall, Travis and Paul (2002, 42-44). Paul's epistles were probably all written between A.D. 48 and 68, whereas the earliest likely date for Mark was between A.D. 55 and 60. Both Matthew and Luke are believed to have been written in the second half of the 60s (as Paul was writing his final epistle, 2 Timothy), and John is believed to have been written in the middle of the 90s, perhaps fifty years after Paul wrote Galatians (Guthrie et al. 1970).

operate with the scholarly consensus that the letter was most probably written prior to the Jerusalem Council (Acts 15) in A.D. 49. Any attempt to figure out the apostle Paul's understanding of how we are to live our lives as believers in Christ cannot do better than to absorb the teaching in this short, powerful, oral polemic,[7] in which Paul pleads with the believers in the churches in Galatia to not submit to life under the Mosaic law. This short epistle, addressed to new believers in the first century who were being asked to follow the Torah as the guide for their new life in Christ, gives valuable insight in helping new believers learn to live in freedom in Christ. This is a vital epistle for believers from a background of Islamic legalism.

Galatians' central theme is that sanctification comes through living by the Spirit. Ever since this letter became one of Martin Luther's favorite epistles, it has frequently been viewed as a glorious statement of the doctrine of justification by faith alone. How can it be otherwise understood, so long as it has such verses as Galatians 2:16? "Yet we know that a person is not justified by works of the law but through faith in Jesus Christ, so we also have believed in Christ Jesus, in order to be justified by faith in Christ and not by works of the law, because by works of the law no one will be justified." Yet, as I have repeatedly reread the epistle over the years, and studied and wrestled with Paul's understanding of the Law,[8] I have become convinced that the question that the believers in

---

[7]In *Grace in Galatia*, Witherington (1998b) demonstrates that Paul uses the conventions of Greek oral discourse in Galatians. The epistle is a brilliantly constructed oral discourse formatted like a letter (see Introduction and 36). It was designed to be "performed" aloud. Seeing the way that Paul used classic Greek oral discourse conventions significantly illumines the content and argument of the text.

[8]Scholarly study of the Pauline literature for more than forty years has been significantly focused on this question of Paul and his understanding of the Torah. Following on from the groundbreaking work of E. P. Sanders in the 1970s and 1980s, N. T. Wright, a prominent New Testament scholar and popular teacher, has built on Sanders's views, accepting his fundamental redefinition of what Second Temple Judaism was all about, and how Paul thought of the law before his conversion, when he was a zealous Pharisee. Wright has argued for new understandings of how the apostle Paul understood and reinterpreted Judaism after his encounter with the resurrected Christ on the road to Damascus. It is outside the purpose of this book to interact with and comment on this New Testament scholarship on Paul and the Torah, or even to fully understand and master the works of Wright, but I will bring Wright's perspectives on Paul and the Torah into the present discussion when appropriate.

Sanders's monumental *Paul and Palestinian Judaism: A Comparison of Patterns of Religion*

Galatia were struggling with was not how one is justified in God's eyes. Rather, they were trying to sort out whether or not the Mosaic law can serve as guide and power for living the Christian life. The central question in this epistle is about sanctification rather than justification.

Making an effort to step out of one's own experience with the text and truly attempt to hear the text speak afresh, as it did to its original hearers,[9] helps considerably in understanding the core issue that Paul wrote this letter to address. Knowing the question Paul was answering helps understand the central teaching of this epistle. Listen to what Paul asks the Galatians:

> Did you receive the Spirit by works of the law or by hearing with faith? Are you so foolish? Having begun by the Spirit, are you now being perfected by the flesh? Did you suffer so many things in vain—if indeed it was in vain? Does he who supplies the Spirit to you and works miracles among you do so by works of the law, or by hearing with faith? (Gal 3:2-5)

The question that the Galatians were struggling with was precisely whether or not they ought to become Torah-observant Gentiles in order to help them bring their new spiritual life to perfection and maturity. Witherington vigorously supports this interpretation: "The most basic contrast that underlies all of Paul's argument in this discourse is not between faith and works of the Law, but between life in the Spirit lived out by faith and life lived on the basis of Torah observance" (Witherington 1998b, 360).

These early believers, many of whom were believing God-fearers, were being taught by zealous Jewish believers in Christ that the best way to live out their life in Christ was through following the Torah. Paul was

---

(1977) set things in motion, and his later works added to the revolution in New Testament scholarship's views of Paul. See, for example, *Paul, the Law and the Jewish People* (1983). Wright has written numerous works on this topic, and the ones I have found most helpful were *What Saint Paul Really Said: Was Paul of Tarsus the Real Founder of Christianity?* (1997) and *Paul in Fresh Perspective* (2005). Wright published *Paul and the Faithfulness of God*, a seventeen-hundred-page treatise on Paul, in 2013.

[9]It is so easy to read our current questions and concerns into a text like this. However, most good commentaries attempt to get at the original intent of the author. Yet, as Silva argues in *Interpreting Galatians* (2001, 15-39), every commentator brings his or her own set of assumptions and questions to the task of interpreting the text.

rightly alarmed. As a former Torah-observant Jew, he knew that following the law did not bring freedom from sin and power over the flesh. Paul wrote this letter in order to persuade the believers in the infant churches in Galatia not to submit to circumcision and not to use the Mosaic law as a guide in their Christian walk. Paul was convinced that a new age had dawned and that all was now focused in and through Christ. To allow the law to guide their New Covenant experience would have been to go back to living as if Christ had never come at all. Moisés Silva (2001, 169-86) believes that this eschatological perspective expresses the core of Paul's theology, especially as it appears here in Galatians. Paul was convinced that if the Galatian believers were to use the Torah as a guide for living, they would find their faith in Christ useless and they would be cut off from their relationship to Christ (Gal 5:2-5). Witherington agrees: "All the arguments in Galatians are intending to convince the Galatians not to submit to circumcision and the Mosaic Law and instead to continue to walk in the way of freedom in the Spirit which Paul had taught them when he first delivered the Gospel to them" (1998b, 27).

Though this is not the place to spell out implications of this point for evangelizing and discipling Muslims, surely the fact that the central message of the first New Testament document so strongly opposes law observance for Gentiles should give us cause to reject radical proposals, such as one that Joshua Massey made a decade ago (2004a, 2004b), that call for Christian missionaries among Muslims to live like Torah-observant Jews in order to better reach and disciple Muslims. How can it be possible that we Gentiles should live like Jews to reach Gentile Muslims? If our apostle, that is, the apostle to the Gentiles, passionately opposed non-Jews submitting to the Torah, how can it serve God's purpose in this final eschatological age of Christ to return to the yoke of the law in order to bring Muslims under the same oppressive yoke under which the Jews struggled?

Living by the Spirit is the best way to nurture spiritual growth. One of the central teachings of the Old Testament is that the way one overcomes the evil inclinations of the flesh is by conforming one's heart and mind to the Torah. Psalm 119 is a well-known example of this quintessential Old Covenant approach to spiritual formation. From its first verse, "Blessed are those whose way is blameless, who walk in the law of the LORD!" (Ps 119:1) to its last, "I do not forget your commandments" (Ps 119:176), this psalm extols the positive effect on God's people of walking according to God's law. One can understand why devout Jews of Paul's day (and devout Christians in our day who, for example, stress the need to teach the Ten Commandments) would not be quick to abandon Torah observance as central to their spiritual growth and holiness after coming to believe in Christ as Messiah.

Paul, that one-time zealous Torah observer, ardently warned his dearly loved new believers in Galatia that continued Torah observance could lead to them losing their faith (Gal 5:4). Why did Paul stress that Torah observance was not the New Covenant path to holiness? He argued that the Torah was given as a concession to the weakness of human flesh and was put in charge until Christ, the fulfillment of God's promise to Abraham, arrived on the scene. Being under the law was being in slavery and under a needed taskmaster (Gal 3-5). In Christ we are now free to live according to the Spirit. In this new era, righteousness comes through living in obedience to the Spirit (Gal 5:5-6). The entire noble and worthy purpose of the law, to transform people into holiness, is now fulfilled in us through the Spirit. The new "law" of Christ is for believers to love one another and thus fulfill the intention of the Torah by means of the Spirit.

The whole operating principle of the spiritual life in this eschatological new age is one of faith and trust in God through Christ and responsive obedience to the Holy Spirit. When believers live according to the Spirit they experience grace and peace through Jesus (Gal 6:13-18). The flesh has been put to death in Christ's death (which we join to in baptism, as explained in chapter one) and the life we now live, we live by faith. Christ himself lives his life through us (Gal 2:19-21). In Galatians, Paul stresses that it is living by the Spirit alone that has power to overcome the pull of the flesh—the Torah cannot conquer the flesh. When we yield to the Spirit, the fruit of the Spirit grows in our lives and we discover that our flesh—the bodily desires and passions that pull us toward sinful thoughts and behaviors—is crucified and we find ourselves able to live, more and more consistently, in righteousness (Gal 5:15-25). Further, this exhortation to live according to the Spirit is never addressed to individual believers. It is only as we live together, loving and helping each other to be led by the Spirit, that we can know consistent victory over the flesh (Gal 6:1-10).

At this point, it is natural to ask whether there is any ongoing place for law or regulations of any kind in the life of the believer. Surely the New Testament is full of new commandments from Christ and Paul and others—exhortations and authoritative guidance as to right and wrong behavior. The answer is, in part, that there is still plenty of room for moral instruction and exhortations to appropriate behavior, but the believers under the New Covenant are no longer under any legal system. They live under the Spirit, fulfilling the law of love by faith.

Before moving to Philippians, it is crucial that we apply the message of Galatians in discipling BMBs. Living according to the Torah is *not* the way to live the Christian life. Greenlee suggests that the use of the Torah could help make believers stronger: "A colleague with many years of experience in Turkey told me that believers he worked with who evaluated their lives in the light of biblical commandments were those who grew spiritually. The Ten Commandments provides a checklist of moral imperative. Those who dealt with sin in these ten areas were those most likely to persevere in the faith" (Greenlee 2007, 26-27). My response to such a use of the Torah is that it is indeed good that BMBs be aware of their sins and repent of them. However, using the Ten Commandments as a rule to measure one's life is less effective than comparing their lives and actions to the lives and examples of Jesus or even of Paul. Going back to the Torah for instruction in Christian living is the strategy for growth in Christ that Paul condemns. It is critically important that those who disciple BMBs continuously strive to keep the focus on the dynamic and life transforming reality of walking by the Holy Spirit.

Islam is often experienced as a religion of works and of outward conformity to an elaborate code of conduct and religious ritual. The new age that God brought about in Christ, into which the BMB has been brought through faith in Christ, leads to inner transformation by the Spirit as BMBs pay attention to the leading of a person, the Holy Spirit. Such transformation never comes through adherence to a legal code or a community standard. The day-to-day reality of how the Christian life is to be lived, according to Paul, is very different from anything that most former Muslims have previously experienced, and so it should not be surprising that there will be a tendency for BMBs to fall into varieties of legalism as they instinctively try to live their new lives as believers the way that they had previously lived as Muslims. The solution is not to give them more law but to teach them how grace works through the power of the indwelling Spirit in their daily lives.

PAUL IN PHILIPPIANS: KNOWING CHRIST AND THE POWER OF HIS RESURRECTION

Moving from Galatians to Philippians takes us ahead some fourteen years to what is believed to be the last letter written by Paul from his captivity in Rome (A.D. 62).[10] The tone, context and content of this letter differ considerably from that of Galatians. What is this short letter all about? When I sought help in discerning the main theme(s) of the letter from commentators on Philippians, I did not find consensus. Hawthorne gives eight reasons why Paul may have written the letter (1983, xlvii-xlviii), and other commentators suggested from two to five main themes.[11] Though many of the themes given by commentators overlap, New Testament scholars appear to find it difficult to agree on Paul's main purpose for writing. Yet, as I read and reread the epistle, two major concerns stood out. It seems to me that when Paul wrote this letter to the believers twelve years after he planted the church there on his first visit,[12] he sought to ensure that they would remain united in love, demonstrating the re-

---

[10]Among the many scholars who believe that Paul wrote Philippians from Rome in A.D. 61 or 62 are Barnett (1999, 341), DeSilva (2004, 646 n. 15), Marshall, Travis and Paul (2002, 43) and Witherington (2004, 278).

[11]DeSilva (2004, 653-55) gives five main reason for Paul's writing. Hendriksen (1962, 17-21) and O'Brien (1991, 35-38) each give four reasons, and Bockmuehl gives two (1998, 33).

[12]I believe that Paul first preached in Philippi in A.D. 50 (cf. Acts 16), twelve years before he wrote this epistle to them. Most believing scholars seem to concur on this dating for Paul's second journey. See, for example, Witherington (2004, 52, 274, 276).

ality of their faith in Christ by resisting divisions and quarrels among themselves; and that they would deal effectively with the opposition and persecution they are encountering from non-believers. These different but related concerns are also among the biggest challenges facing BMBs and their house churches: the challenges of external persecution and opposition from their own families and communities and the infighting within the fellowship coming from lack of trust and inability to get along.

Paul's view of spiritual nurture in four significant passages in Philippians. In order to draw out Paul's understanding of the process of spiritual transformation seen in Philippians, I will briefly examine these four important passages: Paul's opening prayer (Phil 1:9-11), his thesis statement (Phil 1:27-30), his use of Christ as an example for the believers (Phil 2:1-11) and his explanation of how believers are to live the Christian life by faith (Phil 3:2–4:1).

If you want to know what someone cares about, listen to his or her prayers. Paul's prayer for the believers in Philippi gives clear insight into what he desires to see developing in their lives: "And it is my prayer that your love may abound more and more, with knowledge and all discernment, so that you may approve what is excellent, and so be pure and blameless for the day of Christ" (Phil 1:9-10). What kind of spiritual growth process does Paul envision here? He wants to see the outworking of Christ in their lives bear fruit in an overflowing of love that grows in wisdom, spiritual knowledge and discernment. Love is the foundation for everything else. This recalls his statement in Galatians that the only thing that counts is "faith working through love" (Gal 5:6). In his insightful study of the way that the crucified Christ shaped Paul's entire spirituality and theology, Gorman emphasizes the significant role of love:

> Love is clearly central to Paul's spirituality and to his understanding both of Christ and of himself. Love . . . fulfills the Law. . . . The source of this understanding of love is in the cross, which is the expression of Christ's love. . . . Christ's love on the cross is thus the paradigmatic act of love that can give rise to analogous acts by any who are in Christ. (Gorman 2001, 215)

Paul's opening prayer for the believers in Philippi expresses one of his core understandings of Christian spirituality: we are to love as Christ loved us in dying for us. Gorman coins the word *cruciformity* to identify this conscious imitation of Christ's sacrificial love (2001, 4-7).

In the second passage that we are examining, Philippians 1:27-30, we see the central theme of the epistle: "Let your manner of life be worthy of the gospel of Christ, so that whether I come and see you or am absent, I may hear of you that you are standing firm in one spirit, with one mind striving side by side for the faith of the gospel" (Phil 1:27). Paul believes that the believers' manner of life should be a credit to the gospel of Christ. They must remain firm in their commitment to live out the gospel, and they must not allow anything to break their united commitment to Christ and his glory. The gospel is the life-transforming center of life. Paul disciples the believers here by calling them to live their lives in a manner consistent with the gospel. We are to imitate not only Christ's teachings and lifestyle but also his self-sacrificing love and humility exhibited in his taking on human flesh and yielding to death. Paul calls us to live worthy of the gospel of the crucified Christ—to live in "cruciformity" to Christ.

In our third passage, Philippians 2:1-11, Paul begins (Phil 2:1-4) with an emotionally charged appeal to the believers to be united in love:

> So if there is any encouragement in Christ, any comfort from love, any participation in the Spirit, any affection and sympathy, complete my joy by being of the same mind, having the same love, being in full accord and of one mind. Do nothing from selfish ambition or conceit, but in humility count others more significant than yourselves. Let each of you look not only to his own interests, but also to the interests of others.

Notice how Paul motivates them to become united. First, he appeals to their heritage as believers that they are in Christ together, comforted by his love and experiencing the Spirit together in love and sympathy (Phil 2:1). Paul then asks them to love each other out of their love for him (Phil 2:2). He continues by asking them to search their hearts and motivations and to not act out of rivalry or conceit but to have a Christ-like perspective on themselves and others (Phil 2:3-4). His exhortation and loving rebuke reaches its climax in Philippians 2:5-8, where he appeals to them to be like Christ himself who sacrificed himself for others in his incarnation and crucifixion.

Paul takes the fundamental new transforming fact of history—the sacrificial act of God, offering himself in his Son on the cross, which ushered in the new era of the Spirit—and calls on the squabbling believers to emulate God's love in the way they relate to each other in the local church. Much study has gone into understanding every word and phrase of this Christ-hymn (Phil 2:6-11),[13] but the important point for us is to notice how Paul motivates believers to forsake squabbling and infighting. He calls them to imitate Christ's humility and sacrificial obedience to the Father. Gorman points out the significance of Paul's use of this Christ-hymn: *"For Paul, to be in Christ is to be a living exegesis of this narrative of Christ, a new performance of the voluntary renunciation of rights and selfish gain in order to serve and obey"* (2001, 92, emphasis in the original). The apostle Paul's spiritual life is entirely modeled on the example of Christ's life and death. He appeals to the believers in Philippi to live out of the powerful grace that comes to them in the story of Christ. Christ's example of love ought to motivate loving action better than any other conceivable incentive.

Our final passage from this epistle, Philippians 3:2–4:1, is Paul's very personal account of what it has been like to live as a disciple of Christ since his encounter with Christ on the road to Damascus.[14] There has

---

[13]Hawthorne bemoans that "this section is the most important section in the letter and surely the most difficult to interpret. The number of genuine exegetical problems and the sheer mass of books and articles it has called forth leaves one stricken with mental paralysis" (1983, 76). Gorman comments: "Philippians 2:6-11 may well have received more scholarly attention in the modern period than any other Pauline passage" (2001, 89).

[14]Much scholarly discussion is taken up trying to make sense of the structure of Philippians 3–4. Many have believed that the abrupt change in direction between Philippians 3:1 and Philippians 3:2 shows that Philippians is made up of several former letters pasted together by some unknown later editor. However, such a reading is not natural or necessary to account for what is happening in the text. Furthermore, in contrast to their lack of consensus about the central themes of Philippians, all of the commentators I consulted agree that the letter in the New Testament canon is in fact one cohesive letter written by Paul. See Bockmuehl (1998, 20-25, 175-77); DeSilva (2004, 647-49); Hawthorne (1983, 122-23); Hendrickson (1962, 31-37); Marshall, Travis and Paul (2002, 139-40); O'Brien (1991, 10-18); Silva (1992, 165-67).

been much discussion about who Paul was talking about in Philippians 3:2: "Look out for the dogs, look out for the evildoers, look out for those who mutilate the flesh." It seems clear to me. Paul was responding to the same teaching that he encountered in Galatia. In Philippians, fifteen years later, Paul appeared to have much less patience for this kind of false teaching. In Philippians 3:3, he stated emphatically that those who believe in Christ and worship by the Spirit are the true circumcision. Circumcision of the flesh is no longer the point. He presented his own experience as a zealous, Torah-observant Pharisee, prior to his encounter with Christ, as a sufficient case to demonstrate that living according to the Mosaic law accomplished nothing. Righteousness now comes only through living by faith in Christ.

Having recounted how much he himself was the paradigm of the God-fearing, believing Jew who was zealous for law keeping (Phil 3:4-6), Paul stressed that all that he had prior to Christ was worthless (Phil 3:7). Previously, as a devout, Torah-observant Jew, he would have striven to be righteous according to the requirements of the law. In contrast, Paul argued in Philippians 3:7-11, the only thing that counts is knowing Christ. It is only through knowing Christ and living dependent on him through faith that one can be transformed into Christ-likeness:

> But whatever gain I had, I counted as loss for the sake of Christ. Indeed, I count everything as loss because of *the surpassing worth of knowing Christ Jesus my Lord*. For his sake I have suffered the loss of all things and count them as rubbish, in order that I may gain Christ and be found in him, not having a righteousness of my own that comes from the law, but that which comes through faith in Christ, the righteousness from God that depends on faith—*that I may know him and the power of his resurrection*, and may share his sufferings, becoming like him in his death, that by any means possible I may attain the resurrection from the dead. (Phil 3:7-11, emphasis added)

The way to Christian maturity and transformation is to live in the reality of Christ and his death and resurrection. This is what it means to know Christ, and knowing Christ is the goal of Christian maturity. The most powerful source of spiritual transformation is to live in fellowship with

Christ through the Spirit, following him through suffering, and in faith anticipating the resurrection.

The second half of this remarkable chapter (Phil 3:12-4:1) reinforces this lesson. Paul acknowledged it was an ongoing process and that he had not yet died and been resurrected and therefore, he had not yet attained his goal. He pressed on to arrive at the point of full communion with Christ and transformation into his likeness. Paul built on this sense of living in anticipation of future fullness in the end of this passage:

> But our citizenship is in heaven, and from it we await a Savior, the Lord Jesus Christ, who will transform our lowly body to be like his glorious body, by the power that enables him even to subject all things to himself. *Therefore*, my brothers, whom I love and long for, my joy and crown, *stand firm thus in the Lord*, my beloved. (Phil 3:20–4:1, emphasis added)

Paul called the believers to imitate him in keeping their eyes focused on what they will have in Christ, remembering that their heavenly citizenship is their present earthly identity. It is because we have hope for the future, hope that our bodies will be fully transformed at the day of Christ's return to earth, that we can persevere in our obedience in the midst of opposition, persecution and false teaching. This message of forward looking hope is a powerful message to bring to embattled brothers and sisters seeking to live faithfully in Muslim communities.

Spiritual growth comes by living in cruciformity to Christ in community. These four passages in Philippians yield a powerful picture of the spiritual life of those who live by faith in Christ. The gospel is the all-encompassing shaper of our experience as believers. We must strive, with everything that is in us through our being in Christ, to live lives worthy of the gospel. Love is central. Our love must keep growing in depth of insight and spiritual understanding. We must love God and all others with the kind of love that Christ expressed in his self-sacrificing love expressed on the cross. Yet, this is never completed this side of the resurrection. Paul's vision of the spiritual life is that of a life that is ever increasingly being molded by Christ and transformed into Christ's likeness—a life of cruciformity to Christ.

In addition, it must be emphasized that Paul's vision of spiritual life in Philippians envisions transformation happening in community:

> For Paul, the experience of dying with Christ, though intensely personal, can never be private. Fundamentally, cruciformity means community, and community means cruciformity. Paul, we have seen, did not come merely to "save" individuals but to form communities . . . of cruciform faith, love, power, and hope. (Gorman 2001, 366)

This gospel-saturated understanding of the life of believers and the nature of the church will surely have much to offer as we help BMBs to live as faithful disciples. This profound Pauline vision of loving, cruciform communities of believers offers much hope for the effect of Christ's people living transformed lives in the midst of their Muslim communities.

SUMMING UP PAUL'S UNDERSTANDING OF THE SPIRITUAL GROWTH PROCESS

In his earliest preserved epistle to the believers in Galatia, the apostle Paul was adamant that the Gentile believers' lives should not be lived according to the patterns set out in the Mosaic law. The Galatians are to live their new lives in Christ, by walking each day sensitive and responsive to the voice of the Spirit in them and within their community. This new kind of Spirit-led and Spirit-empowered life fulfills the original purpose of the Torah by transforming believers into people who love and serve others and gain power over their flesh as they, together in vital community, bring forth the fruit of the Spirit in the day-to-day realities of their lives.

Then, fourteen years later in his letter to the church in Philippi, when Paul writes to strengthen the believers in their resolve to persevere in their life together as Christians, the goal is the same: that they will grow in their capacity to love with ever-increasing wisdom and discernment. They are to live lives worthy of the gospel by copying Christ even as Paul has copied Christ. Paul calls believers to follow Christ's example in the way that he gave up all of his rights as God and become a man, and then lived as a servant and obeyed God even to death on the cross. This imitation of Christ has been aptly named cruciformity—living our lives conformed to our crucified Lord. Paul also offers himself as a model to follow. Christ crucified was the supreme inspiration for Paul's entire life and ministry. His supreme ambition was to shape his life, his actions and his motivations to be like Christ. Today, as BMBs in turn seek to mold their lives around Christ's example, they will find all the answers they seek and the empowering grace they need to work out how to live in their communities. As they seek to conform to Christ crucified, they will, as Paul himself experienced, become ever more like Christ.

3

DISCIPLESHIP FROM CHRIST TO THE EARLY CHURCH IN LUKE-ACTS

[Jesus said,] "If anyone would come after me, let him deny himself and take up his cross daily and follow me. For whoever would save his life will lose it, but whoever loses his life for my sake will save it. For what does it profit a man if he gains the whole world and loses or forfeits himself?"

LUKE 9:23-25

Spiritual formation and discipleship are all about development of the life in the kingdom of God that comes to us through the risen Christ. As a disciple of Jesus, I am living with Him, learning to live in the kingdom of God as He lived in the kingdom of God. Spiritual formation is taking the explicit statements of Jesus and learning how to live this way. Jesus did tell us, did He not, that we should make disciples, submerging them in Trinitarian reality? Baptizing them in the Trinitarian name doesn't just mean saying the names "Father," "Son," and "Holy Spirit" over them while you get them wet. The name in biblical understanding is reality, and to baptize them is to submerge them in the Trinitarian reality. . . . The gospel is about life with the Trinity.

DALLAS WILLARD,
THE KINGDOM LIFE

WHEN I ARRIVED IN NORTH AFRICA with basic but growing ability to communicate in both French and Arabic, I was eager to get started in discipling and helping plant churches. At the time, one of the most fruitful means that we had to meet serious seekers was through following up on students who had taken a Bible correspondence course. The training we received on how to handle such contacts included the advice that it was wise to meet with each separate individual for a long time before taking the risk of introducing the seeker or new believer to another local believer. I was not convinced by this safe, individualistic approach, so when I made contact with seekers I brought other believers in soon. After having met once or twice, asking for the Holy Spirit to give me discernment about a person's sincerity, I had those people meet both with other seekers (people whom they could trust, preferably their own friends or family members) and with believers who were willing to take the risk of meeting an untested seeker or new believer.

Later, as the house church matured and local leaders took the lead, they specifically asked if our weekly Bible study groups could act as a bridge. They saw our expatriate homes as safe places for seekers to meet local believers before they knew about the house church itself. Then, when the house church members in the group were confident that a seeker had truly come to Christ, they could invite the seeker to their church service with far less risk. From then on, whenever any one of us met someone who seemed to be genuinely interested in learning more, there was a standing invitation for them to bring such a person with them to our weekly group. Frequently, the encounter that such people had with Christ in the group meetings was sufficient for them to soon become disciples of Christ.

The power of corporate worship, honest and vulnerable sharing and caring and praying for each other was often a stronger attraction to Christ than weeks and months of one-on-one conversations and individual discipling. We were not so much inviting them to follow Christ as individuals, but rather inviting them to join a community of those already seeking to grow deeper in their discipleship to Christ. Now, as we turn to explore the nature of discipleship in Luke-Acts, we will see that living together in community is a significant part of the way that the Holy Spirit worked transformation in Christ's disciples in the New Testament era.

DISCIPLESHIP IN LUKE: A JOURNEY OF FAITH IN DISCIPLESHIP TO CHRIST

Growing scholarly consensus dates the writing of Luke-Acts shortly after the writing of Philippians, at about A.D. 63 or a little later (though some put it up to twenty years later).[1] This puts the writing of this book later than most, if not all, of Paul's epistles. Furthermore, in my discussion here, I will assume that the "beloved physician" Luke, Paul's travel companion (Acts 16:10-40, 20:6, and so on), was in fact the author and that he wrote both parts of this two-volume work.[2]

Luke wrote his Gospel in order to give Theophilus[3] certainty that his faith was based on full, accurate and documented information:[4] "it seemed good to me . . . to write an orderly account for you . . . that you may have certainty concerning the things you have been taught" (Lk 1:3-4). Furthermore, from the opening verses of his second volume, it is clear that Luke wrote Acts to show how the church began in Jerusalem,

---

[1]The following New Testament scholars argue for this early date: Guthrie et al. (1970, 888); Wenham (2005, 95-100); Wenham and Walton (2001, 296-97); Barnett (1999, 380); Marshall (1978, 34-35). Witherington (1998, 62) supports a later dating: "All in all, the late 70s or early 80s seems most likely for the date when Acts was composed." Bruce, in the revised edition of his commentary on Acts (1988, 12), concurs with Witherington's position.

[2]All of the New Testament scholars I consulted agree that the Luke mentioned by Paul in Colossians 4:14 is the author of Luke-Acts and everyone also agrees that Luke and Acts were written by the same man.

[3]It is unclear whether Theophilus was a person, possibly the sponsor of Luke's work, or whether the term "Theophilus" was a device referring to everyone who is a believer—a "friend of God." In this discussion, I accept the strong arguments in favor of Theophilus being a well-to-do, educated Greek sponsor of Luke's writing.

[4]Luke's prelude (Lk 1:1-4) leaves little doubt that written and oral collections of Jesus teachings, sayings and miracles existed at the time that he wrote his own "ordered account." Wenham and Walton (2001, 57-70) describe and assess the various theories over the past hundred years that have sought to discern what those written sources were. Along with them, I favor the two-document hypothesis, which holds that Mark wrote his Gospel first, and that in addition to the oral traditions that were strong at the time, both Matthew and Luke drew on Mark, as well as on an additional written document, called Q, which Mark did not have access to, which is no longer extant.

built on the ministry of Jesus the Christ following his resurrection and spread throughout Judea and Samaria and on to the capital of the Roman Empire (Acts 1:8). He wrote to demonstrate that God was working through Christ and his ministry to fulfill the entire Old Testament and that the church spreading throughout the Jewish and Gentile world had its legitimate origin in God's revelations to the people of Israel.

Journeying to the city of Jerusalem plays a central role in Luke's Gospel. Luke mentions three of Jesus' journeys to Jerusalem (two before he began his ministry), and Jesus ended up in Jerusalem and taught in the temple after "journeying" to Jerusalem throughout the central section of the Gospel (Lk 9:51–19:44). Journeys to and from Jerusalem are also significant in Acts. All three of Peter's missionary trips begin and end in Jerusalem, and Paul visits Jerusalem at the end of his three missionary trips as well. Thus, Luke presents Christ going to Jerusalem so that the gospel goes out from Jerusalem to the ends of the earth.[5]

The work that I found most insightful in understanding the structure of Luke's Gospel is the one that Scobie developed in his analysis of Luke's connection to Acts and the function of Luke-Acts in the canon. Scobie shows that Luke deliberately shaped his Gospel using a chiastic structure (ABCBA) in order to emphasize the middle section, C, Jesus' journey to Jerusalem.[6] Here is a condensed version of Scobie's outline of Luke (2005, 336):

Preface (Lk 1:1-4)

A[1]—The birth of Jesus (Lk 1:5–2:52)

    B[1]—Jesus' early ministry (Lk 3:1–9:50)

        C—Jesus' journey to Jerusalem (Lk 9:51–19:44)

    B[2]—Jesus in Jerusalem (Lk 19:45–23:56)

A[2]—The resurrection and ascension of Jesus (Lk 24)[7]

---

[5]This understanding of the journeying motif comes from Scobie, "A Canonical Approach to Interpreting Luke: The Journey Motif as a Hermeneutical Key" (2005, 327-49).

[6]Other interpreters of Luke often also label the middle section of the Gospel something like "Journeying to Jerusalem." Though they begin and end the section in slightly different places, the basic structure of their outlines resembles Scobie's outline reproduced here. Yet they do not give as much importance to the structure of the Gospel in interpreting the content of Luke. See, for example, DeSilva (2004, 311); Marshall (1978, 400-694).

[7]Scobie suggests that Luke is organized with mirror parts in which earlier parts mirror later parts in a chiastic ABCBA pattern. He believes that Luke deliberately used this structure in order to

I believe that a careful reading of Luke confirms Scobie's suggestion that discipleship and Christology are the two primary themes in the central journey section of the Gospel (Lk 9:51–19:44). Our look at discipleship here, following the chiastic structure in Luke, offers a brief synopsis of Jesus' teaching about discipleship in Galilee, goes into some depth in examining the major discipleship lessons in the central journey section and then concludes with a quick look at Jesus' teaching on discipleship in his final days after arriving in Jerusalem.

Jesus' modeling and teaching on discipleship while in Galilee. The appointment of twelve men to be apostles was a significant event that Jesus took very seriously. Luke wants us to see that Jesus was consciously forming a new community to supersede the community of Israel. Just as there were twelve tribes in Israel, so the foundation of this new people consists of twelve men on whom Jesus placed the entire future and growth of the church. Jesus is consciously fulfilling key events and promises in the Old Testament in his actions and his calling as the Messiah. Luke presents Jesus as giving his first extended teaching to the disciples (Lk 6:17-49) only following the appointment of the Twelve (Lk 6:12-16).

There are two collections of Jesus' teachings that Luke places during Jesus' Galilean ministry. The first block of Jesus' teaching (Lk 6:20-49) is about blessings, curses, loving enemies, judging others, trees and their fruit and the necessity of building one's life on Jesus' teaching. Immediately following the appointment of the twelve apostles, as the leaders of the new Israel that Jesus had come to incorporate, Luke presents Jesus giving a set of blessings and woes to the disciples and to the enormous crowd listening in. Anyone familiar with the Torah will immediately see the parallel to Moses, who told the ancient people of Israel to stand on Mount Gerizim before they began to conquer the Promised Land and go through a series of blessings and cursings as a seal of God's renewing the covenant with them (Deut 27:11–28:68). Luke is showing that Jesus was

---

strengthen his argument and to emphasize the importance of the middle section, C, which is the large section, more than one-third of the Gospel, of Jesus journeying to Jerusalem, in which almost half of the material is unique to Luke (and none of it is in Mark).

deliberately giving the people his own version of the covenant pronounce-
ments of blessings and curses for this new covenant (Wright 2004, 71).

In this first block of teaching, Jesus teaches his disciples that though
they may be poor and hungry, weeping and rejected, reviled and spurned,
they are nevertheless blessed because they are with him. Rather than
experiencing the prosperity and material well-being associated with the
covenant blessing to the people of Israel under Moses, Jesus' kingdom
people will often be poor, despised, rejected and persecuted on account
of their association with Jesus in his kingdom. Discipleship to Jesus is
often a road of suffering and struggle in which Jesus' disciples hold onto
the reality that they are being rewarded in God's presence (Lk 6:23), even
though the reward may be not yet visible. Yet, this is good news for them
because in the kingdom of God they will be satisfied and will laugh and
rejoice. Luke continues with a series of Jesus' teachings that give the
disciples a sense of what life in the kingdom is to be like. He begins to
establish the radical new and all-embracing commitment to which Jesus
calls his disciples. In the second teaching section in the Galilean period,
Jesus uses the familiar parable of the sower (Lk 8:1-21) to make it clear to
his disciples that the crucial thing is how people respond to the word that
they receive from him.

Also in the Galilean period, Luke reports Jesus' instructions for the
apostles being sent out on their first mission (Lk 9:3-5) and then debriefs
them after their return (Lk 9:18-27). The instructions Jesus gives for this
first mission are very concise. He tells the apostles to travel light and to
pay close attention to the way they and their message are received. Those
who receive the apostles will be blessed and those who do not will be
under God's judgment.

Understanding that Luke believes that the apostles were the appointed
founders of the church, which was the fulfillment of the hopes and
promises of the Old Testament prophets, helps us avoid the mistake of
expecting that we, or our BMB friends, are expected to do everything
that Jesus trained the apostles to do. Jesus was inaugurating the kingdom
of God, and the apostles were commissioned with a unique role in establishing this new spiritual kingdom on earth.

In summary, then, in the early Galilee material, Luke arranges his accounts to draw attention to Jesus' call to discipleship. This call involves leaving everything and following Jesus. It means living within a kingdom that has radical new values of love and mercy and forgiveness. It is a call to commitment and obedience to Jesus and his teachings at great cost. Yet it is also a call to share with Christ in the glory to come (refer to the transfiguration in Lk 9:28-36). This call is also the fulfillment of Old Testament prophecy and the beginning of the new age in which people transfer their allegiance from the Torah to Jesus.

Jesus' teaching on discipleship during his journey to Jerusalem (Lk 9:51–19:44). It is quite clear that Luke 9:51, "When the days drew near for him to be taken up, he set his face to go to Jerusalem," signals the beginning of this new block of material arranged by Luke to occur during the journey that Jesus takes from Galilee to Jerusalem. A similar expression repeated seven times (Lk 9:53; 13:22, 33; 17:11; 18:31; 19:11, 28) stresses that Jesus has set his face to go to his death in Jerusalem. During this extended journey, Luke draws attention to the growing tension between the Pharisees and rulers who reject Jesus and the disciples who seek to obey him. Both the length of this middle section (a third of the entire Gospel) and Luke's narrative devices suggest that this section is the heart of his Gospel. We will examine two types of texts placed within this journey for insights into the nature of discipleship to Jesus as it is given to us by Luke in his Gospel: Jesus' teaching about the cost of discipleship and Jesus' teaching on possessions.

Luke gives us two main accounts in which Jesus stresses the high cost of following him. In the first (Lk 9:57-62), Jesus teaches three different people that following him demands giving up everything. A few chapters later, when speaking to the crowds, Jesus issues his familiar radical demand of discipleship (Lk 14:26-27): "If anyone comes to me and does not hate his own father and mother and wife and children and brothers and sisters, yes, and even his own life, he cannot be my disciple. Whoever does not bear his own cross and come after me cannot be my disciple." This radical call for total allegiance is followed by two parables that are unique to Luke: the tower builder and the king about to engage in war.

Jesus concludes with this sobering challenge: "So therefore, any one of you who does not renounce all that he has cannot be my disciple" (Lk 14:33). Luke alone among the Gospel writers records Jesus' demanding call to total, non-compromising commitment. Another account of the radical demands of discipleship, given on the journey to Jerusalem, is Luke 12:49-53, in which Jesus declares that his coming divides families.

Another focus of Jesus' teaching during the journey to Jerusalem in Luke is a set of teachings on attitudes toward wealth and possessions. The paradigmatic statement that Luke uses to define the purpose of Jesus' ministry in Galilee (cf. Lk 4:16-30) sets the context for Luke's handling of wealth and possessions in the rest of the Gospel. Jesus said that he was fulfilling Isaiah's prophecy and had come to preach good news for the poor and to free the oppressed. Because two of the four passages in which Jesus deals with wealth and possessions in the central journey section are unique to Luke, it is not surprising that many commentators have identified this as one of Luke's major concerns.[8] Because money is one of the thorniest issues Westerners have to deal with in discipling BMBs, it is helpful for us to examine Luke's presentation of Jesus' teaching on possessions and poverty. We will further examine the practical out workings of this issue for discipling BMBs in chapter thirteen.

Luke is the only one who records the parable of the rich fool who planned to keep expanding his barns to hold his abundant crops (Lk 12:13-34). After telling the parable, Jesus gives an extended discourse (Lk 12:22-34) on anxiety and the folly of using possessions to assure material security. Jesus teaches that it is as we entrust ourselves to our heavenly Father in the new kingdom and seek God and his purposes that we can trust him to look after all of our needs for food, clothing and shelter. As we learn to trust the Father's love and provision, we are freed to use our possessions to bless the needy, rather than hoarding them in fear and self-protection.

Four chapters later Luke tells Jesus' parable of the shrewd manager (Lk 16:1-9) in order to further instruct his disciples on the proper attitude to

<hr>

[8]Wenham (2005, 84-86), for example, identifies wealth and poverty as one of Luke's major themes.

money. One of the points of the story is that the disciples are to use money and possessions in order to serve kingdom purposes. At the same time, the parable also works on another level. For first-century Jews, any story of managers and stewards was understood to be about God the manager and Israel his steward. Read as a parable, the point is that Israel has failed in its stewardship task and is about to be dismissed from its stewardship. Jesus was bringing in a new eschatological order, and the Jews were being removed from their role of stewards of God's purposes on the earth.

Luke concludes this series of teachings on money with the story of the rich man and Lazarus, a story that is also unique to Luke (Lk 16:19-31). As usual in Luke, when Jesus is addressing the crowds he is primarily talking to the Pharisees. Jesus is challenging the Pharisees about their rejection of him and his transforming kingdom message of love and mercy toward all. They continually appeal to Abraham and Moses, but the one who fulfills everything in Abraham and Moses is present; still they refuse to acknowledge him. Jesus issues his prophetic warning that even if someone were to rise from the dead to warn them of their impending fate, they would not listen, precisely because they have refused to listen to Abraham and Moses. This is one of Luke's significant points in Luke-Acts—the Jews did not reject Jesus as their Messiah because he was not the true Messiah. Rather, they rejected Jesus as their Messiah because they had previously rejected the authority of Abraham and Moses.

There remain two more stories to examine to complete our look at Luke's presentation of Jesus' teaching on wealth and possessions. In Luke 18:18-30 we have the account of the wealthy ruler who is drawn to Jesus' teaching about eternal life. Jesus exhorts him to put his trust in God, sell everything and in utter dependence on God, follow Christ (just as he had taught everyone in Lk 12). The rich man cannot give up trusting in the security that his possessions give him, and so he leaves, grieving that he cannot have the eternal life he seeks.

Following the story of the rich man who could not give up his possessions, Luke tells the story of Zacchaeus, the rich man who did release his possessions and follow Christ (Lk 19:1-10). This story, unique to Luke, tells how, in response to Jesus' acceptance and welcome, Zacchaeus joyously gives away half of his wealth and pledges to right any wrongs that he has done to anyone. Truly, Zacchaeus has grasped the attitude toward possessions that Jesus has been teaching. In the kingdom, Jesus' disciples trust that their Father will provide and so they are able to generously use their possessions justly and especially to help those in need.

It would seem that a central theme of Jesus' teaching about discipleship during the journey to Jerusalem is that discipleship to Jesus involves a fundamental posture of strong faith in a loving and merciful God. The call to follow Jesus involves a radical abandonment of dependency on land, possessions and reputation. It is a call to trust God for our lives so that we can treat others as God treats them, in love, mercy and compassion. It is a commitment to enter into the new community of Jesus' followers who live together with complete trust in God. Jesus is bringing something new, and everyone must choose whether to enter into it and follow Jesus or reject it and thus reject God's new order of love and mercy. The call to discipleship is a call to live within a new order, and because this new order challenges the existing order of things, it is also a call to come, suffer and die, as stakeholders of the existing order persecute the members of the new community of love, faith and grace. This typical reaction against the kingdom is especially visible in the way Muslim communities so often reject and persecute any who follow Christ.

Jesus' teaching on discipleship in Jerusalem and beyond. A look at two final stories of Jesus with his disciples following their arrival in Jerusalem concludes this study of discipleship in Luke. Only Luke places the dispute about who would be greatest in the context of the Passover meal. During the Passover meal there is a strong sense that the kingdom of God that Jesus has been preaching is about to be set up (see Lk 22:16-18). Jesus assures them that they would indeed be assigned the leadership of the kingdom that Jesus was about to receive from the Father (Lk 22:30). However, he tells them that leadership in this new kingdom will be radically different from authority as they know it and see it exercised in the

Gentile world around them. In the new kingdom of the heavens, greatness is measured by service to others rather than by authority. In most of the Muslim world, as is increasingly true in the West, leadership is typically about status, power and privilege. This discipleship lesson that the apostles found so hard to learn is a key lesson that BMBs also struggle to learn.

Luke's version of the Great Commission is the final passage to be probed for insights into discipleship in Luke:

> [Jesus] said to them, "Thus it is written, that the Christ should suffer and on the third day rise from the dead, and that repentance and forgiveness of sins should be proclaimed in his name to all nations, beginning from Jerusalem. You are witnesses of these things. And behold, I am sending the promise of my Father upon you. But stay in the city until you are clothed with power from on high." (Lk 24:46-49)

The apostles had just lived through the most momentous days of their lives. They were struggling to understand all that had happened. In *Surprised by Hope*, N. T. Wright suggests that the disciples were stunned by Christ's resurrection and had no idea it was going to happen.[9] Jesus explains to them that everything that had happened had been written about him in the "the Law of Moses and the Prophets and the Psalms" (Lk 24:44). The apostles, once they had received the promised Holy Spirit, were to be witnesses, proclaiming "repentance and forgiveness of sins" to the nations. Jesus had lived with and taught the apostles for three years, and they were now being given the responsibility for which Jesus had trained them. Yet, Luke makes it clear that Jesus spoke these words to everyone in the room. This new task, taking the announcement of forgiveness of sins to the nations, is one of the core tasks of all disciples. Now the journey to Jerusalem had ended and the journey from Jerusalem to the uttermost parts of the earth was about to begin.

Central discipleship lesson from the Gospel of Luke. Discipleship to Jesus in Luke is a radical commitment to live life under the loving care

---

[9]See especially chapter 4, "The Strange Story of Easter" (2008, 53-76). The resurrection alone explains the existence of the Christian faith.

of the heavenly Father in such a way that every attitude and perspective is turned on its head. Following Christ means embarking on a journey of faith in which we learn to live in self-denial, loving others, serving others, forgiving others and trusting God to provide all that we need so that we do not need to be anxious about our security, wealth, health or reputation. As we learn to live in the new realty of the new community that Christ has brought into being, we are also called to share this message with the nations, so that others can enter in and live as disciples who no longer live for themselves but for God and others.

DISCIPLESHIP FROM JEWISH DISCIPLES TO GENTILE CHRISTIANS IN ACTS

Turning from Luke to Acts, one is immediately struck by the different focus. In Acts, Luke is intent to show how the kingdom message of forgiveness through trust in the Messiah, the heir of David's throne, extended from Jerusalem throughout Judea and Samaria and to the "ends of the earth." Because of this central purpose on the part of Luke, there is a nearly complete absence of material that deals with either discipleship or spiritual nurture. Given the paucity of explicit teaching on discipleship in Acts, in our search for insight into the way spiritual transformation occurred in the book of Acts we will examine Luke's description of the nature of the spiritual life in the early community in Jerusalem just after Pentecost, in the Jewish and Gentile churches outside of Judea and then the nature of the spiritual life in the Gentile churches that came about through Paul's ministry as recorded later in Acts. This brief reflection on the life of the early communities will yield insight into how the gospel transformed the earliest Jewish and Gentile followers of the Messiah.

Spiritual life in the Jerusalem church following Pentecost. In several places in Acts 1–7, Luke describes the activities and characteristics of life in the early church (such as in Acts 1:14; 2:42-47; 4:32-35). Other aspects of their lives can be ascertained indirectly through Luke's stories.[10] Fol-

---

[10]In this discussion I draw significantly on Barnett, "The Community of the Messiah in Jerusalem (c. 33/34)," which pulls together all the New Testament material available to give a portrait of the earliest church community (1999, 195-214).

lowing the day of Pentecost, the inner core of some 120 Galileans (Acts 1:15; Lk 24:33; Barnett 1999, 198) quickly expanded through the addition of largely Greek-speaking diaspora Jews who maintained residences in other parts of Jerusalem.

What kind of a picture does Luke give of these early communities of Christ's followers in Jerusalem? The focal point of their time together, meeting daily in the temple and in their own homes, was the teaching of the apostles and fellowship together (Acts 2:42). They shared whatever resources they had among themselves and looked after each other's needs. They were a joyous community that knew the anointing of the Holy Spirit among them. Luke, perhaps somewhat in amazement, reports that "there was not a needy person among them" (Acts 4:34).

The apostles devoted themselves to teaching (Acts 2:42; 4:2, 18; 5:21, 25, 28, 42). From the beginning, the apostles appeared to have given reliable traditions about Jesus that were taught. Characteristic, too, of the early community in Jerusalem was a powerful presence of the Holy Spirit working grace among them all (Acts 4:33; 5:12-16, and so on). Healings and deliverances were common, and the power of God was visibly at work. Within a year, according to Acts, there were many more than ten thousand disciples, perhaps as much as 10 to 15 percent of the one hundred thousand people in Jerusalem (Barnett 1999, 217).

Luke does not paint a completely rosy picture. Ananias and Sapphira were a lesson to the early community that the Holy Spirit did not appreciate hypocrisy (Acts 5:1-11), and there were tensions between the Hebrews (the Aramaic-speaking Judeans and Galileans) and the Hellenists (the Greek-speaking Jews from the diaspora). Yet, in the spirit of Jesus' teaching about wealth and anxiety in Luke, the apostles took immediate action to ensure that the needy Hellenist widows were not neglected (Acts 4:34-35; 6:1-6). It is with good reason that those early days of the Jewish church in Jerusalem have long been looked to by subsequent generations of Christians up to our own day as an ideal of Christian community to emulate. How did they learn the new faith and grow during this era? It is hard to be certain from this distance in time, yet it appears that it was all happening as they lived their lives together in vital

community, in obedience to the Holy Spirit in their midst and in submission to the apostles' teaching.

Spiritual life in the Jewish and Gentile churches outside of Judea. The
brief descriptions of the church in Antioch suggest that as that church
grew, the disciples there experienced similar levels of fellowship and the
power and anointing of the Holy Spirit as did the church in Jerusalem
(Acts 11:19-30; 13:1-3; 15:30-35). Other incidents hint at the spiritual vitality and warm love between the believers. When Paul visited the believers in Troas, they spent the whole night together (Acts 20:7-13).

Luke's general portrayal of discipleship in Acts. Luke presents us with
an inspiring picture of the disciples in Acts. They were eagerly studying
both the Old Testament Scriptures and the apostles' teaching, fellow-
shipping together in vital community, worshiping joyously, praying passionately and boldly proclaiming this new message of salvation wherever
they went, accompanied by many powerful miracles and signs of the
Holy Spirit's presence. A crucial point in the developing church's understanding of the nature of the new community came in the Jerusalem
Council (Acts 15), in which the elders in Jerusalem release Gentile converts from any need to follow the Torah as the pattern of righteous living.
Though Acts lacks examples of the teaching being given to new believers
on how to grow, what we do see reflects the approach taken by the Paul
in the Epistles.

SUMMING UP LUKE'S PORTRAYAL OF DISCIPLESHIP
IN LUKE AND ACTS

Combining the lessons learned about discipleship from Luke with our
observations on the community life in Acts helps us see Luke's overall
portrayal of discipleship and spiritual life: The people of God live in communities that practice radical discipleship to Christ through faith in the
loving and merciful Father of Jesus. Their new life of obedience to Jesus
struck at the root of first-century ways of viewing life. For the Jews of the
New Testament era, so much of the meaning of life was about observing
the Torah. For the Gentiles, life consisted of surviving and gaining power,
influence and prestige. Jesus' call to discipleship overturns the normal

order of both kinds of societies. Disciples, brothers and saints, are called to set aside old allegiances and enter into the community of the Spirit.

For the Jews to whom Jesus and Luke communicated, the exhilarating new reality was that God called everyone, and especially Gentiles, into membership with the Jews in this new Israel of God. There was no longer any difference between Israelites and the uncircumcised. All were united in faith in the same loving God, through trust in the same Lord and Messiah, who had become God's appointed King over all people on earth. Aramaic-speaking Jews, Greek-speaking Jews and Greek- and Latin-speaking Gentiles are all brought together into the same community of the Spirit living in radical commitment to Christ and to each other.

DRAWING ON THIS NEW TESTAMENT VISION FOR DISCIPLESHIP IN MUSLIM COMMUNITIES

Our time spent immersed in the New Testament era has yielded a renewed vision for discipleship and spiritual maturity that holds tremendous promise for believers in the often difficult and oppressive environments of the Muslim world. This radical call of discipleship to Jesus, the dynamic new community that came into being through the Spirit, as documented by Luke, and the potent vision of Spirit empowered living exemplified by Paul in cruciformity to Christ, hold enormous potential for BMBs learning to live in their communities throughout the Muslim world.

This fresh understanding of Luke's and Paul's vision of discipleship and spiritual maturity gives a healthy perspective on our thinking about discipleship. Both Paul and Luke believed that they were privileged to be a part of a new work that God brought about through Christ for the sake of all the nations of the world. Placing the task of discipleship and spiritual nurture into the bigger framework of the purposes of God being worked out in the New Covenant in Christ guards against inappropriate simplistic or mechanistic approaches to discipleship. The special challenges involved in helping disciple BMBs are tied to the bigger realities of God's purposes for the church in this new age of the kingdom.

One of the biggest pressures on believers in Muslim contexts is the social pressure from their families and Muslim communities. This renewed insight into the significance of the new community created in the New Covenant era underlines the importance of BMBs being able to join healthy, growing and dynamic Christian churches. The capacity for new believers to grow and persevere in the challenging conditions typical of the Muslim context is vitally linked to their being welcomed into vital, Spirit-filled groups of believers, which are experiencing the realities of the new covenant community together. This new community identity, the power of the Holy Spirit flowing within the church and the mutual love and care that characterize Christian community are crucial in seeing BMBs transformed in order to influence their Muslim families and communities. The goal is not simply to do what Jesus and the apostles did, in terms of their methods of discipleship, but to call on God to birth the kinds of communities that he created in those early years as witnessed in the New Testament documents. The task of discipleship must be understood in view of the eternal purposes of God in his church and world in which we serve in our generation.

4

CONTEMPORARY WESTERN EVANGELICAL APPROACHES TO DISCIPLESHIP

Have nothing to do with irreverent, silly myths. Rather train yourself
for godliness; for while bodily training is of some value, godliness
is of value in every way, as it holds promise for the
present life and also for the life to come.

1 TIMOTHY 4:7-8

To enable people to become disciples we must change whatever it is
in their actual belief system that bars confidence in Jesus as Master
of the Universe. That is fundamental and must be taken as an un-
shakable conscious objective by any maker of disciples. . . . We
always live up to our beliefs—or down to them, as the case may be.
. . . We understand that our beliefs are the rails upon which our life
runs, and so we have to address their actual beliefs and their doubts,
not spend our time discussing many fine things that have little or no
relevance to their genuine state of mind.

DALLAS WILLARD,
THE DIVINE CONSPIRACY

Twenty-one-year-old Ahmed was invited into our small discipleship group through his friendship with one of the other young believers. A new believer, led to Christ by his friend only a few months before joining the group, Ahmed appeared eager to grow. But although Ahmed was there week after week, he seldom spoke up and participated. He did not pray aloud, and he did not readily make friends with others in the group. He appeared shy and inward-looking, but for months I took little notice. As God began to burden me for him, I asked two men in the group to make efforts to befriend him. This initially proved successful, and the three began spending more time together. Ahmed appeared to be more at ease in our weekly home meetings.

During a weekend fasting retreat with these young men, I learned that Ahmed was being tormented by evil spirits. A couple of years prior to his conversion, he and a friend had invoked the devil to help them pass their very important final exam in high school (he failed). As the months following that invocation passed, the level of harassment from evil spirits had increased. By the time of the retreat, though he had been a believer for some months, he was finding it impossible to sleep at night due to the tormenting night visitations of demons. He resorted to staying up nights and sleeping in the daytime to avoid their visits. As a result, he could not hold any kind of a job. I arranged for one of his new friends to stay on at the retreat house with Ahmed for a couple more days following the retreat so that they could together confront the demons. They were not successful in seeing him delivered, and I did not attempt any other intervention. From then on Ahmed came to the meetings less frequently and eventually disappeared from fellowship.

Looking back at this sad example of failed discipleship, it is clear to me that I, as a Western discipler, was inadequately equipped to deal with such challenges to the authority of Christ in the lives of my BMB friends. My discipleship experience and understanding of discipleship did not go deep enough to be able to bear good fruit in such cases. Such failures convinced me that in addition to finding more effective practical solutions to the discipling challenges we face, we must also reflect deeply about the nature of spiritual transformation.

The evangelical tradition to which I belong persistently tries to ground everything it does and thinks in the Bible. Most books about discipleship develop their scriptural understanding of discipleship from a study limited to just Jesus and the Gospels.[1] Yet, the immense complexity of the challenges involved in discipling BMBs means that a simple study of discipleship based on how Jesus trained the Twelve will not yield an adequate understanding of biblical perspectives on spiritual growth. That is why I examined the New Testament more broadly in the last two chapters. In them, I attempted to provide a more robust vision for discipleship flowing from the practice and understanding of spiritual transformation in the New Testament. In beginning with this study of the Scriptures, I follow the pattern of other evangelicals writing on spirituality who all seek to base their perspectives on a study of the Scriptures.[2]

But studying the Scriptures is not enough. We must also explore how other Christians have understood and practiced discipleship, both in our time and throughout the history of the church. The current chapter examines contemporary approaches to discipleship practiced and advocated by evangelicals. Then, in the next chapter, I explore how discipleship and spiritual formation have been understood and practiced throughout the history of the church. I believe that taking the time to consider contemporary and historical approaches will help us develop a theologically and historically informed understanding of this important topic.

MODERN PROTESTANT APPROACHES TO DISCIPLESHIP

When I began this study of discipleship I realized that I had read very little material on discipleship. Though I had been a committed and growing Christian for thirty years, had been discipled (mostly indirectly through churches, books and friends) and had discipled others (espe-

---

[1]See, for example, Coleman ([1987] 1998); Coppedge (1989); Eims (1978); Hadidian (1979); Hull (2006); Petersen (1993).

[2]Comprehensive surveys of spirituality throughout church history also attempt to ground their studies in the Scriptures. For example, in *The Story of Christian Spirituality* (Mursell 2001), the first chapter argues that Jesus is the source of spirituality. Similar patterns can be found in other surveys such as Woods (1989); Holt (1993); Thornton ([1963] 1986, 31-43).

cially in North Africa), I had read very little on the topic. In examining
both classic Protestant understandings and contemporary evangelical
approaches from the past forty years, I have been both disappointed and
encouraged. Most contemporary books on discipleship present a view,
popularized by organizations such as the Navigators and Campus
Crusade for Christ, teach an understanding of discipleship that I think
is best described as modernist.[3]

Evangelical modernist discipleship. So, what is modernist discipleship? It typically concentrates on a very individualized course of
either one-on-one or small-group teaching, Bible study and mentoring
that is designed to train evangelists and leaders in local churches or
strong Christian leaders in society. In describing the discipleship processes taught in the modernist approach to discipleship, I will present the
teaching in three books typical of the genre.[4] All of these books present
a vision of the discipleship process that draws on study of the way in
which Jesus trained his disciples as recorded in the Gospels and how they
in turn trained others, as seen in the book of Acts. There is usually strong
optimism about the astonishing potential of multiplication in discipleship. In addition, all of these men speak from extensive experience in
discipling and training disciplers. I want to be clear that I am not suggesting that these books have no value: one can learn much of value from
them and their discipleship model that is of potential application for
discipling BMBs.

This is Hadidian's definition of discipleship in *Successful Discipling*:
"Discipling others is the process by which a Christian with a life worth
emulating commits himself for an extended period of time to a few in-

---

[3]More recent books published by NavPress suggest that the Navigators, at least, are moving toward a more historically informed and nuanced approach. Recent examples of this trend in
NavPress are *Satisfy Your Soul: Restoring the Heart of Christian Spirituality* (Demarest 2001),
Renovation of the Heart: Putting on the Character of Christ (Willard 2002), *The Complete Book of
Discipleship: On Being and Making Followers of Christ* (Hull 2006) and *The Kingdom Life: A Practical Theology of Discipleship* (Andrews 2010), all of which engage the interface between discipleship and spiritual formation.
[4]The three books are Eims's *The Lost Art of Disciple Making* (1978), Hadidian's *Successful Discipling*
(1979) and Coppedge's *The Biblical Principles of Discipleship* (1989). Robert E. Coleman, known
for his early books *The Master Plan of Evangelism* (1963) and *The Master Plan of Discipleship*
([1987] 1998), forwarded both Eims's and Coppedge's books.

dividuals who have been won to Christ, the purpose being to aid and guide their growth to maturity and equip them to reproduce themselves in a third spiritual generation" (1979, 28-9). Hadidian's book is full of lists. He lists five marks of spiritual maturity, nine marks of a person who can be a discipler and four stages in training a disciple. He puts the whole process of teaching and training that leads to individual transformation in figure 4.1. The book advocates what appears to me to be a mechanistic approach (if one follows these steps one will get these outcomes) to spir-

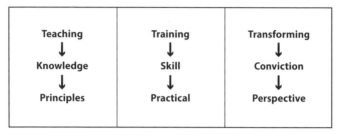

Figure 4.1. Hadidian's teaching, training and transformation model (92)

itual nurture and then enthusiastically organizes and manages in order to accomplish the desired outcomes. It is businesslike in its efficiency and optimistic about the amazing multiplying outcomes for evangelism and leadership that will occur if the formula is carried out.

In a similar way, in *The Lost Art of Disciple Making* (1978), Eims produces a straightforward manual for discipleship and leadership training. It covers a lot of ground in quick summaries. He gives a model for training people in local churches in the United States. Eims too has a number of lists, including thirty suggested topics to cover in the training of disciples (74), ten qualities to aim for in training disciplers and five qualities to look for in choosing people to train as leaders. Eims also offers a number of suggestions for training workers and training leaders.

Coppedge's *The Biblical Principles of Discipleship* (1989) is more of a theology of discipleship than a manual. Coppedge spends most of his time looking at the Old and New Testaments in order to explain the theological and biblical foundations for discipleship. He then draws his material on discipling from a study of the Gospels and Acts. Coppedge

expresses biblical and theological foundations for the model of discipleship taught by people like Eims, Hadidian and Coleman. In ways
similar to these men, Coppedge lays out a model for making disciples
and training leaders, "just as Jesus has made them" (114), based on the
pattern of Jesus with his disciples. Coppedge believes that the key principle in discipling is multiplication. He asserts that the heart of Jesus'
approach to finding sufficient disciples to do the work of the harvest is
to multiply disciples (83).

Coppedge's study is a good example of a thoughtful analysis of the
biblical foundation for this discipleship model. Much of the content and
shape of this model is clearly drawn from observing and directly applying
patterns and principles that he finds in the Old and New Testaments.
Nevertheless, Coppedge also displays a consistent weakness of this genre
of discipleship material in that he does not refer to any previous Christian
experience in his discussion and theology of discipleship. His thinking
displays no influence of other streams of Christian experience other than
this modernist, managerial approach to spiritual formation.

Recent developments in modernist discipleship. In *Conformed to His
Image: Biblical and Practical Approaches to Spiritual Formation* (2001),
Kenneth Boa covers the entire range of approaches to spiritual formation
that have been practiced throughout the many traditions of the church
up to the end of the twentieth century. Boa organizes his book into
twelve "facets" of spiritual formation that include almost every imag-
inable form of spiritual nurture. He treats every approach to spiritual
formation with fairness and offers generous critiques of their downsides.
He argues that all these approaches are facets of the gem of spiritual life
which we Christians have known and experienced through the centuries.
He places discipleship in his eleventh facet, entitled "Nurturing Spirituality: A Lifestyle of Evangelism and Discipleship" (367-87). Boa develops
a biblical philosophy of discipleship, which he articulates in eleven
helpful principles, as follows.

1. We must be disciples to make disciples.

2. Discipleship is a dependent process.

3. Concentration is crucial to multiplication.

4. People are not our disciples.

5. Reproduction is a mark of discipleship.

6. There is no maturity without ministry.

7. We cannot measure our ministries.

8. Discipleship is more than a program.

9. Discipleship requires a servant attitude.

10. Spiritual friendship is a component of discipleship.

11. Effective discipleship requires more than one method. (2001, 370-76)

Further, Boa believes that levels of development in discipleship relate to the changing needs, goals and focus of the disciple, as well as the changing roles of the discipler (see table 4.1). This chart could be used as a guide to help disciplers follow progress in their discipleship relationships with BMBs. Boa believes that the main dynamics in the discipleship process are exposing, equipping, encouraging and exhorting. Boa is one of the few contemporary writers on discipleship who takes into account lessons learned in previous eras and other traditions of Christian experience. He has a nuanced understanding of the relationship between teaching and training and argues for balance: "Since there is a reciprocal relationship between thinking and habits, attitudes and actions, belief and behavior, it is important to avoid the extremes of all theory or all technique" (380).

Table 4.1. Boa's Levels in Discipleship Maturity (2001, 373)

Developmental Level	Developmental		Role of Discipler	Developing Spiritual Focus
	Needs	Goals		
Babies (new converts)	Love, protection, nourishment	Health, growth	Mother	New life
Children (disciples)	Boundaries, obedience	Training, learning	Father	Life in Christ
Young adults (workers)	Growing independence and activity	Contribution, maturity	Coach	Christ's life in us
Adults (leaders)	Relationships	Multiplication	Peer	Christ's life through us

One more recent work on discipleship merits discussion: Jim Petersen's *Lifestyle Discipleship: The Challenge of Following Jesus in Today's World* (1993). Petersen writes from long experience discipling in the modernist model as a leader with the Navigators. He struggled with the failures of the modernist model. In this book, Petersen seeks to improve his approach to discipleship so that it meets the demands facing the church at the end of the twentieth century. His opening sentence in chapter one is striking: "Thirty years of discipleship programs, and we are not discipled." He describes how he went from his initial experience of being discipled and discipling others on an American university campus where there was an overabundance of Christians wanting to be discipled, to Brazil, where no one was interested in religion let alone in being discipled. He had to rethink his assumptions. Prior to his experience in Brazil, he had viewed discipleship as a system of information and disciplines that resulted in mastering a body of knowledge and a set of skills, which the discipler organized and regulated. He had to learn to explore the Scriptures with people and talk about what they meant—this was true whether it was evangelism or discipleship (15-21). This change in Petersen's approach was needed because the context had changed and people were no longer responsive to the original approach, but he does not seem to question seriously whether the original model might have been deeply flawed in both its method and assumptions.

Petersen advocates a new model of discipleship in which the person stays or becomes an insider with his non-Christian friends and acquaintances and relates to them naturally, bringing to them the resources in Christ that he or she has discovered. Abandoning a managerial model of discipleship, he replaces it with a relational approach, which expects God to work in unexpected and varied ways. Petersen criticizes the modernist model of discipleship, which he long advocated and practiced:

> Do you really believe managing by goal setting is compatible with the affairs of the kingdom? Jesus said, "My kingdom is not of this world." Can you measure the mustard seed, the yeast in the dough? How do you evaluate an hour spent in prayer? Virtually everything of major importance in God's workings stands outside the reach of our management mechanisms. (1993, 51-52)

I find Petersen's approach refreshingly true to life and to my own experience discipling BMBs. He presents a vision of discipleship that gives hope of being relevant in our postmodern society. Yet, a central shortcoming of the book is that Petersen seems to think and live in a historical vacuum in which he makes no reference to alternative models of discipleship learned and used in any other church tradition apart from the American evangelical Protestant tradition of the latter half of the twentieth century. The vast wealth of traditional resources on the spiritual disciplines, spiritual formation and devotion is left untapped. His own approach, like the managerial model that he abandoned, is too much a child of its own age.

Early modern Protestant approaches to discipling. Before offering final assessment of the modernist discipleship models just discussed, we need to pause and look at a few older Protestant approaches to spiritual nurture that could be called early modern. Scougal's well-known little classic, *The Life of God in the Soul of Man* ([1677] 1946), speaks freshly as from another time and yet does not significantly address the question of the process of spiritual transformation. His basic thesis is one that has recently been argued compellingly by Dallas Willard (especially in 1988 and 1998), namely, that the Christian life is God's life being lived in human experience. Scougal argues that "the difference between a religious and a wicked man is that in the one divine life bears sway, in the other the animal life doth prevail" (35). He goes through a list of nineteen things that we ought to do to encourage the growth of God's grace in our souls. Apart from a call to regular prayer and participation in the worship of the local church, almost all of what Scougal advocates are actions of the mind—disciplines of thought. It is as if Scougal believes that everything of importance in the spiritual life takes place in the mind. He stresses such valuable things as watchfulness, self-examination, reflection and meditation on key spiritual truths. Living in an age that downplays the life of the mind, this approach could make for a refreshing change. However, replacing an inadequate mechanistic approach with another from a different era that is overly intellectualist is not a solution. One needs to do more than change one's thinking to bring about transformation.

These things are typical of what I understand to be Puritan and Reformed approaches to maintaining spiritual vigor.[5] However, more recent Reformed efforts to understand how transformation takes place, as represented in the work of Timothy Lane and Paul David Tripp, in *How People Change* (2006), are encouraging. Lane and Tripp have a strong emphasis on thinking correctly and living out of one's convictions well (the life of the mind). However, as they probe the nature of spiritual formation more deeply, they also add helpful reflection on such things as the nature of behavior, the role of the community and the need to have one's heart transformed through a living experiential relationship with Christ.

A quick look at a revivalist tradition is also instructive. Charles Finney, the nineteenth-century American revivalist, offers counsel for discipling new believers in *Instructions for Young Converts* ([1835] 1948). Here is the goal of discipleship according to Finney: "Our object should be to exhibit the character of God more and more, to reflect as many of the rays of the image of God as possible" (7). This is a worthy goal. Yet, Finney's material consists of numerous lists of things to teach and things not to teach young converts. He appears to give little thought as to how to teach all of these things in such a way that they become part of the character of those being discipled. It is assumed that head knowledge will automatically become life changes. He appears to expect that new Christians will adopt the things that they are taught and grow over time into mature Christians automatically as they understand their new faith well.[6]

---

[5]J. I. Packer is a contemporary writer who advocates learning from the wisdom of the Puritans. *A Quest for Godliness* (1990) holds up the Puritans as good models for us to learn from in seeking to live lives of holiness in the late twentieth century. In a later article, Packer (1992) holds up Richard Baxter as a good example of the Puritan approach to godliness and spirituality. Baxter's main insight was that we must have the mental discipline of keeping heaven always before us. This is very much like Scougal's approach discussed here. Alister McGrath also points to the spirituality of the Reformers as a valuable model in *Roots That Refresh: A Celebration of Reformation Spirituality* (1991). A similar Reformed understanding of "correct thinking" as key to spiritual vitality is argued in Packer's *Keep in Step with the Spirit: Finding Fullness in Our Walk with God* ([1984] 2005).

[6]With a title like *The Training of the Twelve* ([1871] 1971), one would expect A. B. Bruce's work to be full of wisdom and practical lessons for the discipleship process. However, Bruce's work is essentially a biblical exposition of much of the Gospels and of Jesus' teaching to the twelve dis-

This brief look at Henry Scougal and Charles Finney as representatives of Protestant writers from earlier times contributes very little in rounding out our understanding of discipleship. Unfortunately, the shortcomings of these three works are often reflected in the discipleship programs that are exported from the West to the Muslim world. They often consist of doctrines and Bible study methods that need to be taught with no reflection on how people grow and change their habits and inner attitudes, and no questioning as to whether such programs bear lasting fruit in transformed lives when they are used in the West.

Strengths of the modernist discipleship model. Clearly, the concerns that the authors bring to the subject are relevant. They are seeking to do a scripturally sound and effective job of growing new believers into maturity in Christ. Their goals are generally exemplary in that they are seeking to see each discipled believer become mature in faith and obedience and able to disciple others as well (2 Tim 2:2). There are definite strengths in the modernist approach to discipleship. (1) Their intentional organization and planning toward the goal of developing mature disciples of Christ is very important. They accept that spiritual growth does not happen because one is alive—growth must be nurtured. (2) They seek to ground everything they do in a careful study of the Scripture. (3) They exhibit an exemplary zeal for obedience to Christ and growth in holiness. (4) They are vitally concerned that the gospel be preached and multiplied to the ends of the earth. There are, however, several serious weaknesses inherent in the modernist approach to discipleship.

Problems with the modernist discipleship model. First, this model of discipleship functions as if nothing has been learned about discipleship in the nineteen centuries between the writing of the New Testament and when contemporary authors sat down to write about their own experience. Though these works are admittedly founded on Bible study and reflection, they are only minimally informed by biblical scholarship, theology and church history. There is no analysis of previous ways that godly men and women have sought to nurture their faith. Even Petersen, in his

---

ciples. He has much rich insight into what it means to follow Christ but does not offer anything in the way of guidance for how to go about discipling others.

rejection of the modernist model, does not draw on outside resources beyond his own experience when revising his approach. This almost universal disconnectedness from any of the rich traditions of the past is a serious flaw in this model.

Second, everyone seems to betray an almost naïve acceptance of the assumptions of modernity about the way people change. The approach seems to assume that if one gives persons a task to do, they will not have difficulty doing it, and when they do it, they will be changed through it. None of these authors takes time to explore what one does when the expected change does not occur (except Petersen, who advocates patience and faith in response). There seems to be a strong optimism that if one carries out the prescribed program (a program invented by the author as an imitation of the practice of Jesus in the Gospels), one will grow and become a strong, faith-filled Christian able to lead others to faith and disciple them. The profound mystery of the life of God in the soul of a person is little explored. The Holy Spirit is not really needed— except theologically. The mechanistic expectations of modernism have been applied to the spiritual domain.

The modernist approach appears to operate on the basis of an entirely unsatisfactory understanding of the process of human change. The basic philosophy of change appears to be "if at first you don't succeed, try, try again." There seems to be only a limited appreciation for the way bad habits are formed and broken. There is almost no quest to understand the mystery of sanctification as something deep inside a person. We probably all know people who have tried to implement such a model. They have tried hard to live in obedience for years, and then one day they drop out of the church and the Christian life. They have not experienced deep transformation in spite of having tried very hard. Often such people eventually become convinced, through their experience of ongoing failure, that Christianity must be unworkable. The modernist discipleship model has serious weaknesses that help to explain why it has often not worked well when applied in the extraordinarily difficult spiritual context in which BMBs seek to live as disciples. This challenging discipleship context needs an approach that is biblically, theologically and psychologically reliable. Simply teaching BMBs a series of Bible lessons has seldom led to deep transformation, nor has setting up a set of objectives and seeking to manage people's lives to perform according to the plan. This is an obvious oversimplification of what has been attempted, but it does explain one of the primary reasons for the distressing failure in discipleship too often experienced in Muslim communities—our models of discipleship have been distressingly inadequate.

THE ROLE OF THE SPIRITUAL DISCIPLINES IN DISCIPLESHIP

Richard Foster's *Celebration of Discipline: The Path to Spiritual Growth* (1978) had a profound influence on many evangelicals thirty-five years ago. Ever since, evangelicals have been increasingly waking up to the value of some of the ancient traditions of the church with respect to the classical spiritual disciplines.[7] I first encountered Foster's book thirty years ago in the context of my local church. During the years living in North Africa and discipling BMBs, I sought to apply a number of his insights in our ministry there. When I visited Canada from North Africa, I began to notice a growing interest in spirituality among my acquaintances in Christian circles, as well as a growing number of evangelicals writing books on spirituality and the spiritual disciplines, which continues until now.[8] And more recently evangelicals are increasingly exploring other aspects of ascetic and contemplative theology and practice as known and taught through the centuries in Orthodox, Catholic and

---

[7]Foster has continued to be one of the most influential evangelical writers on Christian spirituality. His subsequent books, *Money, Sex, and Power* (1985) and *Prayer* (1992), further developed the application of the classical spiritual disciplines to the challenges of living lives of holiness in our contemporary society. His most recent work, *Sanctuary of the Soul* (2011), moves further into the contemplative traditions with an exploration of meditative prayer.

[8]For example, the former pastor of my sending church, J. Paul Stevens, of Regent College, Vancouver, has written several books on spirituality in the past two decades. See, for example, Stevens (2001, with Charles Ringma; 2003, with Michael Green). Another great book is *Satisfy Your Soul* by Bruce Demarest (2001), already mentioned. Reformed Baptist John Piper has written a number of books on spirituality, starting with his landmark and profoundly influential *Desiring God* ([1986] 2011) and, more recently, for example, *When I Don't Desire God: How to Fight for Joy* (2004). A number of writers are grappling increasingly with how to create churches that nurture spiritual growth and health. See *Spiritual Formation as If the Church Mattered* (Wilhoit 2008). Even former evangelists are writing excellent books on living contemplatively: see Ford 2008.

some Protestant traditions. There is no longer any doubt that learning how to grow in one's spiritual life is important to evangelicals.

As part of this process of assessing resources to help inform and guide the nurture of spiritual life in BMBs, I am going to look first at three evangelical teachers on the spiritual disciplines: Gordon Smith, Donald Whitney and Douglas Rumford. Then I will conclude this section with a presentation and analysis of the significant contribution of the late Dallas Willard.

Smith, Whitney and Rumford on the spiritual disciplines. Whitney and Rumford are pastors and Smith was a seminary professor and former missionary and pastor who became the president of Ambrose University College in Calgary, Alberta, Canada, in 2012. All three men cover much the same ground, yet each has a distinctive contribution. Smith's reflection on *Essential Spirituality* (1989) covers a broad range of aspects of spirituality. When he discusses the spiritual disciplines, he breaks them into five groups: the renewal of the mind, personal encounter with God, vocation and Christian service, spiritual authority and accountability, and play. I am struck by how much cheerful, happy wisdom and balance there is in this little book. Indeed, this book could be translated and simply adapted for to help guide BMBs into a full and healthy spiritual life. Smith views the spiritual disciplines as one essential component among many that are needed to develop healthy and strong spiritual lives.

Whitney's *Spiritual Disciplines for the Christian Life* (1991) is a comprehensive instruction in the nature and practice of the spiritual disciplines adapted for life in North America at the end of the twentieth century. Whitney argues that "the Spiritual Disciplines are *the* God-given means we are to use in the Spirit-filled pursuit of Godliness" (15). Of the three primary things that God uses to change us into Christ's likeness (people, circumstances and the disciplines), it is only the spiritual disciplines that are under our control. We have little or no choice about the people and circumstances in our lives, but we do have a choice as to how much we engage and practice and grow through the use of the spiritual disciplines. Whitney is adamant that the spiritual disciplines are the primary path to growth. "The Spiritual Disciplines then are also like a channel of God's transforming grace. . . . That's why the Disciplines must become priority for us if we will be Godly" (17). The bulk of Whitney's book is his exposition and presentation of eleven central disciplines: Bible intake, prayer, worship, evangelism, service, stewardship, fasting, silence, solitude, journaling and learning. He readily acknowledges that there are many other disciplines that could be added (15). His final chapter helpfully tackles the challenge of carrying out the disciplines.

Douglas Rumford's *SoulShaping: Taking Care of Your Spiritual Life* (1996) takes the image of body fitness and health and applies it to the soul. He provides a spiritual health program and diagnosis that, if followed, will yield a healthy and strong soul. Rumford begins with a list of ten symptoms to look for in diagnosing soul health.[9] After a perceptive discussion of getting the soul back on track to health, he discusses the spiritual disciplines in four sections and concludes with a look at seven vital signs of a healthy soul: a continuing experience of grace, expectancy that is rooted in faith, resilience, compassion, zeal—holy energy, integrity and gratitude (439-54).

Unlike Foster and Whitney, who both devote only their first few pages to a discussion of the reason for the spiritual disciplines and how they are vital to spiritual growth, Rumford devotes his first five chapters to working through to a clear understanding and theology of change (part one, 3-114). In this section he exhibits a refreshingly clear understanding of the human personality and how it is that we can change and grow, develop new habits and become new, substantially changed people: "Spiritual life is a living thing; it is not mechanical. . . . The soul will not be manipulated like a thermostat or turned on and off like a switch. If we are going to cultivate true spiritual growth, we must respect the natural movement of the spirit" (65).

Throughout the book Rumford seeks to elucidate the way that spiritual growth happens and change is nurtured. He develops the physical

---

[9]Here is his list of poor soul health indicators: low-grade "depression fever," busy but bored, loss of control over life's routine, loss of responsiveness to others, withdrawal from responsibility and leadership, preoccupation with projects of lesser importance, restlessness and dissatisfaction, resurgence of unhealthy habits, diminished impulse control and diminished resistance to temptation, guilt and shame and a hard heart (Rumford 1996, 12-26).

analogy of sports ability and muscle performance to illustrate how character strength and resilience grow through the spiritual disciplines.

> Spiritual discipline, then, is developing *soul reflexes* so that we know how to live. We discipline ourselves to develop *soul memory* so that we'll be equipped for the times of high demand or deep crisis. . . .
>
> Spiritual Disciplines are a tool that the Holy Spirit uses in our lives to work growth. *Spiritual vitality grows out of our relationship with the Lord Jesus*. . . . Even though the process of spiritual growth is in many ways mysterious, *there are steps we can take* to . . . put ourselves in touch with God's power. (87, 98, emphasis in the original)

Rumford groups twenty disciplines according to their respective objectives: those that connect us to God's presence (repentance, confession, preview, review, prayer and worship); those that give us the eternal perspective (Bible study, meditation and spiritual reading); those that release us from the power of evil and sin in us (fasting, silence, solitude, battling temptation and prayer for spiritual battle) and those that give us a life of purpose (building character, building relationships, spiritual direction, spiritual friendship, stewardship and spiritual service through gifts). He concludes with the counsel that we prayerfully focus on the disciplines that we need to exercise to grow in a few areas at any given time and then make some concrete commitments and make ourselves accountable to carry them out (430-33).

Willard on discipleship and spiritual formation. In the past twenty-five years Dallas Willard, the late professor of philosophy at the University of Southern California in Los Angeles, has rightly become one of the most influential evangelical writers on discipleship and spiritual formation. His six books on the spiritual life and discipleship (1984, 1988, 1998, 2002, 2006, 2014) provide a profound explanation of the potential of the transforming power of God's life lived through us. Ever since first encountering Willard in 1995, through his first book (*In Search of Guidance*, 1984), his teaching has had a profound effect on my walk with God and on my understanding of discipleship and spiritual transformation. Any attempt to understand contemporary evangelical writing on discipleship must consider Willard's contribution. In order to do so, I will summarize the content of his books and then examine in greater detail the model of discipleship and spiritual formation that he presents in *The Divine Conspiracy* (1998) and *Renovation of the Heart* (2002).

In his first book, *Hearing God: Developing a Conversational Relationship with God* ([1984] 2012), Willard presents a nuanced description of the nature of the Christian's spiritual life as an ongoing relationship characterized by conversation of the disciple with God. He describes the stages that people normally pass through on their journey to maturity and presents a biblically grounded and beautiful vision of what spiritual maturity and intimacy with God looks like. In his second book, *The Spirit of the Disciplines: Understanding How God Changes Lives* (1988), Willard develops a spiritual psychology of Christian spirituality and provides a persuasive apologetic for the use of the classical spiritual disciplines. In his 1998 masterpiece, *The Divine Conspiracy: Rediscovering Our Hidden Life in God*, Willard presents "discipleship to Jesus as the very heart of the gospel" (xvii). Based on a fresh, rich and controversial exposition of the Sermon on the Mount, Willard elucidates a comprehensive understanding of discipleship that encompasses all of life as a life of following Jesus. Then, in *Renovation of the Heart: Putting on the Character of Christ* (2002), Willard narrows his focus somewhat to provide a handbook for personal spiritual transformation—a guide to show us that the way into the soul rest that Jesus offers (Mt 11:18-20) is pervasive inner transformation, and that there are specific small steps that "quietly and certainly lead to it" (10). Taken together, Willard's four books on the spiritual life provide[10] those of us seeking to nurture the spiritual growth of BMBs with invaluable insight into both the nature of the spiritual life and the processes that God has designed for nurturing and deepening

---

[10]Willard's *Living in Christ's Presence* (2014) was published several months after Willard's death. Though this book contains some valuable insights, it covers much the same ground dealt with elsewhere, so I will not consider it here. Similarly, *The Great Omission: Reclaiming Jesus' Essential Teachings on Discipleship* (2006) covers much of the same ground as his earlier books, though in different format. And though *Knowing Christ Today* (2009) is an insightful philosophical argument demonstrating that spiritual knowledge is real knowledge, it does not add to our understanding of spiritual transformation, so I will not deal with it here either.

the supernatural life of God in all of us, regardless of our pre-Christ background. I believe that the truths about human nature and spiritual reality elucidated by Willard can apply in any cultural or religious context.

The central thesis of *The Divine Conspiracy* (1998) is that being a disciple of Jesus in "the Kingdom of the Heavens" is what the Christian life is all about. We live our lives on earth in the kingdom, which we enter into and live in by grace. In living this life of supernatural grace we are steadily transformed into the likeness of Christ. We become the kinds of people who naturally do the deeds characteristic of kingdom life. "The teachings of Jesus in the Gospels show us *how* to live the life we have been given through the time, place, family, neighbors, talents, and opportunities that are ours" (284). Willard suggests that there are three things that we must do to become disciples: ask, emphatically and repeatedly, to see him more fully as he is in order to become like him; dwell in Christ through the Gospels and put into practice everything we learn; and decide that we are going to become disciples (295-99). He further suggests three necessary elements if we want to be disciplers of others. (1) We must be intentional disciples ourselves. (2) It must be our conscious, implemented objective to help others become disciples. (3) We must enthrall people with a powerful vision of life in the kingdom in fellowship with Jesus (299-305). Willard then underscores a crucial task: "*To enable people to become disciples we must change whatever it is in their actual belief system that bars confidence in Jesus as Master of the Universe. That is fundamental and must be taken as an unshakable conscious objective by any maker of disciples*" (307, emphasis in the original). This advice is particularly important in discipling BMBs. We must understand what they believe (as a result of their Islamic heritage and cultural background) and then guide them in a process of learning that effectively deals with their inappropriate understandings.

Several things distinguish Willard's approach to discipleship from that of those we have discussed so far. Willard has a sophisticated spiritual and psychological understanding of what it takes to empower real and lasting change. He stresses that discipleship is a process of learning to walk by grace in relationship with the Father. In his emphasis on the need for people to have the actual hindrances to understanding and loving God removed, Willard advocates an approach to discipleship that is adaptable to any cultural context. Willard does not give much specific guidance (he avoids, happily, long lists of things to do and teach) on what to do in discipleship programs. He avoids getting bogged down in practical questions which, in any case, need to be dealt with uniquely in each context. Willard imparts a positive vision for the potential of fruitful discipling and empowers disciplers to work out the specifics in their particular contexts.

In *Renovation of the Heart* (2002), Willard goes one step further and lays out a simple, clear design for personal and corporate spiritual transformation through spiritual formation. The intention of spiritual formation is to "bring every element in our being, working from inside out, into harmony with the will of God and the kingdom of God" (93). In the first third of the book, (chaps. 1–5) Willard explains that spiritual transformation encompasses all of the six basic aspects of the person: thoughts, feelings, choices, body, social context and the soul (30). Willard has a good deal of insight into the nature of the soul:

> [The soul] is the deepest part of the self in terms of overall operations; and like the body, it has the capacity to operate (and does, largely, operate) without conscious supervision. . . . The soul is that aspect of your whole being that *correlates, integrates,* and *enlivens* everything going on in the various dimensions of the self. It is the life-center of the human being. (37, 199, emphasis in the original)

The reliable pattern of spiritual change: Vision, intention and means (VIM). One of the most helpful things Willard elucidates is what he calls "the reliable pattern" of spiritual change. This is the general pattern of personal transformation that applies to every area of human endeavor, including that of spiritual transformation (2002, 85). We must, first, have an accurate vision of life in the kingdom; we must, second, decide or intend to become Christ-like; and, third, we must know the way to do it—we must have the means (85-91). He suggests using the acronym VIM (meaning strength and vigor) to remember this unvarying pattern, which is vision, intention and means. VIM thus gives us an organizing framework for designing the components of any program of spiritual formation, including those that are cross-cultural. The key element in discipling BMBs, which has, in my experience, too often been lacking, is an accurate understanding of the means that are needed in order to yield fruit in ongoing, long-term transformation.

In the second section of *Renovation of the Heart* (chaps. 6–13), Willard offers rich insight and helpful practical suggestions on how to pursue and experience transformation in every part of our beings (thoughts, feelings, choices, body, social context and the soul). He fleshes out how VIM works in our lives and communities. Although this guide to personal and community transformation is addressing Western contexts, Willard is dealing with the essence of spiritual processes that are, I believe, transferable to Muslim contexts.

The interpretation of spiritual development that Willard presents in *Renovation of the Heart* is not mechanistic or minimalist and differs profoundly from the perspectives characteristic of the modernist discipleship paradigm that dominated the last half of the twentieth century. He does not ignore the need to be practical and detailed, but he insists that the details of living a life of obedient discipleship are to be worked out in each context. Rather than setting out a discipleship program, Willard challenges us to individual and corporate self-examination in order to discern which areas need to be transformed and then encourages us to figure out, with the help of the Holy Spirit, what needs to be done to change, and then get at it, empowered by grace (254-55). This is a transferable strategy for spiritual change rather than a non-replicable program.

The value of the spiritual disciplines for discipling BMBs. Our examination of recent evangelical treatments of the spiritual disciplines and of Willard's vision for spiritual transformation provide important resources in understanding how to help BMBs grow into spiritual maturity. Any psychologically sound approach to discipleship ought to include use of the spiritual disciplines. As is true with most approaches to discipleship, the spiritual disciplines do not function well when they are understood to be a program of spiritual formation. Sadly, lack of understanding of and instruction in the spiritual disciplines has for far too long constituted one of the primary weaknesses of most contemporary evangelical and modernist approaches to discipleship.

At the same time, however, a significant limitation of both modernist discipleship and spiritual disciplines is that neither of them appears able to deal with the challenges of spiritual warfare and demonization. One of the primary concerns I have about the discipleship vision developed by Willard is that he seriously underestimates the power of demonic oppression and, perhaps due to lack of direct exposure to it, does not directly address this spiritual challenge in any of his books. In the late 1990s, I taught a group of workers about the value of the spiritual disciplines. A response from one experienced colleague was that many BMBs are so bound by demons at the time of their conversion that they are unable to exercise the self-control needed to practice any of the disciplines. He suggested that the disciplines could be of value only after a process of deliverance and inner healing had brought about some degree of psychological and spiritual freedom. The story of Ahmed, told at the beginning of this chapter, suggests that in some cases at least, my colleague was right. We did not have the authority in Christ necessary to deliver him from serious demonization.

I devote chapter twelve to the topic of demonic oppression, but it is important to point out here that the strong spiritual opposition sometimes encountered in Muslim contexts can put a significant constraint on the fruitful practice of the spiritual disciplines. In *God at War: The Bible and Spiritual Conflict* (1997), Gregory Boyd develops a compelling theology of spiritual warfare in which he contends that conflict between God and the powers of darkness is a dominant theme throughout the Scriptures: "Where the Kingdom of God is being spread, the kingdom of darkness will be most at work. . . . The atmosphere of the world is diabolical, with the enemy persistently seeking to find an entrance into the believer's heart" (278, 279).

How then does the practice of the spiritual disciplines relate to deliverance ministry? Though deliverance is often crucial in setting believers free to grow in their faith, I believe that lasting deliverance for individuals best occurs in the context of a vital corporate experience of spiritual nurture, which includes the spiritual disciplines. A community of disciples that is strengthened through appropriate exercise of the spiritual disciplines will possess the spiritual authority and discernment needed to deal effectively with any demonization encountered. Furthermore, it is the prayer and support of a vibrant Christian community and the establishment of good individual disciplines that enable a formerly demonized person to grow strong in faith and permanently overcome demonic oppression.

5

Historical Understandings of Spiritual Formation in the Church

And they devoted themselves to the apostles' teaching and fellowship, to the breaking of bread and the prayers. . . . And all who believed were together and had all things in common. . . . And they were selling their possessions and belongings and distributing the proceeds to all, as any had need. And day by day, attending the temple together and breaking bread in their homes, they received their food with glad and generous hearts, praising God and having favor with all the people.

ACTS 2:42, 44-47

[Spiritual] theology is Christian doctrine interpreted and applied by a teacher of prayer, together with the mental and physical disciplines which nurture and support it. . . . It is the key to the art of living as fully, creatively, and indeed joyfully, as mankind is capable.

MARTIN THORNTON,
ENGLISH SPIRITUALITY

TWICE NOW I HAVE BEEN A PART of academic communities in which the regular chapels contributed in quite powerful ways to my own and our community's spiritual health and vitality. Twenty-five years ago I was part of an Episcopal academic community, and part of the student life there were daily morning chapels that used readings and prayers from the Book of Common Prayer. As the weeks progressed during that year, I found that the daily prayers and Scripture helped form a strong sense of being in a community that was conforming itself around Scripture in humble believing prayerfulness. Now at Houghton College I am once again in an academic community that pauses three times a week for chapel services. Participation in these thrice-weekly times of worship, in addition to our regular weekly worship in our local church and weekly small-group meetings, are shaping me in ways that I am increasingly seeing as significant. In both cases, being a part of intentional Christian communities has profoundly deepened and enriched my Christian experience.

In North Africa I also saw the spiritual impact of weekly meetings containing warm fellowship, worship, Bible study and prayer. In my second year in the country, I made contact with two young men who had studied the Bible by correspondence and had identified in some way as new believers. A young believer and I began spending eight to ten hours every Saturday with these two men. We would drive and find a private spot in a nearby forest or beach and would spend two or three hours together. We would sing together, do an inductive Bible study and then share needs from our lives and pray for each other. After several weeks, one of these men asked if his friend Ali could join us, even though he was a self-described atheist. Ali was a law student in university, and he joined us every week for four or five weeks as we continued the routine just described. He said very little and asked no questions but fully participated, looking up the texts and reading them himself as we discussed them.

Then one evening, after we had just completed studying 1 John for a month, we were visiting in a café and Ali told us that he wanted to join and become a disciple of Jesus with us. He explained that in Islam he had never seen love, respect, openness and genuine seeking after truth that he saw in our little weekly group. He simply knew that the message of the gospel *had* to be true because it bore fruit in such loving ways in the lives of four young men. As Ali joined in with the regular weekly meeting of the body of Christ he encountered the Holy Spirit present in our midst. That weekly time of intimate sharing, study and worship affected him as he recognized the presence of God in our midst.

How does my experience in intentional Christian communities and Ali's story relate to this chapter's topic—historical understandings of spiritual transformation in the church? As we will see, one of the biggest lessons I learned from my study of the ancient traditions of spiritual transformation was that individual participation in regular, carefully planned corporate worship has, for centuries, been one of the cornerstones of spiritual transformation for Christians across Orthodox, Anglican and Catholic traditions. In a small and informal way together with Ali, we experienced the spiritual power of corporate gatherings with the written Word open and our hearts open to God together. The power of corporate worship learned well since the earliest centuries of the church was experienced by a little group of five men sitting on a blanket in a forest in North Africa.

Opening the door into the history of Christian spirituality unveils a vast literature and wealth of Christian learning and spiritual experience. Suddenly the superficiality of much of our (especially my own) contemporary understanding and spiritual experience is revealed. My initial introduction to much of this material was Richard Foster's survey of what he calls "The Great Traditions" in *Streams of Living Water* (1998). Foster arranges the centuries-rich array of Christian traditions into six main streams of devotion: contemplative, holiness, charismatic, social justice, evangelical and incarnational. Further understanding of the vast historical panorama of diverse approaches to nurturing spiritual maturity has been gained through studying historical overviews and analyses of Christian spirituality and reading some of the ancient and contemporary writers in these traditions.[1] We will limit our exploration to representative perspectives from Orthodox, Benedictine and Anglican traditions. These approaches to spiritual nurture have profoundly influenced major branches of the church for multiple generations. As I hope will become evident in what follows, our efforts in discipling BMBs can be enriched as we draw upon the time-tested ways that these often ancient traditions have understood spiritual transformation and practiced spiritual formation.

SPIRITUALITY IN THE EASTERN ORTHODOX TRADITIONS

Writers within Eastern Orthodox traditions see the first six or seven centuries following the end of the New Testament era (that is, the patristic period) as the time in which the correct, or orthodox,[2] understanding of both theology and spirituality were developed. Thus, contemporary Orthodox writers believe, with somewhat plausible historical merit, that their Orthodox theology and understanding of spirituality is, in fact, the correct understanding because it was developed by the early church fathers who were close enough to the time of the apostles to have authority to make permanent judgments on many matters—decisions that should hold for all subsequent developments in the church. Orthodox writers go back to what they view as the authoritative theology and practice developed and affirmed in the seven truly ecumenical, or international, church councils held in the fourth through eighth centuries.[3]

Bulgarian Bishop Photti of Triaditza describes Orthodox spirituality as a living tradition that supports ongoing authentic experience of Christ in his people through its correct doctrine (Siromahov 2012, 7). Orthodox spirituality's vision is that every man and woman living their normal

---

[1]The historical surveys by Boa (2001), Chan (1998), McGrath (1999), Holt (1993), Mursell (2001), Thornton ([1963] 1986; [1959] 1988) and Woods (1989) were helpful in understanding these historical currents in spirituality.

[2]The English word *orthodox* appears in the 1580s via late Latin *orthodoxus*, from the Greek *orthodoxos* ("having the right opinion," from *orthos*, "right, true, straight").

[3]Delegates from all branches of the church participated in these seven ecumenical councils (the later councils also included the Celtic and Irish churches). These councils spanned 450 years and were as follows: Nicea in 325, Constantinople in 381, Ephesus in 431, Chalcedon in 451, Constantinople II in 553, Constantinople III in 680-681 and Nicea II in 787 (Holt 1993, 52-53).

lives will experience the power and transforming presence of Christ through the Holy Spirit as their ordinary experience. The main characteristics of Orthodox spirituality are that it is Christ-centered, trinitarian in emphasis and experience, church-centered (one can know Christ only within the church) and mystical and ascetical (Hierotheos 1996, chap. 1).

Having adopted many of the traditions developed in monastic communities in the early centuries, Orthodox worship and devotion is closely tied to the liturgical prayers and traditions in the church community. The idea is that a disciplined and regimented corporate and individual prayer life enables people to keep focused on Christ and his will. One is taught to pray throughout the day, at set times and in set ways. Private personal prayer is informed by and surrounded by public liturgical prayer. There is a daily cycle of prayer[4] that is integrated into a weekly cycle,[5] which is itself all part of an annual cycle of prayer and Scripture reading[6] that has been passed on from the early centuries. This pattern of public and private prayer built around the reading and praying of the Scriptures is often known as a rule.[7] The expected fruit of this structured corporate and personal prayer and Scripture reading is that the normal Christian, living in such an intentional community, will experience the transforming presence of the Holy Spirit throughout each day.

An important part of the Orthodox approach to individual spiritual

---

[4]This consists of the evening service of Vespers, the morning service of Matins, the four services of the Hours (sunrise, 9 a.m., 12 p.m., 3 p.m.), the Compline service (before going to sleep) and the midnight service. Each of these prayer services focuses on a different aspect of the life of the biblical revelation and the church and Christ. For example, Vespers focuses on creation, sin and salvation in Christ, the Hours focus on the coming of the true Light (Christ), descent of the Holy Spirit at Pentecost, the crucifixion, and the death and burial (based on Salmas 1998, 1-2).

[5]The weekly cycle sees each day having a special focus for the daily prayer cycle in it. For example, Sunday focuses on the resurrection, Tuesday honors John the Baptist and all the prophets and Saturday focuses on the martyrs and ascetics and all who have gone before in the race of the faith (Salmas 1998).

[6]The annual cycle begins September 1, a tradition begun by Constantine in the early fourth century. Similar to the perhaps more familiar Anglican church calendar, the liturgical year has movable and immovable feasts.

[7]The term "rule," derived from the Latin word *regula,* as used in works on spiritual theology, refers to this regular daily, weekly and annual pattern of devotion and work, which is used to guide a monastic community or other group of Christians seeking to work together to bring spiritually guided order to their daily routines.

life and devotion is the "quiet" contemplative tradition.[8] Mether explains how a central aspect of this contemplative tradition, centered prayer, is meant to operate:

> One is to try to pray with all one's thought, feeling, and attention focused on the prayer even at the stage of verbal prayer. But such as we contra-naturally are, we do not have the power to attend fully . . . nor the right attitude or feeling and any attempt on our part to emotionally try to feel the right feeling is imagination. We must work solely with focusing our thought (by stilling) and attention, and then, the prayer will teach us what to feel, how to worship, and elicit the appropriate response from us if and only if we are participating seriously in the ethical [action] and liturgical life of the Church as prior and contextual conditioning. . . .
>
> Make no attempt to feel what one thinks one should feel. That is the role of the Holy Spirit through the Services, Psalms, Prayers, and Hymnography of the Church. Instead, noting one's distraction, irritability, pain, (pseudo-spiritual) passional concern over what to feel, and inattention, try again to just attend. Listen. (Mether 1998, 6, 7)

According to Mether, Orthodox, biblically true, spiritual experience is relational to the core—it is "ultimately and inescapably interpersonal communion. . . . The entire substance of the spiritual life of the Christian is relationships. It is all about improving the quality of how well you relate to others: God or neighbor" (4-5).

A distinctive of Orthodox spirituality in this quiet contemplative tradition is the important role that the Jesus Prayer—Lord Jesus Christ, Son of God, have mercy on me a sinner—has in spiritual experience. The use of the Jesus Prayer as a tool for centering in on Christ is consistently advocated as a way to calm and focus the mind to attend to Christ's presence. The Jesus Prayer works correctly only when it is used within the context of ethical action and in participation in the life of the church. Further, the Jesus Prayer is in itself a plea for mercy that encapsulates the core reality of our spiritual condition as understood through Orthodox

---

[8]This contemplative tradition is known by its Greek name, Hesychast (pronounced "hessy-cast"). The word *Hesychasm* means "quietness," so I call this the quiet contemplative tradition in the discussion in the text here to avoid confusion that may come by using the Greek terms.

biblical doctrine. We are forgiven sinners who are now in relationship through Christ with our neighbors and with God. Used rightly, in the context of ethical action and the church community with its correct doctrine and worship, it is a powerful tool to help produce valid personal encounter with Christ through the Holy Spirit (Mether 1998, 6).

As a way of wrapping up this brief introduction to Orthodox understanding of spiritual growth processes, I want to mention some of the ways in which Orthodox writers distinguish their approach to spiritual nurture from Protestant and Catholic traditions. According to Hierotheos, the central difference between Orthodox spirituality and all Protestant and Catholic spiritualities is that, put bluntly, "Orthodox spirituality is God-centered, whereas all others are man-centered" (1996, 1). Hierotheos argues that Western theology is based on rational thought whereas Orthodox theology emphasizes direct encounter with God. "We accept faith by hearing it not so that we can understand it rationally, but so that we can cleanse our hearts, attain to faith by [a 'vision of God'] and experience the Revelation of God" (Hierotheos 1996, 2). Hierotheos describes Protestant tradition as salvation obtained through believing in God, as a matter of accepting truth. In contrast, Orthodox theology sees salvation as transformation and becoming like Christ by grace. Unless faith cures the soul, it is not true faith. Salvation is experiential participation in the uncreated energy of divine grace. It is far more than right belief (Protestantism) or rational faith (Catholicism) (Hierotheos, 3-7).

According to Orthodox quietness spirituality, spiritual experience has to be grounded in both orthodox doctrine and membership in the right (Orthodox) church, and it is nurtured through active worship, prayer and participation in the daily, weekly and annual life of the liturgically shaped Christian community. It is inconceivable that true spiritual growth and maturity could be attained by anyone apart from the church and from the true experience of the Holy Spirit that alone comes through participation in the living church tradition. A valid Orthodox psychology of spiritual growth is only conceivable as the experiential outworking of living and worshiping within the community of the (Orthodox) faithful.

What lessons from Orthodox spirituality can be applied to discipling

BMBs? It is clear that in the Orthodox vision of spiritual life the idea that a convert to Christ could grow strong apart from the true Christian body is unthinkable. Thus, spiritual nurture, growth and survival for all BMBs in Muslim contexts would be assured only for those believers who join themselves to Orthodox communities. Although, as a Protestant, I do not accept the distinctive "rightness" of the Orthodox traditions and doctrine, I believe that the teaching that the spiritual life can exist and grow only within small "o," orthodox Christian community is of vital importance. Further, I agree with the Orthodox understanding of spiritual nurture, which teaches that Christian spiritual growth and maturity must be inherently trinitarian, and thus communal and relational, and grounded in the local Christian community. And because the Christian life is so much more than merely right belief, it would be valuable to draw on the tradition of the Jesus Prayer in teaching BMBs how to regularly enter into the presence of Christ in individual private prayer. Such encounters with the living God will help bring about the kinds of individual transformations that the Christian life promises.

AUGUSTINE'S RULE AND MONASTIC COMMUNITY

Augustine of Hippo (354–430) is primarily known among Protestants for two remarkable books, his *Confessions*, the autobiographical account of his conversion, and *The City of God*, his magisterial exposition of the relationship of the kingdom of God to the world and its systems. He is less often renowned as the author of his own monastic rule and for being the founder of several monastic communities (see Augustine [397] 1984).[9] Yet, the Rule of Saint Augustine is the oldest extant Western monastic rule, written in about 397, predating that of Saint Benedict (c. 530) by 133 years. It had a major impact on the Rule of Saint Benedict, and in many ways it established the foundation for much that followed (Van Bavel 1984, 4-6).

So what does Augustine's rule consist of? The rule is short (only twenty-four pages in the masculine version and fourteen pages in the

---

[9]Thornton firmly places Augustine together with Saint Benedict as the founder of Western monasticism, although he makes no specific mention of Augustine's rule ([1963] 1986, 44-47).

feminine), saturated with scriptural texts and reads like an oral summary of already familiar guidelines for living in community. The goal is to create a community where people share everything in common and there is no needy person among them (as in Acts 4:32-35). Augustine sets forth principles by which a Christian community can successfully operate according to the practice of love. "According to Augustine, therefore, a monastic community should offer an alternative by striving to build up a community that is not motivated by possessiveness, pride and power, but by love for one another" (Van Bavel 1984, 8). The tone of the rule is fatherly and gentle. Augustine is setting forth a series of exhortations, many of which are quotations of Jesus and the apostle Paul, which, if followed, will enable all of the members of the community to live in harmony. Augustine himself lived as part of the community that he ran, even while he was a bishop. He lived a very simple lifestyle in community with others called to live in Christian community.

The sole aspect of the Augustinian monastic ideal that I want to highlight is the strong emphasis placed on community. The hope that Augustine brought to the creation of his monastic community was that those who are serious about following Christ and obeying his teachings can be considerably helped by living together in a community where everyone is striving together to live according to the truth and power of the gospel. He believed that when people live in an intentional community, they would be constantly challenged to live in such a way that their natural sinful bent toward selfishness would be thwarted. He believed that living in a committed community helps individual growth in personal holiness. This stress on community as the locus of spiritual formation is something that we have not encountered in the contemporary literature on discipleship. It is this emphasis on the importance of living in community that also marks the Rule of Saint Benedict, to which we now turn.

BENEDICT AND THE BENEDICTINE APPROACH TO SPIRITUAL NURTURE

Who was Saint Benedict, and what kind of a rule did he establish?

Benedict (c. 480–547) lived in Italy as the Roman Empire was falling apart. Disgusted with the paganism he saw in Rome as a young man, he renounced the world to live in solitude in a cave. Some monks asked him to be their abbot, and the development of Benedictine communities followed. The rule has had an incalculably huge impact on Western Christendom up to our own day. The rule is known for its balance and moderation. Emphasis is on building community, and the role of an abbot is more that of a father than of an autocrat. Saint Benedict's rule is longer than that of Saint Augustine, yet it is still quite short, with an introduction and seventy-three short chapters in just seventy pages. The first seven chapters cover spiritual doctrine, the next thirteen concern liturgical form and the remaining fifty-three chapters are concerned with practical matters pertaining to living in community (in the Fry edition, 1998).

Benedict established a daily rhythm of prayer, study and work that was permeated with the Scriptures and prayer. Most believe that the reason that the Benedictine way continues to attract so many and be so influential is that it sets forth a positive vision of a community focused on Christ. Esther de Waal, in her application of the rule of Benedict to twentieth-century urban Christians, says that the rule's aim "is to establish a life that can be lived after the Gospel . . . a life that is earthed in Christ" ([1984] 2001, 34). In reading the rule, I was struck by how devotedly Benedict sought to live every detail of his daily routine in a way that glorified Christ. Though I do not expect many BMBs or evangelicals to be called to monastic life, the central themes of the rule are of value to every Christian, regardless of their life calling: community, obedience, humility and contemplation.[10]

It is impossible for one who has not lived in a monastic community to appreciate fully the power of living according to a rule such as that of Saint Benedict. In a monastic community, the Benedictine rule

---

[10]This summary of the central themes of the rule is taken from Thomas More's preface to the rule (xv-xxv). Other summaries focus on such things as listening to God, balance between work and prayer and the three vows of obedience, stability and daily conversion (Parish of St. Benedict Ealing Abbey, 2012).

structures daily life around five to seven corporate times of prayer and Scripture reading.[11] Between the daily sessions of corporate worship, the community carries out its life of work and study. Each monastic community finds its own way of being self-sufficient through the work or industry it pursues. Silence is generally kept apart from when the monks gather for worship. The life of a Benedictine monk is shaped outwardly by Scripture, worship and work, in loving cooperative community.

The community life sought, and sometimes experienced, in this kind of monastic tradition can be very attractive. Yet, the kind of set-apart community that is created in a Benedictine monastery is beyond the reach of most Christians, whether living in the West or in the Muslim world in the twenty-first century. It is in adapting the Benedictine rule to everyday life that the value of the Anglican spiritual tradition, which we now turn to, can best be seen. It is an application of the Benedictine ideals to the normal life of a working person encumbered with work, family and community responsibilities.

THE BOOK OF COMMON PRAYER AND ANGLICAN UNDERSTANDING OF SPIRITUAL GROWTH

As mentioned at the beginning of the chapter, during my year studying in an evangelical Anglican seminary I experienced daily chapels in which we used the prescribed prayers and Scripture readings of the Book of Common Prayer to shape and give content to daily worship. Seldom have I experienced such a rich and expanded prayer life (corporate and personal) as I did during that year. We prayed ancient prayers aloud in unison with reflective reverence, read Scripture devotionally organized according to the liturgical calendar, celebrated festivals such as Advent, Pentecost and Lent and generally found our

---

[11]The websites of two communities suggest some of the variation among Benedictines and Trappist abbeys. One Benedictine monastery in England has its seven prayer times at 6:00 a.m., 7:35 a.m., 9:00 a.m., 12:45 p.m., 4:00 p.m., 6:35 p.m. and 8:00 p.m. (Parish of St. Benedict Ealing Abbey 2012). The Trappist Abbey of the Genesee, close to my home in New York, meets to recite a similar set of prayers and Scripture chanting at 2:25 a.m., 6:00 a.m., 11:15 a.m., 4:30 p.m. and 6:40 p.m. (Abbey of the Genesee 2012).

lives shaped around the events and truths of the Gospels in a way I had never previously experienced. In my attempt to understand and better appreciate Anglican approaches to spirituality more fully, I studied the writings of Martin Thornton. The following discussion draws primarily on three of his principal works: *English Spirituality* ([1963] 1986), *Christian Proficiency* ([1959] 1988) and *The Heart of the Parish* (1989).

What then are the significant features of Anglican spirituality according to Thornton? As was the case with the Orthodox understanding, Thornton argues that all spiritual practice must be based on correct biblical theology and understanding of God and human nature. Following Saint Benedict, Thornton also stresses the trinitarian nature of God and spells out the practical consequences of the incarnation for Christian spiritual experience. Here is his description of spirituality: "A 'spiritual' life is one in which the spirit of God, sought and nurtured in prayer, controls its every minute and every aspect" (Thornton [1963] 1986, 16). Thornton teaches that every truth flowing from the incarnation must have a practical outcome in human experience such that correct doctrine will result in authentic spiritual experience. His definition of "spiritual theology" stresses this relationship between creed and deed: "[Spiritual] theology is Christian doctrine interpreted and applied by a teacher of prayer. . . . It is the key to the art of living as fully, creatively, and indeed joyfully, as mankind is capable" (Thornton [1963] 1986, 24, 25).

What does this spiritual proficiency look like, and how is it achieved in Thornton's version of Anglican spirituality? Echoing much that is found in Orthodox and Benedictine teaching, Thornton argues that the framework for growth in Christian proficiency consists in living within the church's authoritative rule of the spiritual life (Thornton [1959] 1988, 17-24). Thornton repeatedly stresses that private prayer (the third element) can work only as a means to grow in grace when it is a part of Christian community experience balanced with both corporate worship of the body of Christ, which has the daily morning and evening prayer services, and the celebration of communion with Christ (Thornton 1989,

205-7). Thornton explains how these three essential elements interrelate in the intriguing analogy of a fence:

> We are constructing a fence—to keep the devil out of the garden of the soul.... This carefully constructed fence of the spiritual life is built around a series of big strong posts, firmly embedded in the ground, and placed at regular intervals; these represent the . . . [regular communion services], which acts as the central support of all else. A more numerous series of smaller stakes, embedded in the ground and placed at more frequent intervals between the main posts are the . . . [daily corporate prayers and reading of Scripture]. Finally there are a number of horizontal, parallel cross-pieces which may vary in number, size, strength, or material, which link up the verticals and which are dependent upon them: this is private prayer. (Thornton 1989, 206)

In his discussion of the Anglican rule, Thornton stresses that the daily liturgical worship must be followed carefully. He believes that the organization of Psalms and other Scripture reading, and the prayers that go with them, must be kept according to the prescribed content, order and shape of the Book of Common Prayer with no alteration.

To complete this concise portrayal of English spirituality several further points need to be noted. First, it needs to be emphasized again how strongly Thornton teaches that it is orthodox theology that is the root and ground of all orthodox spiritual practice. Thornton shows how the three core doctrines of the Christian faith (the Trinity, the incarnation and the church) point to and effectively demand a specific and structured practical approach to Christian spiritual growth and nurture. Spiritual practices are grounded and determined by who God is (triune), what Christ did (incarnation and cross) and who we are as members of the redeemed body (the church). It is these central truths that determine how we are to practice our Christian faith and grow in holiness and purity as members of the divine body of Christ on earth (Thornton [1959] 1988, 5-16).

Thornton's second main point is that local pastors (parish priests) need to be equipped to be effective spiritual directors—what we would call disciplers. He sees that the central responsibility of every pastor is to be a spiritual director—someone who can competently and wisely, under the leading of the Holy Spirit, equip, guide and mentor those who are willing so that they can grow mature and proficient as Christians. Such spiritual direction is essential if individual Christians are to grow in their local church community. In the final chapter of *English Spirituality*, Thornton offers a series of instructions as to how an Anglican spiritual director ought to go about the job ([1963] 1986, 290-302). This set of instructions shows a profound understanding of the nature of spiritual nurture, as well as a deep and determined commitment to ensure that a young Christian is nurtured within the tradition and teachings of the church. This spiritual guidance is done from within the church.

The final point from Thornton's approach, which is worth mentioning because of its application to the nurturing of BMBs, is his emphasis on the idea of a remnant.[12] Thornton develops the strategy of prayerfully choosing a core group of Christians who evidence a desire to grow deeper and then doing extra levels of training and mentoring with them (Thornton 1989, 248-54). For Thornton, this remnant focus is the central way that he sees the church being renewed. The remnant is "the very heart which recapitulates and serves the whole; in fact the complete Body of Christ in microcosm, and its relation to its environment is the relation between Christ and the twelve, to their world. This palpitating heart pumps the blood of life to all the body as leaven leavens the lump or salt savors the whole" (Thornton 1989, 23). In a very real sense, with Thornton's concept of the remnant we come full circle to where we began this chapter—to discipleship. Thornton's model is a tradition-enriched and theologically profound model of discipling a group of keen believers to grow into strong mature Christians who then become disciplers and influencers of others. Thornton advocates that this remnant group commit about six hours a week to devotional activities and to service in the community above that of the regular participation in the services of the local church. In so doing, they will grow mature and be models and influencers in the local church.

---

[12]In *The Heart of the Parish: A Theology of the Remnant* (1989).

Assessing the Contributions of the Three Orthodox Traditions

This discussion of Orthodox, Augustinian-Benedictine and Anglican approaches to spiritual formation has uncovered remarkable congruence on what I believe are the three major contributions that these traditions add to our understanding of the way that Christian spiritual growth and formation takes place. These three new elements are the strong emphasis on the close link between correct doctrine and correct spiritual practice, the insistence that true spirituality only exists within authentic Christian community (within the church) and the understanding of corporate spiritual discipline, or the rule, which systematically organizes one's day, week and year into regular corporate, church governed and centered patterns, by which the individual is saturated with Scripture, taught profound prayer and immersed in Christian community.

These three new, yet ancient, emphases combine to pull spiritual formation strongly away from the dangers inherent in unhealthy individualism that has often marked Protestant spirituality since the Reformation. The determination of correct biblical doctrine is based not so much on individual exegetical insight (though of course the Bible is the source) as on the received doctrine developed in the first centuries of the church. Right practice is arrived at through submitting to the wisdom of the first six centuries of Christian experience guided by the Holy Spirit, which is seen as normative for all three streams of the church. Community relational experience and commitment are at the heart of Christian spirituality, and it is impossible for anyone to experience this apart from being part of a local church that stands in theological continuity with the church universal. The third new element is the importance of a pattern of doctrinally coherent and liturgically shaped daily individual and corporate prayer, Scripture reading and worship. Participation in community worship according to such a rule means joyfully submitting oneself and one's praying to the accumulated wisdom of Christians through the ages. None of these three elements, which are clearly central to all three of these ancient traditions, were even hinted at in the evangelical understanding and practice of discipleship of the twentieth century, which has formed the foundation for our unsuccessful efforts to disciple BMBs. With these lessons from our reflection on these three ancient traditions in mind, we next seek to understand more clearly what kinds of processes need to be in place in order to help BMBs grow to maturity in Christ in the midst of their Muslim communities and societies.

6

CONTEXTUALIZATION AND DISCIPLESHIP
WITHIN MUSLIM COMMUNITIES

But you are a chosen race, a royal priesthood, a holy nation,
a people for his own possession, that you may proclaim the excellencies
of him who called you out of darkness into his marvelous light. Once you
were not a people, but now you are God's people; once you had not
received mercy, but now you have received mercy.

1 PETER 2:9-10

Those who say that Muslims cannot separate religion
and culture are ignoring over thirty years of successful C-4
contextualization throughout the entire Islamic world that has proved
that MBBs' new identity in Christ is so powerful that it does, in
fact, provide a new religious identity without the need to
sever their former cultural identity.

TIMOTHY C. TENNENT,
THEOLOGY IN THE CONTEXT OF WORLD CHRISTIANITY

WHEN MIKE ARRIVED WITH HIS young family in our North
African city, he was exceptionally well trained, having had considerable field experience prior to getting advanced theological and mis-

siological training. When he joined our multi-agency fellowship of expatriate church planters, Mike eagerly shared his vision for ministry. While doing graduate studies, he had researched Sufi brotherhoods in the country.[1] His church planting vision was to shape the fellowships of Christ followers that he expected God to give him into worshiping groups that shaped some of their devotional practices and group dynamics in imitation of those found in Sufi brotherhoods. He dreamed of seeing "churches" that would develop into thriving, multiplying groups, with a cultural-religious identity that closely resembled Sufi brotherhoods, while also being thoroughly Christian in theology and in identity with Christ. In short, Mike hoped to launch "Sufi-like" house churches that would be able to flourish and multiply as Sufi brotherhoods have flourished in North Africa.

It was not long before he was connected with a handful of young men in his neighborhood, who were already new believers, and he set to work discipling them and forming them into a "Sufi-like" house church. When he began sharing his vision with these young men, they were both unaware of the existence of Sufi brotherhoods and uninterested in trying to follow their devotional or group practices. They simply wanted to study the New Testament and grow in their understanding of what it meant to follow Christ. Thankfully, Mike laid aside his contextualized "Sufi" vision for the church and focused on teaching them how to learn from the Scriptures and how to live as Christians in their community.

This encounter with a more radicalized vision for ministry within Muslim society taught me that typically the dangers apparent in some radical experimentation in contextualization quickly fade when faced with on-the-ground ministry realities. However, I have since come to realize that in certain situations something does need to be said and done to address these dangers. Sometimes correctives must be attempted, and we need to clarify appropriate and inappropriate approaches to con-

---

[1]"Sufi" is the Arabic term used to identify Muslim groups that emphasize mystical aspects of faith, often stressing love for and mystical union with Allah. Sufis have rites that, with music, dance and chants, sometimes take them into a state of unconsciousness (ecstasy). Their rites are often secret and the brotherhoods often operate secretly. Sufism is a very widespread form of folk Islam.

textualizing.[2] Given the current controversies surrounding which approaches to contextualization are both biblical and missiologically sound,
it is important to explore the debated issues and clarify the approach to
contextualization that explicitly shape this book's vision for effective
BMB discipling in Muslim communities.

THE CONTROVERSY ABOUT APPROPRIATE CONTEXTUALIZATION

So many articles were devoted to and promoted insider approaches to
ministry in the *International Journal of Frontier Missiology (IJFM)* in the
first decade of this century[3] that the current editor decided that *IJFM* had
to limit considerably the number of articles devoted to insider movements (IMs). In early 2012 the website Biblical Missiology posted a controversial petition asking Wycliffe and SIL to stop removing the terms
"Son of God" and "Father" from their translations for Muslim languages.
SIL responded shortly afterwards denying that they supported such
translations (*Biblical Missiology* 2012a, b; SIL 2012). Further, in an unprecedented move in 2012, both SIL and Wycliffe asked the World Evangelical Alliance to mediate in the growing dispute about their translation
practices. They called for an external audit of their translation practices
in Muslim contexts (Hansen 2011, 2012). Clearly these issues are far from

---

[2]In early 2011 I helped assemble a small international team of missiologist and mission leaders
to begin what has turned into a series of Bridging the Divide consultations (BtD). At the time of
writing, the work of BtD continues, with the fourth annual consultation having been held in
Turkey in 2014. BtD is seeking to bring together face to face those who have radically differing
perspectives on how we are to minister inside Muslim communities. Our many goals include
de-dramatizing the emotive language that too often characterizes this debate; providing a safe
place where those with strongly opposing viewpoints can discuss the issues together and seek
better understanding; removing unhelpful misunderstandings; healing relational rifts; ensuring
that people born Muslims are fully involved in these discussions; preventing worse polarization,
and as much as is possible, working toward ministry models that remain, or return to, faithfulness to the Bible and historically informed and well-grounded principles of cross-cultural ministry. For more information, visit the Bridging the Divide website at www.btdnetwork.org.
[3]Nearly every issue of the *International Journal of Frontier Missiology (IJFM)* in 2006–2007 had at
least one article on contextualization in Islamic contexts. The majority were written by people
committed to or experimenting with more radical approaches to contextualization, such as
Brown (2007, 41-42) and Travis, Parshall, Hoefer and Lewis (2006, 124-26). *IJFM* also published
critiques of this perspective by Tennent (2006, 101-15) and Corwin (2007a, 5-20; 2007b, 53-55).
For further perspectives see the multiple published responses to both articles in *IJFM* 23:3; 24:1;
24:2 (2006, 2007).

being resolved. It is beyond the scope or purpose of this chapter to assess, let alone review, the various arguments in this ongoing and sometimes divisive debate.[4]

So, what is the debate about? There has long been debate between those who see the primary reasons for the difficulties in missionary efforts among Muslims to be the result of the ideology of the Islamic community, versus those who see the challenges as coming primarily from inadequate missionary methods. The first group argue that it is not surprising to see meager results and a high rate of attrition among BMBs, given the nature of Islamic communities and their built-in ideological resistance to the gospel and often violent opposition to all those who choose not to believe in Muhammad or who leave Islam. The second group tends to believe that a more thorough adaptation of approaches to the Islamic contexts will yield far more lasting fruit in ministry. Their conviction is that the primary cause for the limited response of Muslims to the gospel comes from approaches to Muslims, such as extractionism, that are not sufficiently adapted to Muslim social and ideological concerns.

Despite strongly differing perspectives on the cores issues, proponents in both camps agree that there must be appropriate contextual adaptation, in Islamic contexts, of both the way that the gospel is communicated and the shape of the church. They also agree that it is important for

---

[4]The earlier *Evangelical Missions Quarterly* (*EMQ*) discussion on contextualization (see below) continued, with a bit less intensity than in the *IJFM* in the first half of the first decade of the new millennium. See, for example, "A Biblical Look at C5 Muslim Evangelism" (Woods 2003) and "Lifting the Fatwa" (Parshall 2004). Also see "Misunderstanding C5: His Ways Are Not Our Orthodoxy" (Massey 2004c).

For more recent *EMQ* articles, see a provocative short article on some of the core contextualization questions, "Contextualization: A Few Basic Questions" (Waterman 2008). In one article, "Muslim-Friendly Christian Worship" (Hoefer 2009), one leading proponent of radical contextualization issues a deeply disturbing call for Christians to abandon vital Christian identity distinctives in public worship and rewrite the creeds so as to avoid offense to Muslims who misunderstand Christian beliefs and practices. He is calling for Christians to shape their worship as Dhimmis (those in submission to Islam)! In welcome contrast, Hyatt offered some helpful questions to ask to help missionaries to avoid syncretistic practices in "Christian Witness in Muslim Settings" (2009). Irwin expresses gentle but clear and uncompromising opposition to IMs in "Muslim Churches? Another Perspective on C5" (2011). In 2012 *EMQ*'s new Point/Counterpoint series published two articles together, one expressing strong opposition to IMs thinking and in particular, a strong critique of common ground consultants (McNeil 2012), and the other a response by Higgins (2012). Publishing these articles together helps to clarify some terms and positions. The debate continues within the pages of the *EMQ*.

the BMBs themselves, under the guidance of the Holy Spirit, to make the decisions about how to adapt their Christian faith to their local Islamic context. Everyone is striving to provide theological frameworks that will undergird flourishing, contextualized, Christ-centered communities inside Muslim societies.

Clearly, one's perspective on what is appropriate contextualization will influence the emphasis that one has in discipling and the way one disciples BMBs. This is borne out when reading the literature on ministry to Muslims. For example, Parshall (1985, 2003), Love (2000), Blincoe (1998) and Daniels (2005) all tend to emphasize the need for quite radical contextualization in order to help limit hostile reaction from the Muslim community and make possible some sort of a movement to Christ within the Muslim community. They are aiming for the creation of a significantly contextualized church community or insider movement and typically expect the discipleship to be taken care of without much outside involvement. They report, with considerable praise to God, whenever they believe that this has begun to happen.

In contrast, though acknowledging the importance of sensitively contextualized witness and church life, people such as Adeney (2001, 2002), Garrison (2004), Hawatmeh and Muller (2003), Jabbour (2007), Livingstone (1993), McCurry (2001), Muller (2006) and Sinclair (2006) emphasize the need for effective teaching and support to help BMBs through the inevitable hardships that their conversion to faith in Christ will bring. They generally view Islam in a more negative light and believe that one of the primary tasks of discipleship is to help Muslims leave behind the teachings and habits of their old faith and replace them with appropriate, mature discipleship to Christ, while staying as closely connected to their Muslim family and communities as possible.

Reasons for Not Embracing Insider Movement Approaches

In practice, it seems that the goals of missionaries across the contextualization spectrum are very similar, even though it is sometimes expressed in very different language. All are seeking to help establish followers of

Christ and see churches or movements of BMBs sensitively adapted to the local culture by the BMBs themselves. I profoundly empathize with all efforts to see communities of Christ followers flourish within Muslim communities. All of us work and pray toward seeing flourishing communities of Christ followers inside Muslim lands. This emphasis on believers creating new communities is vital. As I have already stressed, an essential component for fruitful discipleship is that new believers immediately become part of strong, believing communities (churches) because much of the discipleship process takes place uniquely within community. Those in all contextualization camps agree that the formation of communities of believers that relate in healthy ways to their Muslim context is crucial for seeing multiplication of churches.

It is also true that, regardless of ministry model, everyone stresses the importance of yielding to and being guided by the Holy Spirit and continuing to be shaped by his written Word in one's mission practice. People in both camps also affirm that we can and must trust the Holy Spirit to look after and mature those who are truly seeking to obey Jesus. Gilliland exhorts us to look primarily at the long-term direction of worshiping communities in evaluating their soundness:

> But in time, the direction these churches take will help to remove ambiguities. Those who are captive to Satan will be seen for what they are, blatantly syncretistic. If in time they resist fellowship with redeemed people, do not accept the greater message of the Bible, or refuse to enter into or participate in biblically valid power ministries, they have identified themselves as outside of the kingdom. (2000, 336)

Though I agree with Gilliland, that ultimately the outcomes of our methodologies will eventually be seen in how the Holy Spirit chooses to bless or abandon the ministry, I do not thereby believe that we cannot decide which approach best lines up with scriptural teaching and healthy missiological precedent. I believe that unhelpful syncretism is more likely to develop, because it is already there in the theoretical foundations, when one adopts an insider movement approach.

For example, in a visit to the Middle East in 2008, I talked with a few people who are trying to launch a new insider movement in one country. These men studiously avoided suggesting to the new believers that they are forming churches, and they did not discourage them from continued involvement in the mosque or from continuing to identify themselves as Muslims. Though I was much encouraged at the apparent rapid growth in numbers of conversions to Christ (more than a dozen in just a few years) and the readiness that the new believers demonstrated to share their newly discovered love of Jesus with members of their social networks, I had a number of deep concerns. They were the high esteem that the workers had for the Qur'an and for Muhammad, the efforts to dissuade new believers from all contact with local churches and the adamant assertions they made to Muslims they dealt with that they were not seeking to have anyone leave Islam. In light of mission practices such as these, I continue to have strong hesitations about radical approaches to contextualization and attempts to launch insider movements. This chapter concludes with three reasons for being cautious about embracing such radical approaches to contextualization.

An inadequate understanding of the nature of conversion. First, I believe that this approach has an inadequate understanding of conversion, both in the sense that they are sidestepping clear New Testament teaching and models about the nature of conversion and that they are ignoring the very typical psychological reality of what conversion means for a Muslim who encounters the living God in Christ. In his doctoral study of conversion, Greenlee pays particular attention to how conversion works in the Muslim world. He is generous in his assessment of insider movements, suggesting that it is difficult to judge such movements from the outside. Nevertheless, Greenlee presents a strong vision for conversion and how the biblical account of conversion works in the real world (2007, 67-84). Greenlee reminds us that

> we cannot fully understand Christian conversion. It is a mystical, miraculous, merciful work of God. Coming to faith in Christ is not something that can simply be boxed away as a psychological phenomenon or a social function characteristic of certain societies, as some secular observers might suggest. It is something that can only be comprehended with the insight and revelation given by the Spirit of God. (2007, 98)

In my experience it is quite rare to find people who have chosen to believe in and obey Christ who want to continue to call themselves Muslims or continue to attend a mosque. None of the twenty-three BMB leaders whom I interviewed continued to think of themselves as Muslim in any way. Most Muslims I have known who have come to Christ walk away from Islam without much more than a backward glance. The only two men that I knew deeply who had trouble letting go of Islam following their conversion proved in time to have not been solidly converted and eventually reverted to Islam or lost their faith. Most BMBs see themselves as having been liberated from an oppressive religious system that they suffered under for years. While church planting in North Africa, all suggestions made to BMBs that it might be a good idea to attend their local mosque in order to reach out to their Muslim neighbors were met with incredulity.

Of course, not all former Muslim followers of Christ have this perspective. Insider advocates often argue that the reason that BMBs see things this way is due to the way they have been discipled. John Travis is typical:

> A growing number of MBBs and CBBs are now favorable towards insider movements, but few of them are able to attend missions conferences, discuss missiology in English, or write English-language articles. My understanding is that they support insider approaches, not because some missionary pushed the idea, but because they sense the Lord's leading in this direction. We have met a number of MBBs who say that if they had known, when they came to faith in Christ, that it was possible to retain their official religious identity, then they would have gone in that direction. Many of these Christian MBBs are now working in support of existing [insider] communities or to help new ones be birthed. (Corwin 2007a, 17-18)

Yet, all the Muslims I have known who have come to faith in Christ have instinctively felt that they had to leave the religious life (not their social and cultural identities) of their community because it contained core values that were no longer consistent with their new identity in Christ.[5] They felt that the light of their new faith in Christ could not

---

[5] Through the Bridging the Divide consultations, mentioned earlier, I have recently met a handful of Muslims who have preferred to remain a part of their Muslim religious community as believers in Christ. These personal acquaintances are a result of our ongoing efforts to bring such be-

remain inside the darkness of continued Muslim religious practices. One BMB, originally from Saudi Arabia, expressed his hesitations about insider movements to me in a private email. He concludes his long biblical critique of IMs with these penetrating words:

> There is a line between being in your culture and engaging your culture, and crossing the line to bow down to your culture and putting the priority on that above God's Word and his name. From what I can see, the line is getting crossed or at the very least blurred.
>
> I know this is a very touchy topic with many. I am not attempting to dishonor those who poured out their heart and life to serve the Lord among Muslims, rather, I am questioning the new methods and new approaches being utilized among them. It almost seems that we elevate Islam above all other belief systems in such a way that we almost want to please them.
>
> When I left Islam, I paid a heavy price. I lost everything. However, I gained my salvation and eternal life. I am not ashamed of the gospel of my Lord who took my shame on the cross. I am not weak, for his strength is all I have. He is an able and willing God, and ALL things are possible for him. (email to the author, October 22, 2008, name of the writer withheld)

What is more, most disciplers working with BMBs have found that believers must totally renounce the religious system of Islam and everything associated with it in order to obtain freedom in Christ to live as whole and healthy human beings. Writing in response to Chandler's portrayal of Mazhar Mallouhi as a Muslim pilgrim of Christ who seeks to preserve his Muslim social identity (Chandler 2007), Mostafa S., another Middle Eastern BMB, responds:

> Seeking to continue to live inside the Muslim family structure is commendable, but it also tends to weaken my new Christian identity. When I try to do that, I end up living as an alien: I am neither a Muslim nor a Christian. Trying to keep the old identity makes you lose both identities. I will need to sacrifice something very important. *Islam never provides a personal identity like the one Jesus Christ gives.* Islam provides a murky and

---

lievers into the conversation about contextualization. Nevertheless, these few personal connections have not influenced my sense that such attitudes are rare and unnatural.

nationalistic identity that does not bring about any good, even though we have searched for its value for years! (2008, 30, emphasis in the original)

The spiritually dark and oppressive nature of Islam. The second reason that I hesitate to endorse the view that it is good for believers in Christ to continue to identify themselves as Muslims and remain within the religious community of Islam is that Islam is a false religion and people need deliverance from it, not help to remain within it. Islam is simply not true: it is not a revelation from God and Muhammad was not a prophet. Nor is it good for anyone to remain within this oppressive religious system once he or she has seen the light of Christ and has a way out. It sometimes happens that in his mercy God works in people while they are still Muslims to give them some truth through the Qur'an, which he then uses to lead them to Christ and to the God of the Bible and then out of Islam. For example, God often uses the incomplete and inaccurate portrait of Jesus given in the Qur'an to give people a desire to know more about this amazing prophet, Isa, who healed the sick and raised the dead. This is all good, but I believe that in balance, the harm wrought by Islam to most Muslims far outweighs the good that God can bring about in using it to draw some Muslims to himself.

Let it be clear when I say that there is very little good in Islam, I am *not* saying that there is very little good in Muslims. Islam is the religious ideology and orthopraxy that Muslims generally follow, but it is not them. Neither am I denying that which is very clear to all observers— that Islam is not monolithic or the same everywhere. Indeed, we are witnessing, in our time, a growing struggle among Muslims to determine which vision of Islam has most authority in representing true Islam. Understanding this battle for the soul of Islam is increasingly the concern of Western political and intellectual leaders because jihad is one of the central driving forces behind Islamic terrorism. BMB humanitarian and scholar Patrick Sookhdeo argues persuasively that jihad is central to the nature of Islam:

Unless the militant interpretation of Islamic sources is recognized as the basic cause of Islamic terrorist activities, there is little hope of a lasting solution. . . . As long as moderate Muslims do not acknowledge that there is a problem within Islam itself, not just with a small minority of Islamic radicals, there is little hope of change. . . . If Western politicians, media, church leaders and others continue to acquiesce with the assertion that religion is not a factor in terrorist violence and therefore that Islam need not change; it is difficult to see how peace can be achieved unless the whole world is under the rule of Islam. (Sookhdeo 2007, 424, 427,428)

More moderate Muslim spokespersons, who are usually based in the West, try hard to persuade Westerners that Islam need not be characterized by violence, lack of civil rights, the oppression of women, and so on. The title of one book well expresses the struggle that moderates face: *The Great Theft: Wrestling Islam from the Extremists* (Abou El Fadl 2005); they need to assert that true Islam is not extremist and convince everyone, and especially most Muslims, that true Islam is not what the Islamists say it is.[6] However, they face an uphill battle because the actual text of the Qur'an, along with centuries of mainstream Sunni and Shiite traditions (in both Hadith and commentaries), support the Islamist version of Islam much more than they do the modernist pro-democracy versions of Islam taught by moderate Muslim imams and academics. Even if it were granted that moderate versions of Islam have a more solid Qur'anic basis than Islamist versions, they still promote deeply anti-Christian principles, which when followed faithfully (as in countries like Jordan and Morocco), yield deeply-rooted social and political oppression of all minorities. One BMB expressed this succinctly: "Both radical and moderate Islam kill; one kills the body and the other kills the mind."

Things appear even worse when we read some of the books critical of Islam by former Muslims, such as Ibn Warraq's *Why I Am Not a Muslim* (1995) and *Leaving Islam: Apostates Speak Out* (2003). Here is one

---

[6]In this book, Abou El Fadl presents a penetrating historical analysis of how the groups whom he calls "Muslim puritans" have become so influential in recent decades. He argues that the strong influence of these puritans is a new and rare phenomenon: "This is perhaps the first time in history that the center of the Islamic world, Mecca and Medina, has been under the control of a puritanical state for such a prolonged period of time" (2005, 102). Though his interpretation of Islam is much more reassuring than Islamist alternatives, it has plenty of significant problems as well. Few non-Muslims would want to live under the vision of humanity and human life that his version of moderate Islam mandates.

statement from this articulate Muslim apostate and atheist that illustrates the often merciless nature of Islamic civilizations:

> The horrendous behavior toward women, non-Muslims, heretics and
> slaves manifested in Islamic civilization was a direct consequence of the
> principles laid down in the Koran and developed by the Islamic jurists.
> Islamic law is a totalitarian theoretical construct, intended to control
> every aspect of an individual's life from birth to death. (Warraq 1995, 2)

I find Ibn Warraq's critique of Islam, the Qur'an and Islamic civilization
quite compelling. Other books written by moderate Muslims (e.g., Manji
2005), BMBs,[7] other atheist apostates (Ayaan Hirsi Ali 2007, 2010) and
non-Muslim scholars who are opposed to Islam[8] all point to the same
disturbing truth about Islam's pervasive dark side and negative impact
on people under its influence and control. Given the often disturbingly
dark nature of Islam as an ideological and social system, one cannot
justify encouraging believers to remain submitted to the ongoing abusive
power of Islam in their lives. It is difficult to approve of insider approaches that encourage followers of Christ to remain within the
mosques and under the authority of their Islamic communities for a
prolonged period.

Insider vision for discipleship does not align with the New Testament.
The third and primary reason for rejecting the thinking of insider proponents is that so much of what they are advocating seems to go against
a reasonable and responsible reading of the New Testament. Tennent has
argued that the exegesis and application of key New Testament passages
by insider movement proponents in support of their approaches is very
often unsuccessful. He suggests that key texts that proponents use to
defend pro-insider positions can be read as possibly supporting an ap-

---

[7]Refer to Caner and Caner (2002); Gabriel (2002, 2003); Solomon and Alamaqdisi (2006). These
BMBs have penned strongly written critiques of Islam. All of them were imams and Muslim
academics before their conversion to Christ. They have very little sympathy for Islam and portray
it in a very negative light. I believe it is prudent for those who know Islam only from the outside
to listen well to the voices of those who were once Muslim leaders.

[8]Though not focused exclusively on Islam per se, Pryce-Jones's analysis of what is wrong with the
Arabs, in *The Closed Circle* (1989), shows that most of their problems can be laid at the feet of
the religion that most live by.

proach that does not attempt to give Muslim forms new meanings (2007, 202-10). He further argues, with considerable justification, that (1) many such writings tend toward theological reductionism by embracing a minimalist understanding of the gospel; (2) the theological analysis of pro-insider writings tend toward an individualized and privatized faith, rather than expressing a robust biblical ecclesiology; and (3) they tend to elevate the personal experience of Muslim believers' experience of Christ over the content of the apostolic proclamation (210-16).

I have found that the examination of discipleship in Islamic contexts clarifies many of the issues around contextualization in ministry to Muslims. Studying discipleship, rather than merely conversion, helps clear up the fog surrounding this debate. Miriam Adeney helpfully explains that the necessity of discipleship ought to influence our theology of religion and view of contextualization:

> If discipleship is central in our Lord's last words, a Christian theology of religion surely must ask whether religions enhance discipleship of Christ. . . . As long as evangelicals remain fixated on the question of whether someone can be "saved" through another religion, our theology of religions will remain superficial. After all, who knows what God's Spirit does or does not do in human hearts? But if we enlarge the question to whether someone can grow to maturity in Christ in another religious context, whether someone can become a full-fledged disciple of Christ while worshipping in another faith, then the limitation of other religions and value of missionary work become clearer. Does Islam facilitate discipleship? I suggest that Islam impedes discipleship in doctrinal, communal and sacramental areas. (2001, 77, 79)

This critical truth will be seen clearly as we discuss some of the biggest obstacles to effective discipleship in Muslim contexts, and how to help BMBs flourish within their Muslim communities in the face of these challenges.

In addition, it is crucial to observe that the picture presented in the New Testament is of people joining churches that stand out because of their countercultural public commitment to Jesus Christ as Lord. Though primarily operating as house churches, and thus, at times, somewhat below the radar of the Roman authorities, the typical picture we have of churches in the New Testament was that believers strongly identified themselves as members of Christian communities, and in so doing experienced frequent persecution and opposition from the community stakeholders (refer to 1 Peter). Building one's mission ecclesiology on an overarching desire to have believers in Christ maintain their Muslim community identities in order to extend their witness for Christ in their communities seems to me to be an unhelpful and biblically unsupportable church planting objective.

Again Adeney helpfully articulates the significance of Christian community for the discipleship of believers coming out of Islam:

> Disciples are not lone rangers. Relationship is at the heart of the doctrine of God. . . . A call to fellowship is at the heart of the doctrine of the church. . . . How profoundly Muslim-background believers yearn for inclusion in the people of Christ! They long for brothers and sisters. They ache to be members of that great company of faith that has stretched down through the ages. . . . Christians dare not bring a gospel of individualism. They must bring a gospel of kingdom community. Whatever form it takes, discipleship needs community. . . . Religion is more than what happens within oneself. Religion requires relationships. To pass the faith to the next generation requires a vital community. And Islam itself clearly cannot provide a Christian the community she needs. (2001, 80-81)

It is because of the need to disciple BMBs into strong Christian communities that I am hesitant to endorse insider approaches to contextualization. Though many of these brothers and sisters are highly esteemed, one is led to conclude that their approach to ministry among Muslims is not consistent with the New Testament and presents too many serious risks to commend as a suitable approach to ministry.

THE GOAL SHOULD BE CHURCHES WITHIN MUSLIM COMMUNITIES, NOT INSIDER MOVEMENTS

For these three reasons, then, I cannot go along with Insider approaches to ministry among Muslims: their unsatisfactory theology of conversion, the oppressive and ideological nature of Islam and an understanding of discipleship and the church that I believe is inconsistent with the biblical witness[9] and the experience of the church throughout history. Therefore, I am firmly in agreement with Schlorff when he states:

> The emergence of "a people movement to Christ that remains within Islam" is not a legitimate objective from the biblical standpoint. . . . I believe that the future of evangelical missions to Muslims lies with that approach that views the objective in terms of bringing Muslims into the kingdom of God as Jesus preached it; including leading them to faith in Christ, training and mentoring them in Christian discipleship and leadership, and gathering them into distinctly Christian flocks that retain social and cultural ties with Muslim society as much as possible, but without outwardly remaining Muslim. (2006, 146-47)

It is this goal of evangelism, discipleship, church formation and leadership training, in ways that are appropriately adapted culturally by the BMBs themselves, that forms the missiological foundation for this present study of discipleship. The discipleship in Islamic contexts that undergirds this research is one that sees our ministry task as evangelizing and then discipling BMBs into thriving, multiplying churches that stand boldly in authentic culturally appropriate witness for Christ inside Muslim communities and societies.

The goal is not to start insider movements. The explicit discipleship goal envisioned in this book is to disciple in such a way that BMB disciples are able to stay within their networks of families and the Muslim communities in which they live whenever possible. The vision of this book is the discipling of new believers and the planting of churches that express uncompromisingly bold and culturally appropriate witness for Christ by believers and churches that remain inside Muslim communities.

---

[9]It is outside the scope of this chapter to explicitly argue the case for this claim that the insider approaches are *inconsistent with the biblical witness*. There are many Scripture texts (such as 1 Corinthians 9:19-23; John 4:1-42; Acts 15) that proponents of insider movements cite in seeking to find biblical support. It is *very important* to them, too, that they not base their ideas on mere strategies of convenience or utility. However, I remain convinced that IM proponents are, perhaps inadvertently, mishandling and wrongly applying these texts. I cannot accept that their ideas find compelling support in the Scriptures. For the biblical case for this conviction I refer you to the numerous published articles that deal with the details of exegesis and hermeneutics of the key texts under dispute, beginning with Tennent (2007, 202-16) cited above.

7

The Goals, Processes, Roles and Stages in Discipling BMBs

But we were gentle among you, like a nursing mother taking care of her own children. So, being affectionately desirous of you, we were ready to share with you not only the gospel of God but also our own selves, because you had become very dear to us. For you remember, brothers, our labor and toil: we worked night and day, that we might not be a burden to any of you, while we proclaimed to you the gospel of God. You are witnesses, and God also, how holy and righteous and blameless was our conduct toward you believers. For you know how, like a father with his children, we exhorted each one of you and encouraged you and charged you to walk in a manner worthy of God, who calls you into his own kingdom and glory.

1 Thessalonians 2:7-12

There is risk of every kind involved in the cause of winning and discipling new believers. . . . To say it is costly is too trite; it might cost you your life. The result of your love and commitment to your disciple is that a bridge of trust is established and the disciple will respond to your leadership and teaching. . . . The most important thing in the life of the discipler is to have the heart to do it. Where there is such a heart, there will be a way. You will find a way.

In discipling, we know the ultimate goal is God Himself, being recreated in His image, yes, being indwelt by Him. . . . All other aspects of discipling revolve around this central goal of Christ living in us. This is what we communicate, to teach, and to build into the lives of young disciples. They must see the radiancy of the indwelling Christ in us. We, by the power of the Spirit, engender this in our disciples.

DON MCCURRY,
HEALING THE BROKEN FAMILY OF ABRAHAM

IN 1993 MY NEXT-DOOR NEIGHBOR Adam suddenly came to faith in Christ after having had dreams and visions of Jesus (Isa) over a five-year period. I immediately launched into an intense discipleship relationship. For a few years, my life seemed scarcely my own as I walked alongside Adam and several other BMB friends, seeking to encourage them into maturity as together we helped launch a BMB house church. Those years of intense ministry, sustained and guided by the Holy Spirit, were anything but orderly and reasoned. Through that experience discipling Adam, I have learned that discipling a BMB is often like teaching someone to swim in the ocean in the middle of a fierce storm.

Successful discipling is much more art than science, but the best disciplers are themselves disciples who have a profound understanding of what they are about as they disciple in the midst of the storm. Everyone's approach to discipling BMBs is profoundly, and often unconsciously, shaped by what one thinks discipleship is and how one understands the spiritual growth process. Much of our failure in discipling comes from flawed, often implicit, understandings of discipleship that lack biblical, spiritual, psychological, social and cultural validity. We need to reflect on the nature of discipleship in order to move from somewhat flawed implicit assumptions to explicit studied understanding that can improve our practice of the art of discipling.

The biblical, historical and missiological perspectives on the meaning and processes of discipleship discussed in the first six chapters set the stage for this chapter's examination of discipleship that draws on analysis of face-to-face interviews with seventy-five seasoned disciplers with extensive experience in discipling BMBs in diverse Muslim communities.[1] We first consider the nature and goal of discipling and examine how it is that BMBs mature—what kinds of processes are involved? We then consider the roles of disciplers and conclude with an exploration of the stages through which BMBs often pass on their journey to maturity.

THE GOAL AND MEANING OF DISCIPLESHIP

Many have offered helpful definitions of discipleship and the goal of discipleship in the life of a believer and in the fellowship of believers. As was seen in chapter four, Dallas Willard believes that being a disciple of Jesus in "the Kingdom of the Heavens" is the essence of the Christian life. He teaches that we live our lives on earth in the kingdom, which we enter into and live in by grace. Over time, we become the kinds of people who naturally do the deeds characteristic of kingdom life (1998, 284).

Horst Pietzsch, writing out of his experience discipling BMBs in Africa, stresses the central role of Christian community when he says that the goal of discipleship is "to integrate them into Christian fellowship and to lead BMBs to become mature disciples of Christ, so that they accept responsibility for themselves and make wise spiritual and practical decisions" (2004, 11).

Roland Muller also stresses the importance of community in discipling BMBs. He points out that, for Muslims, conversion to Christ and joining the new community of believers is an intertwined experience. "Many of those from shame-based culture . . . will want to be accepted by the community of believers in Christ. They usually want to check out this aspect of following Christ before they make any rash decisions. And so they will start to check out the Christian community" (2006, 323). Ac-

---

[1] Interviewees had an average of eleven years of experience and have discipled, on average, forty-four BMBs. A full description of the demographics and experience of interviewees, as well as a description of the research design and methods of analysis, can be found in appendix A.

cording to Muller, personal faith and discipleship must develop in the context of community or it does not occur at all. "The message and the community are usually one and the same" (328).[2]

Most of those writing on church planting are less explicit about what they see as the objective of BMB discipleship. Gene Daniels (2006) views the objective as having communities of BMBs who live in obedience to Isa within a new Christian community that bears witness to the surrounding Muslim community as being authentically local and yet spiritually attractive.[3] Greg Livingstone sees the objective as a mature community of believers who demonstrate Christ by their Christ-like lives and mutual love. They are to be contextualized in their expression of faith so that they seem normal and natural, yet demonstrate a supernatural reality not found in the culture (1993, 203). Phil Parshall does not deal with individual discipleship. Instead, he focuses his attention on ways of ensuring that the believers and the local church are able to be as naturally "Islamic" as possible. His goal is to have groups of believers who blend in significantly into Muslim society but who exhibit godliness and love that draw Muslims to them.[4]

David Garrison's understanding of discipleship is part of his vision for local, multiplying churches within movements. The goal is to produce reproducing disciples who evangelize fearlessly, disciple new believers and grow into becoming pastors and trainers of pastors (2004). Kevin Greeson, who also focuses on launching church planting movements among Muslims, sees discipleship as part of the process of equipping

---

[2]Though Muller strongly emphasizes the need for Muslim seekers to be welcomed into the believing community prior to their conversion, he does not call this welcome into community discipleship. The person is still a seeker and will remain so until he or she makes a personal faith commitment to follow Christ. At that point, people become insiders in the community rather than merely warmly welcomed outsiders. As was noted in the introduction, both evangelism and discipleship need to be community focused and carried out in community. But they are not the same thing.

[3]This summarizes Daniels's perspective in his narrative on church planting among Muslims in Central Asia.

[4]Parshall's work is immensely valuable to all of those seeking to see the church established in the Muslim world. However, he focuses more on cultural and theological issues related to implanting contextualized groups of Christians effectively into Muslim societies than on individual discipleship (see Parshall 1980, 1985, 1994a, 1994b, 2003). In his book on ministering to Muslim women written with his wife, Julie (2002), there is one chapter on discipling BMB women.

new believers to understand their faith and share it with others as they plant churches.[5]

With these understandings of discipleship having set the stage, let us turn now and look at how experienced disciplers understood discipleship. The first thing I asked was that interviewees give their functioning definition of discipleship: "Give me your quick one- or two-sentence definition of what it means to disciple someone."[6] Quite a few people stressed that it was not primarily doing Bible studies with someone, but rather, it was living one's life as a friend of and model for the BMB. As can be seen in table 7.1 below, the definitions of discipling BMBs given most were ones that stressed whole life involvement of the discipler with the one being discipled. The most frequently given definitions were: investing one's life and time in the BMB disciple and modeling Christ to them, teaching the basics of the Christian faith and life and how to live as a Christian disciple and helping change their behavior so that they live increasingly in ways consistent with the call of Christ. The expectation expressed is that disciplers will share their lives with their BMB friends with the aim of seeing new believers learn how to live like Christ and demonstrate significantly transformed and increasingly Christ-like behavior.

Probing the demographic details of the answers suggests,[7] somewhat surprisingly, that there was little significant difference between the answers given by Westerners and non-Westerners, or between answers given by BMB disciplers compared with other disciplers. There appears

---

[5]In his first book, *Camel Training Manual*, Greeson devotes an appendix to discipleship (2004, 118-38). In his second book, *The Camel* (2007), he has no discussion of discipleship.

[6]The complete list of questions asked during the interviews is in appendix B.

[7]Interviewees sometimes gave several definitions. The answers in table 7.1 cover 95 percent of the definitions offered. In this and all other tables in this book, it is important to understand my method of analysis. Most questions were open-ended, and when people give three or four different responses, they were all noted. In analyzing the responses and arranging them in tables for presentation, I analyzed the range of answers given and categorized them according to meaning. This means, for example, in table 7.1 that 149 responses were given in the nine slightly different definitions offered even though only 75 people were interviewed, and not everyone answered every question. The analysis was of the answers given, and there was little attention paid to what percentage of all interviewees gave particular answers. The total number of given answers is different in each table because the number of answers given varied from question to question and person to person.

to be a slightly nuanced but interesting difference in the answers given by men and women. In each of the top three definitions, men had a slightly higher percentage of the answers than women. In addition, women more often than men offered the two definitions at the bottom of the table (being a friend and persevering with BMBs). These defini-

Table 7.1. Definitions of Discipleship

Definitions of Discipling	Total	Regional Background		Religious Background		Gender	
		Global South	West	BMB	Other	M /50	F /25
1. Investing one's life and time and modeling Christ	36	19	17	13	23	25	11
2. Teaching basics of Christian faith and life and how to live	29	16	13	9	20	21	8
3. Change behavior, to live in the way of Christ	27	14	13	11	16	21	6
4. See BMBs through to maturity and ministry	13	7	6	4	9	8	5
5. Teaching them to study the Bible and apply it	11	8	3	6	5	7	4
6. Growing toward mature dependence on God	11	5	6	4	7	8	3
7. Help see them well integrated into a fellowship	11	6	5	3	8	8	3
8. Persevering with BMBs and never giving up	6	4	2	3	3	2	4
9. Being a friend who encourages growth and trust	5	2	3	2	3	1	4
Total Who Chose Answer	**149**	**81**	**68**	**55**	**94**	**101**	**48**

tions stress the relational side of discipleship. Though this indicates that women, not surprisingly, evidenced a slightly greater sensitivity to the need for discipleship to be built on strong, supportive relationships, there is nevertheless quite strong agreement by both men and women that discipling BMBs involves pouring one's life into one's newly believing friends. In examining the definitions from the perspective of the years that interviewees had spent discipling,[8] there was an overwhelming

---

[8]There were numerous angles from which it was possible to do comparative analysis of responses. Effort was made to make comparisons that would be more valuable in providing insight for disciplers. Tables included in the text are chosen for their perceived value in elu-

pattern of more experienced people giving the first three definitions more than twice as often as those with less experience. Together, these patterns show a strong consensus that discipling best happens in the contexts of strong, intimate personal relationships.

One particular discipler, a non-Western woman who had discipled women for more than a decade, many of whom are now playing active roles in several BMB house churches, expressed this quite passionately:

> Discipling is pouring your life into new believers, sharing everything, to form them into Christ's image. You need to transmit what you have received until Christ is formed in them. In the Muslim world, it is not merely a matter of a program to run, but an intensive living your life with them. We have to do it as Jesus did, living with them and discipling them in the activities of their daily lives.

This is life-on-life mentoring. Because BMBs have not normally lived among people who model what it means to be a disciple of Christ before their conversion, the only way they can figure out what it is like to follow Christ practically is to get to know a disciple well enough that they can see how it works in a flesh-and-blood person. This BMB reality has given me a better understanding of what Paul was talking about when he called the believers in Philippians to "join in imitating me, and keep your eyes on those who walk according to the example you have in us" (Phil 3:17). As McCurry put it, "They must see the radiancy of the indwelling Christ in us. We, by the power of the Spirit, engender this in our disciples" (2001, 311). We can disciple others only as far as we have gone ourselves, and we must point those we disciple to Christ, even though they learn what it means to follow him initially by following our example.

THE PROCESS OF SPIRITUAL FORMATION AS UNDERSTOOD THUS FAR

What produces spiritual growth? Because we desire to encourage spiritual development and maturity in the lives of the BMBs with whom we

---

cidating key points of comparison. Including tables of every category analyzed would be a distraction.

walk, it is vital that we understand the kinds of teachings, activities and processes that result in growth. Inaccurate and unhelpful understandings of what contributes to growth can lead to much frustration and wasted time—both our time and the time of those whom we seek to disciple.

Before discussing the perspectives of experienced disciplers, let us recall some of the lessons learned in our earlier reflections on Scripture and church history. We saw that Paul believed that transformation occurs as we walk with the Spirit in loving fellowship with others in conscious imitation of Christ crucified, living lives of self-sacrificing selfless love together in community, even as Christ did. Luke sets out a similar vision of disciples trusting the Father and living their lives in loving community together, freely proclaiming the liberating gospel. This New Testament picture of the spiritual growth process envisions people growing by living together in Spirit-led and Spirit-graced communities.

In examining the spiritual disciplines, we saw that they can serve as a vital channel of God's grace flowing in us and transforming us. Spiritual disciplines are most effective when believers are living together in communities whose members have experienced deliverance from demonic bondage, when necessary, through the powerful work of the Spirit. Practice of the spiritual disciplines is vital in helping achieve genuine individual and corporate transformation when people live in genuine, loving, Spirit-empowered community.

We also discovered three valuable emphases in our survey of ancient and Orthodox understandings of spiritual transformation. First, it is important to adjust our life practices so that they are consistent with correct scriptural doctrine. One example is that our spiritual experience must be consistent with the relational reality of a triune God. Second, spiritual transformation happens only when people join communities and submit to the corporate life of a local body that is seeking to follow Christ together. The third insight was that it can be helpful to spiritual growth if we shape our individual and corporate lives around the events of Christ's life, in creating a rule, a structured rhythm of daily prayer and work.

While the first two lessons from church history are valuable, I believe that the transformation that the ancient traditions were seeking to create through living according to a rule is accomplished only among people who live as members of communities empowered by the Holy Spirit in which they love and serve under the leading of the Spirit. Seeking transformation through living according to a structured rule is putting the focus on an ineffective agent for transformation. God does not transform us primarily through our structuring our daily and weekly and yearly routines around the events in Christ's life. Individual and corporate transformation occurs in us when we live in joyous, mutual submission to the Spirit in the living body of Christ in a local church. Therefore, our efforts should be on nurturing genuine, Spirit-honoring communities, rather than on artificially structuring the use of our time around the events of Christ's life and ministry.

Bringing all these earlier lessons together, we arrive at a vision of a Spirit-empowered, individually disciplined and truly loving shared life, which experiences the rich flow of God's grace in and through the members of a loving community living together in imitation of Christ. We now turn to our discussion of spiritual transformation processes as they are understood by seasoned disciplers and see how much their insights express and endorse those seen thus far.

ELEMENTS IN THE SPIRITUAL GROWTH PROCESS VALUED BY EXPERIENCED DISCIPLERS

Conversations with disciplers sought to discover what people understood about the growth process. This was sometimes hard to get at because in many cases people had never previously thought about the issue of process. In asking about the growth process, I sought to elicit their underlying, often intuitive, understanding of spiritual growth processes. Not surprisingly, there were many kinds of answers—twenty-three in all. The analysis here focuses on only the twelve most frequently mentioned responses, which are given in table 7.2.[9] It is not surprising to see that the

---

[9]There is much rich data in the tables that present the outcomes from the interviews. The analysis of the data given in the text is often quite general and broad-stroke. The rich nuances among the responses seen in the tables, and later, the specific recommended practices received from interviewees, are often very helpful. Unfortunately, space does not permit much elaboration of the rich information summarized in the tables. The reader is encouraged to pause and examine the

two most frequently mentioned components of the discipleship process stressed relationships with others in a church. Eighty-one percent of interviewees stressed that BMBs must be in a church group whose members, preferably including other BMBs, know and trust them. It is intriguing

Table 7.2. Primary Factors Cited in the Growth Process

Primary Growth Processes	Total	Regional Background		Religious Background		Gender	
		Global South	West	BMB	Other	M /50	F /25
1. Committed to and in a church group, loved by other BMBs	61	32	29	21	40	41	20
2. Has a trusted discipler who models and mentors	45	26	19	16	29	32	13
3. Personally values, reads, studies and applies the Word	36	18	18	11	25	22	14
4. Learns to pray individually and daily	27	11	16	6	21	17	10
5. Receives targeted teaching in ethics and doctrine	23	10	13	8	15	18	5
6. Reaches out, witnesses and disciples others	22	13	9	5	17	15	7
7. Develops own walk with God in prayer, Word, etc.	20	10	10	4	16	13	7
8. Committed to grow and obey Christ at all costs	18	8	10	4	14	14	4
9. Understands and uses spiritual gifts in service	16	11	5	7	9	10	6
10. Confesses sin, has right relationships, reconciles	15	5	10	4	11	8	7
11. Embraces opposition and hardship as part of growth	14	6	8	3	11	11	3
12. Experiences that God is love — Christ gave his life!	10	8	2	7	3	5	5
Total in Category	**307**	**158**	**149**	**96**	**211**	**206**	**101**

to note how closely this ties in with the high importance given to living in community observed in our earlier reflection on discipleship in the New Testament and church history. Similarly, 60 percent also stressed that spiritual growth happens when the BMB has a trusted discipler or

---

detailed content of many of the tables. Some of the tables could be profitably used as the basis for ministry team discussions.

mentor modeling the Christian life for the new believer. The activities so often thought to be the main contributors to spiritual growth in Western evangelicalism, such as personal prayer, reading of the Bible and witnessing, do appear as a high priority here as well (points 3, 4, 6 and 7). However, they appear after the need for BMBs to be in relationship with other believers in a church community and the importance of being individually mentored by a more mature discipler.

Nevertheless, it is also important to appreciate the high priority that these experienced disciplers gave to BMBs developing their personal walk with God in prayer and in the written Word. In fact, responses 3 and 4, 7 and 8, and 10 through 12 all deal with personal encounter with God and with the truths of the Christian faith. Putting these seven responses together we find that experienced disciplers highlight the importance of developing a strong, intimate and personal walk with God. This personal spiritual life entails personal prayer, study and meditation in the written Word, a deep commitment to persevere in obeying God at all costs, readiness to confess sin and be reconciled with others, willingness to accept opposition and embrace hardships and a deep personal encounter with God as a God of love. Thus, even though this stress on individual and personal walk with God did not top the list as the most frequently mentioned element in the growth process, this aspect of the discipleship process accounted for more than half of all of the responses given.

This resounding emphasis on the importance of developing one's personal intimacy with God corresponds to what we will see (in chapter nine) as being one of the major challenges to effective discipling in Muslim contexts—the spiritual nature of the Christian life. For most Muslims, with the possible exception of Sufi Muslims, the experience of their Muslim faith is less about personal intimacy with God and internal heart transformation than it is about conformity to religious practice and care to not shame one's Muslim family and community by avoiding "un-Islamic behavior." As a result, when Muslims initially encounter Christ and begin their journey as disciples of Christ, the central role of a personal relationship with the Creator of the universe is often hard to understand. Most have few instincts to know what to expect or how to shape this new intimacy with God. It is therefore not surprising that experienced disciplers stress the vital importance of new believers developing personal and individual intimacy with God, as well as the importance of corporate experience of God within the church community.

As we saw in chapter five, this stress on the vital reality of personal encounter with God is also a central emphasis in Orthodox spiritual traditions, which teach centering prayer and contemplation as vital means of focusing on Christ. Orthodox spirituality expects individual personal encounters with Jesus Christ, by means of individual and corporate contemplation of Christ, to be the normal experience for Christians. This strong emphasis in the interviews on a personal intimate walk with God strongly resonates with the Orthodox teaching that the way to sustain and deepen personal intimacy with God is to practice centering prayer and other contemplative forms of prayer.

Continuing our reflection on the significance of the responses given in table 7.2, it is intriguing to notice, especially for those of us who tend to view discipleship as primarily teaching, that only four responses stress the importance of understanding the faith (3, 5, 9 and 12) and only one of these four involves instruction or teaching (5). Dallas Willard often stressed that an essential component in growing into maturity is having one's actual errors in thinking addressed and corrected through creative teaching that carefully targets specific misunderstandings of Christian teaching and the Christian way of living. One-third of the interviewees stressed this need to teach specifically to areas of typical weakness and common Muslim misunderstanding (response 5), and some even said that former Muslims need "de-programming" to unlearn Islamic misunderstandings. One important Christian truth that needs to be experienced in Muslim contexts is that God is really a God of love who personally loves the believer (response 12). BMB disciplers, in particular, laid emphasis on the importance of helping BMBs to encounter the God of love.

A few fascinating observations can be made about the demographics of the interviewees and the nature of their responses. Realizing that they were split equally among Westerners and non-Westerners, it is encouraging to note that there are very few differences in emphasis that would lead one to think that Westerners see things substantially differently from non-Westerners. It is true that I did notice slight differences in emphasis between the two groups, such as the slightly stronger emphasis given by non-Westerners to the importance of relational elements like being in church and having a personal discipler (points 1 and 2 in table 7.2). Yet, Westerners put a slightly stronger emphasis on the need for BMBs to learn how to keep strong relationships and be reconciled to each other by confessing their sins to one another (point 10). Non-Westerners put a slightly greater stress on the need for BMBs to put their faith to work in witnessing, teaching and using their spiritual gifts (points 6 and 9), although this was usually stressed by Easterners who worked in Western groups known for their emphasis on witnessing, such as Love Agape and Navigators.

This finding about the similar perspectives of Western and non-Western disciplers challenges the commonly repeated claim that Western missionaries impose a Western mindset and their cultural baggage on the people with whom they share the gospel. There is little in my research to support this oft-repeated charge. In contrast, it appears that the Western disciplers interviewed, most of whom had taken the time to learn the language and adapt to the culture of their host country, were so effective in adapting their approach to discipleship that it was virtually indistinguishable from the approach of their non-Western, Arab and Muslim background co-laborers.

That being said, did BMBs express different perspectives on what contributes to transformation than disciplers from Christian backgrounds? The only discernible difference was the already mentioned increased stress that BMBs put on believers needing to understand the love of God (point 12). There also appeared to be little difference between men and women as to how they understand the spiritual growth process. Men mentioned the importance of teaching (point 5), commitment (point 8) and willingness to persevere through persecution (point 11) more than women did, but the slight differences in emphasis were not marked.

What, then, according to the experienced disciplers interviewed, are the key elements that lead to spiritual maturity in believers coming to faith in Christ in Muslim contexts? For growth to continue strong the BMB needs to be part of a warm, nurturing and trusting group of believers who understand where they come from. Further, they do better when they have a close relationship with a mature believer who can model Christ to them and show them, through life and example, how to live as a believer. It is also vitally important for BMBs to develop a strong personal relationship with God and learn how to be in the Scriptures and in prayer personally. They must also share their faith with others from early on, taking every opportunity to tell others what they have learned, and they need to develop their spiritual gifting in serving others. They also need to receive teaching that enables them to renew their minds according to the truth of Scripture so that they are able to endure hardship and persecution knowing that God is a God of love who cares for them in the midst of their trials.

The final question pondered, in reflecting on the perspective of experienced disciplers, was whether those with more experience had different perspectives than those just getting started in discipling BMBs. Surprisingly, when I correlated the data according to discipling experience, there was almost no difference at all in their understanding of the discipleship process.[10] All three groups put church involvement, having a personal discipler and learning to grow through engaging the Scriptures as the top three factors. However, there were four items that experienced disciplers emphasized more than others: knowing and exercising one's spiritual gifts, practicing the confession of sin, keeping right relationships and sharing the gospel from early on.

Those who write about ministering to Muslims have not always recognized the vital elements of the spiritual growth process uncovered through this research and reflection.[11] However, several have highlighted some of

---

[10]Refer to appendix C, table A.3, for the table of comparisons based on discipling experience.

[11]When describing the spiritual growth process, many tend to assume the mechanistic process operative in what I have called (in chap. 4) modernist approaches to discipleship. It is one thing to have a clear objective for discipleship, but it is quite another to use the right means to develop maturity in new believers that reveal valid psychological and spiritual processes of growth and development. Having the right set of objectives does not mean that one will reach them simply

these key dynamics in their writing about BMB discipleship. Daniel Sinclair, for example, stresses both relationship and community while also emphasizing teaching and training. In a list of eight keys to effective discipleship, he includes the relationship that the discipler has with the disciple and the fact that BMBs must be discipled *into* communities:

> A discipler is not a substitute for the body of Christ. A vital component of a new believer's growing in obedience to Christ is obeying Him in regard to His teachings on the community of faith. Over the years, I have observed discipleship plans that involve working one-on-one only, keeping believers isolated from one another. I have never seen that approach succeed. (2006, 114-15)

Looking at it from a slightly different but very helpful perspective, Roland Muller also stresses the importance of community when he argues that for a BMB to survive and grow to maturity there must be a shift of identity from the old Muslim community to the new Christian community. The BMB must "come out"[12] and be known as one loyal to Christ within his or her family and community. A key part of the discipleship process is helping the BMBs bring the two parts of their lives together. Their new identity through membership in a Christian community must be reconciled with their former Muslim identity. They need to integrate their two parts into one so that they are known both as followers of Jesus by the Muslim family and as committed believers by the Christian community. BMBs' identity in their community significantly influences their own sense of core personal identity. Eventually, their personal faith commitment must line up with their public identity within their Muslim family and community. Muller exhibits a profound understanding of the community dynamics of discipleship and the necessity of ensuring that the BMB becomes closely identified by at least some

---

because one tries hard. To see examples of this prevalent tendency among missionaries to Muslims, see Love (2000, 210-11) and the third section of Jabbour (2007).

[12] This term is used here and elsewhere in the book in conscious reference to how this term is used by those who unveil their homosexual preferences. The sense of shame and dishonor that is often still associated with such an exposure of previously hidden sexual preference aptly expresses the shock and deep sense of shame that most Muslim families feel on learning that one of their members has become a follower of Christ.

from his or her own Muslim community as a member of the community or church of followers of Jesus out of Islam (2006, 93-106).

In situations where there is a highly visible ethnic Christian community, or some other publically visible Christian community (whether a minority or the majority, as in the West), I do not think it is necessary for believers to join or become publically associated with *this* community. When I speak of the importance of BMBs being identified as committed members of their Christian community by both their Muslim family and by their church, I am thinking especially of the community of believers. Such a community could be an underground house church or a larger movement of BMBs known only by those closely associated with it, even though it might not be widely known to the Muslim community generally.

A central imperative of appropriate discipleship in Islamic communities, then, is ensuring that BMBs can identify with, belong to and be discipled in a caring, believing Christian community. As was discussed in chapter one, baptism is a rite of passage into membership in the new creation community. If baptism takes place without resulting membership in a real community, then the transfer of identity is unlikely to hold for long. This is one of the main reasons why individual converts are best sustained in a Muslim society when there is effective church planting occurring at the same time. For the discipleship process to work well in the Muslim world, it has to include an effective and profound way of ensuring that the new believer makes a transfer of allegiance and identity into the new creation community of a local church. There is much debate about how to make this happen. However, most agree that authentic community is vital for discipleship to be effective in the Muslim world.

FIVE ESSENTIAL PROCESSES THAT ENSURE ONGOING SPIRITUAL GROWTH

Pulling all of these rich strands of experience and reflection together leads to the identification of five essential elements that enable BMBs to grow to maturity in their faith in Christ. Foundational to spiritual growth is each individual developing a strong relationship with God in which he or she experiences the power and guidance of the Holy Spirit who works ongoing transformation through a personal relationship with God. The next most important element for individual discipleship and growth in Christ-likeness is involvement in and commitment to a living local expression of the body of Christ. It is vital that this local church, led and empowered by the Holy Spirit, functions as a welcoming, loving community in which the corporate gatherings of the community express core biblical truths in the form and content of their larger and smaller gatherings each week and throughout the year. Added to personal relationship with God and vital community engagement, in Muslim contexts it is also vital to encourage the creation of personal mentoring relationships by which newer believers have intimate access to a more mature believer or believers from whom they can learn what it means to follow Christ. The fourth essential element is that believers ought to be individually and corporately obedient to the living Word through reading of and submission to the written Word. Fifth, believers need to be encouraged to identify and use their spiritual gifts and share their faith and serve others as soon as possible following their entrance into the body of Christ.

THE ROLE OF THE DISCIPLER

From the beginning of my discipling of BMBs twenty-five years ago, I often looked to the apostle Paul as a model and sought insights from the way he discipled or trained believers to shape my own role as a discipler. The passage in 1 Thessalonians that heads this chapter has been a primary source of inspiration in my understanding the role of a discipler.

> But we were gentle among you, *like a nursing mother taking care of her own children.* So, being affectionately desirous of you, *we were ready to share with you not only the gospel of God but also our own selves,* because you had become very dear to us. For you remember, brothers, our labor and toil: we worked night and day, that we might not be a burden to any of you, while we proclaimed to you the gospel of God. You are witnesses, and God also, *how holy and righteous and blameless was our conduct*

toward you believers. For you know how, *like a father with his children,* we
exhorted each one of you and encouraged you and charged you to walk
in a manner worthy of God, who calls you into his own kingdom and
glory. (1 Thess 2:7-12, emphasis added)

The highlighted phrases in Paul's self-description have been particularly
important in shaping my understanding of the roles of disciplers as they
walk alongside BMBs in their faith journey. Similarly, as seen in the quotation that heads the chapter, Don McCurry also understands the costly
nature of discipling in the way that the apostle Paul discipled.

In the interviews I did not directly ask about the role of the discipler.
However, the responses to my first question, asking respondents to
define discipling, elicited quite a number of definitions that addressed
the role of the discipler (see table 7.1). Three of the top nine responses
given (table 7.1, responses 1, 8 and 9) point to the role of the discipler as
one who invests one's life and time, modeling Christ and persevering
with BMBs as a friend and never giving up on them (51 of 157 responses).
One Arab pastor put this simply: "One must help the person know how
to follow Christ practically through sharing one's life and personally
demonstrating what it means to follow Christ."[13] An international BMB
leader from the Middle East, who has personally helped disciple more
than a hundred other BMBs, emphasized the need to invest one's life in
the BMB, seeking to mentor godly character in the disciple. He believes,
for example, that the discipler should spend a year with a new believer,
modeling and teaching him or her how to pray, read the Scriptures, live
according to the Word, make Spirit-led decisions, live lives of integrity,
and so on. He believes that a major weakness in the BMB movements for
which he is providing mentoring and leadership training is the lack of
personal discipling. Similarly, another experienced Arab BMB discipler
went so far as to suggest that a disciple must voluntarily submit himself
or herself to the influence of the discipler. Thus, the discipler is exercising
a kind of leadership over the disciple that has an enormous amount of

---

[13]This Christian-background Arab pastor in the Middle East has been discipling BMBs for more
than twenty years and has helped disciple some fifty BMBs.

influence. This relationship of authority is essential in seeing a new believer well discipled in the way of Christ. The disciple must be accountable to a mentor, or discipler.

The other primary role of the discipler that comes out in this first interview question is that of a teacher and trainer who passes on vital knowledge and trains BMBs to be disciplers and leaders themselves (47 of 157 responses). The stress in the teaching is on how to live as a Christian, rather than on Bible or doctrinal knowledge. Thus, there is an organic and natural relationship between investing one's life in the disciple and teaching him or her how to live as Christ would have that person live. The emphasis in this teaching is on how to walk with God and live together with other believers. Furthermore, those who mention the need to teach biblical truths and doctrine usually mention this after they have first stressed the need to be a personal mentor who knows the disciples well and is teaching them how to live as Christians. The context for teaching biblical knowledge is within a very personal mentoring relationship with a disciple. Thus, the role of a discipler is one of life-on-life transfer that includes instruction in how to read and grow through the Scriptures. The role of a teacher who teaches Scriptures is not typically viewed other than as a part of a fuller role as a personal mentor and model for the new believer.

This strong stress on the importance of the role of life-mentor is also emphasized by those who have written about BMB discipleship. Horst Pietzsch, the author of the only work devoted entirely to the subject of discipling BMBs, says that the discipler's role is to walk alongside the BMB, being a true brother or sister, friend and counselor. Like McCurry, and many of those with whom I spoke, Pietzsch also stresses the high level of commitment required from someone who disciples BMBs: "Once you decide to be involved in ministry to BMBs, be in it wholeheartedly. Commit yourself to make a difference in the life of a BMB for the Lord's sake. Reschedule your life and adjust your priorities to accommodate this ministry" (2004, 12). Haines expresses a similar sentiment: "True discipleship is friendship and mutual trust. Discipling finds its roots in Christ's love. The path to the mountain of success may cross the dark forest of the unexpected. Faithful prayer and persistent friendship, however, bring great fruit for God's Kingdom" (1998, 126). Similarly, Ron George stresses the need to walk with the disciple and vulnerably model what a true Christian is like: "Few of us are willing to open up our lives and live a transparent life so that the younger ones in the Lord see us in all our weaknesses and yet also see 'Christ in us, the hope of glory.' It is not our success and strength that reveal Christ, but the weakness and pain that we go through that show His life in us" (2000, 81).

Stages in the Spiritual Development of BMBs

Are there recognizable stages that BMBs go through as they mature that are similar across diverse Muslim world contexts? In one of the language schools where I worked, we shaped our teaching curriculum around four broad stages of language ability: beginner, intermediate, advanced and proficiency. There would have been no value in trying to teach the finer points of essay construction and complex sentences to low-level beginners. One had to wait until the students were in the more advanced levels before tackling such nuanced levels of the language. Similarly, I believe that there is potential value in understanding the stages that are typical in the spiritual development of BMBs. The discipling process will be more helpful when it matches its activities and priorities to the stages through which believers often progress as they mature in their new faith in Christ.

As a part of my visits with experienced disciplers, I asked them whether they had observed stages in the growth of the people they discipled. I was surprised that very few could identify distinct stages. However, seventeen people identified stages that BMBs passed through as they grew to maturity. I have synthesized the stage categorizations given by the seventeen people who had observed clear stages (from three to seven distinct stages). My understanding of the markers that indicated that people were passing from one stage to another, and what made a particular stage different from others, yielded the following set of four stages. I believe that these stages are typical of the development process through which BMBs pass as they mature.

These stages are not prescriptive but descriptive. People pass through these stages at very different rates and very inconsistently. Some will loop back to an early stage and, sadly, many never get beyond the first or second stage before fading away or reverting to their Islamic faith. What is more, everyone with experience discipling in non-Muslim contexts will recognize elements here that are typical for all disciples regardless of their contexts. A distinguishing factor in Muslim contexts is the extent and severity of persecution that new believers often face. The nature and extent of such oppression and persecution will significantly affect the way in which theses stages are shaped and experienced by both the disciple and the discipler.

> *Stage 1: Honeymoon*: The period of initial euphoria and joy, zeal and great hunger and thirst to grow and mature.
>
> - Must learn more of the differences between Christianity and Islam and have their prejudices against Christianity removed.
> - Women in particular feel valued through their new identity in Christ.
> - They are eager to learn how to pray.
> - They read and absorb the Scriptures rapidly.
> - They often also have fear and keep their faith hidden.
> - This stage ends when the first major testing hits them.
>
> *Stage 2: Consolidation and deepened commitment*: The period of testing and trials in which BMBs have to choose to persevere in their faith regardless of the cost.
>
> - They have to count the cost of continuing as a disciple of Christ.
> - The most common tests or spiritual attacks are disappointment with other believers whether expatriate, BMB or Christian-background local believers; opposition to their faith in Christ from friends and/or family; persecution, mild or severe, from family, society or police and government.
> - They may not say a lot about their faith to others during this stage.
> - The emotional high has gone and the believer is learning the disciplines of faithfulness to Christ and remaining committed regardless of trials.
> - Sometimes there needs to be some deliverance from demonic strong-

holds during this stage, to enable the breakthroughs needed for continued growth.

- Many BMBs do not survive this stage and back off from their new faith.

Stage 3: Looking beyond themselves: They develop a heart to witness to and serve others, often including their family, and they begin to minister to others.

- Their walk is increasingly steady, and they grow through perseverance. They are developing habits and attitudes that can take them through to maturity.
- They are active in their local fellowship serving wherever they can. They are increasingly active in sharing their faith with others.
- They can, and often do, begin to disciple other new believers at this stage.
- If not yet done, this is the stage where they finally "come out" and acknowledge their faith to their family and selected members of their close circle of friends.
- This stage may often have further trials and tests, but the BMBs are more able to handle them and are less shaken by social and spiritual opposition.

Stage 4: Life of ministry and service: For some, there is a further development to the point that their lives become increasingly focused on ministry and service.

- This is the stage that BMBs can remain in for the rest of their lives.
- With time and experience, BMBs learn to better discern their spiritual gifts and serve with increasing fruitfulness in their areas of gifting.
- Some step into leadership roles within the church and help advance the cause of Christ and the purposes of the kingdom.
- Others exercise spiritual leadership in their family, work and communities.
- Many develop a passion to help others grow through the stages in maturity that they have been through.

Those of us who walk alongside BMBs recognize that our role in their lives changes as they progress through the stages. The very intense life-on-life mentoring, discussed above, is particularly important in the earlier stages. However, as believers progress into the third stage, the discipler's role shifts more to that of a friend, encourager and occasional advisor. As believers move into the latter stages, the discipler becomes increasingly a friend and fellow servant in life and sometimes, in ministry. One's role as a discipler has ended, and one's role as a brother or sister, as an encouraging and supportive friend, may continue indefinitely.

A VISION STATEMENT FOR DISCIPLING BMBs

At the beginning of this chapter, we discussed the goal and nature of discipleship in order to present a compelling vision for BMB discipling. When we set out to disciple we must know what it is that we are seeking to accomplish. The vision statement that concludes this chapter pulls together much of what has been learned about spiritual growth and discipleship from study of the New Testament, contemporary teaching on discipleship, church history, contextualization and from interviews with seasoned disciplers.

A Vision Statement for Discipling BMBs

We will work hard to see BMBs trusting their heavenly Father, discipled personally and living in loving submission to one another within churches whose members individually and corporately experience the transforming grace of God through the presence and power of the Holy Spirit in community.

BMBs will continue to grow as they live together in submission to the teaching of Scripture and in obedience to their Lord, developing individual and corporate disciplines and routines that fortify their faith in order to transform their perspectives and beliefs in ways increasingly faithful to the great biblical story of creation, fall and redemption.

Further, BMBs will live out their Christian faith in ways sensitively adapted to their culture and society. Growing increasingly into Christlikeness, they will serve and reach out with the gospel to people in their families, social networks, communities and beyond, as they grow in individual and corporate maturity and multiply to the glory of God.

Of course, all of this can be very idealistic. The constraints of time, character, family and society will influence the specific shape that this vision of transformation will take in each situation. When one is struggling to help a new believer survive in the midst of the storm, the full-orbed scope of this vision may seem far off. However, to take this image one step further, this vision helps the instructor to know which strokes to teach swimmers so that they have a better chance of surviving and flourishing over the long haul.

8

The Living Pyramid of Relational Communal Discipling of BMBs

His divine power has granted to us
all things that pertain to life and godliness, *through the*
knowledge of him who called us to his own glory and excellence.
. . . For this very reason, make every effort to supplement your faith
with virtue . . . *knowledge . . . self-control . . . steadfastness . . . godliness*
. . . brotherly affection and . . . love. For if these qualities are yours
and are increasing, they keep you from being ineffective or
unfruitful *in the knowledge of our Lord Jesus Christ.*

2 Peter 1:3, 5-8 (emphasis added)

The heart of being a disciple involves living in intimate
union and daily contact with Christ.

Bill Hull,
The Complete Book of Discipleship

Healthy spiritual formation happens
only in a communal context.

Bill Thrall and Bruce McNicol,
Kingdom Life

People need to see the gospel lived out in us if they
are going to understand what it really is.

JIM PETERSEN,
LIFESTYLE DISCIPLESHIP

There is no other path to Christian spiritual formation
than through meaningful interaction
with the Word of God.

BILL HULL,
KINGDOM LIFE

Jesus never gave the idea that we could
walk in fellowship with Him and not be engaged
with Him in mission. . . . He is bringing the good news
of the kingdom to those who are outside.

PAULA FULLER,
KINGDOM LIFE

As CHURCH PLANTERS IN NORTH AFRICA we had become
rather discouraged and were at a loss as to how to move forward.
For the second time in a decade, a growing house church with increasingly mature local leaders had collapsed and the local believers had not
met together for regular worship in almost eighteen months. For seven
or eight years several expatriate couples had labored together, encouraging, discipling and modeling, and we had seen the development of
what we thought was a growing, healthy house church, under the leadership of two national couples. Yet, when the church was functioning
well and numbered almost twenty committed members, two crises one

after the other led them to stop meeting—and that decision to stop meeting for "a few weeks" had expanded well beyond a year.

During the long months that the church ceased regular corporate meetings, several expat men continued in weekly small-group meetings with a handful of younger men and continued in one-on-one discipling relationships with some of these men. Similar low-key relationship based activities were also continuing among the women. Some months into this period, we decided to do a several-month study of the church in the New Testament with the group of young men. The study inspired several of the young men with a fresh and exhilarating vision of what they were called to be as members of the local church in their city and country. This new vision compelled them to approach the former older leaders of the house church, and together they relaunched the church. That was about twenty years ago, and that church has since planted several other churches and led a group of churches in church planting and social ministries in several cities across the country. Several of the young men who caught a vision through that Bible study are today among the main leaders in the national church.

The catalyst to this restart of the church in the city was vision, which gave them motivation. The means for transformation were already present. From then on they met together regularly, and for many years their key leaders continued to be individually discipled and trained, and together they committed to living from the Scriptures and engaging in mission. They had vision, intention and means (VIM), and God continues to grace them with his Spirit as they press on in faithful ministry.

The five citations that head this chapter emphasize different yet ultimately complimentary paths to spiritual maturity. In the first half of the book we have explored a number of significant elements in discipleship and the spiritual growth process. Now it is time to lay a foundation on which everyone seeking to help disciple BMBs can build. In laying such a foundation, this chapter draws together the most significant theological, biblical, historical, contemporary and missiological insights in chapters one through seven to create a model for BMB discipleship that integrates these insights into a cohesive portrayal of the crucial elements needed for fruitful disciple making among Muslims.

MISSIOLOGICAL INSIGHTS FROM REFLECTIONS
ON CONTEXTUALIZATION

The conclusion reached in chapter six was that the discipleship objective should be the effective discipling of believers so that they are able to remain within their Muslim families and be part of appropriately contextualized local churches that flourish within Muslim societies. In distinct contrast, it is *not* appropriate to keep disciples inside the religious institutions and traditions that characterize Muslim communities. BMBs must have a clear identity as Christ's followers that is distinct from the religious identity of those who honor Muhammad and seek to fulfill the religious and legal obligations of the Qur'an and Islamic ideology and law. While not desiring that BMBs be religious insiders, every appropriate effort must normally be made to make it possible for believers from Muslim families and communities so that they can continue to live and serve Christ within their families and as ongoing members of their Muslim communities.

Furthermore, efforts ought to be made to avoid actions that lead to the extraction of followers of Christ from their Muslim contexts. However, given the often ideologically determined self-identification of Muslim communities as consisting only of those who can truthfully pray the Shahada, and the natural tendency in the honor cultures of the Muslim world for a shame-triggered rejection of all who apostatize, it is not surprising that many followers of Christ will be forcefully expelled from their communities. Nevertheless, the research outcomes discussed in chapter ten point out a number of significant things that can be done by evangelists, disciplers and the disciples themselves to defuse potential hostile response considerably. In this way, believers are more likely to be able to remain within their communities even after they are identified irrevocably with Christ, rather than Muhammad. Accordingly, for BMB discipleship to bear the desired fruit in maturity, witness and reproduction, disciplers must consistently strive to practice insider discipleship that integrates new believers successfully into culturally and socially insider churches.

This missiological conclusion serves as the fundamental context for what I am calling the Living Pyramid Model. In figure 8.1 this missio-logical conclusion is visually represented by the large circular plane on which the whole model rests, labeled "Living for Christ inside Muslim family and community." Extraction is not the goal; insider discipleship is the normal intent. Yet, we must be realistic and understand that far too often, the ongoing residence and witness of BMBs within their own families and communities is impossible, at least in the short term, and disciplers must not force new disciples to carry burdens heavier than they can bear.

Figure 8.1. The missiological foundation of the Living Pyramid Model

INSIGHTS FROM EXEGETICAL REFLECTIONS ON DISCIPLESHIP IN THE NEW TESTAMENT

Concerned that part of the reason for the frequent failure observed in BMB discipling may well be due to inadequate understanding of biblical perspectives on discipling, in chapters two and three we took a fresh look at discipleship and spiritual formation in Galatians, Philippians and Luke-Acts and sought to discover afresh how Paul and Luke, the two primary and representative writers in the New Testament, understood this vital topic. I believe that the conclusions reached contribute helpfully to the unfolding Living Pyramid Model for discipling BMBs.

As we saw in chapter two, the picture of the spiritual life given in Galatians is of a life of corporate dependence on the Holy Spirit for everything that is needed for godliness and fruitful living. For Paul, it is only as we learn to walk by the Spirit together that we will experience power over the flesh and a flowing of the fruit of the Spirit into our lives, our homes, our churches and our communities. In many Muslim contexts, where conformity to a religious legal code is the norm, effective discipleship must be grounded in radical dependence on the Holy Spirit for all believers living in community together rather than on a new legal code. This central Pauline lesson from Galatians is represented visually in figure 8.2 by the circular plane labeled "Living in mutual dependence on the Holy Spirit."

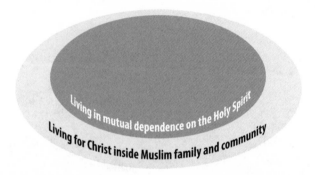

Figure 8.2. Spiritual lesson from Paul in Galatians: Living in mutual dependence on the Holy Spirit

But what about the innumerable situations where there is no church of any kind for new believers to join? In such circumstances, what does one do about this Pauline belief in the importance of being in a believing community? When it is not yet possible for believers to join with others, there will be a much higher degree of attrition, as lone individuals will find the pressures overwhelming. Even so, the Holy Spirit will give special grace to those who persevere and remain loyal when they are forced to survive on their own. A mature BMB recently commented to me that he cherishes his first four years following his conversion, when he knew no other believers. During those years Jesus was his constant companion and the Spirit his source of strength. God provides grace for unavoidably isolated believers, but our aim ought always be to see them belonging to caring local gatherings of believers as soon as possible.

Another vital aspect of the Pauline vision of the Christian life is expressed in Philippians. Not only are we to live in conscious dependence on the Holy Spirit, but also the gospel itself is to shape our core identity as people who are redeemed by and devoted to our crucified Lord. The supreme example of Christ and his self-sacrifice not only bought us salvation and new life but also provides a model for us to emulate as we seek to conform our life to that of the crucified Savior. Seeking to express clearly how Christ's crucifixion shapes our identity, Gorman coined the term "cruciformity" and defines it as "conformity to the crucified Christ" (2001, 4-7). Living one's entire life in conscious imitation of and conformity to Christ, who, in love, sacrificed all and died on the cross for us, is living in cruciformity to Christ. This central Pauline understanding of conformity to Christ is placed at the heart of the pyramid in an effort to show that BMBs' central new identity is found through living in cruciformity to their crucified Lord.

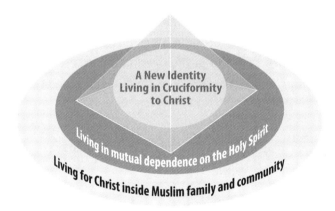

Figure 8.3. Spiritual lesson from Paul in Philippians: Living in cruciformity to Christ

Our study of discipleship in Luke-Acts in chapter three explored a number of rich discipleship themes. In Luke, discipleship to Jesus is a radical commitment to live life under the loving care of the heavenly Father in such a way that every attitude and perspective is turned on its head. Such discipleship is characterized by prayerful trust in the heavenly Father that empowers disciples into lives of self-sacrificing service and self-giving, even to death. This picture of disciples living out a radical trust in their heavenly Father seen in the Gospel of Luke is fleshed out further in the lives of the believers in Acts. Their lives were characterized by deep fellowship and profound love, selfless sharing of their resources, care for the needy, the powerful presence and working of the Holy Spirit in their midst in healings and proclamation and zeal to share the truth and reality of the gospel. This understanding of discipleship in Luke and Acts is put in the banner at the top of the Living Pyramid Model declaring that "Trusting in God the heavenly Father sustains corporate discipleship to Christ." Placing this spiritual reality as a banner over the Living Pyramid intends to suggest that BMBs' entire individual and collective lives are lived oriented in this direction—looking up in trust to the Father in order to persevere in faithful, radical discipleship to Jesus along with other believers in one's local church community.

According to Paul and Luke, discipleship is a corporate life in which everyone lives together in complete dependence on the Spirit. Such disciples trust profoundly in the love of their heavenly Father revealed to them in Christ, and they in turn live lives of sacrificial love and service to their fellow believers and in their communities, empowered by the Holy Spirit for Christ's sake. This New Testament vision of discipleship

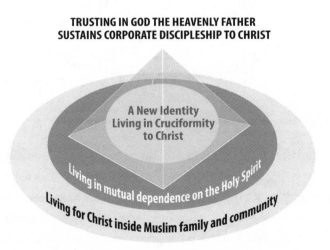

**TRUSTING IN GOD THE HEAVENLY FATHER
SUSTAINS CORPORATE DISCIPLESHIP TO CHRIST**

A New Identity
Living in Cruciformity
to Christ

Living in mutual dependence on the Holy Spirit

Living for Christ inside Muslim family and community

Figure 8.4. Lesson from Luke-Acts: Trusting in the heavenly Father sustains corporate discipleship to Christ

provides the foundation and central core of the Living Pyramid Model that is portrayed in figure 8.4.

The Living Pyramid Model of Relational Communal Discipleship

The image of a living pyramid is inspired by the apostle Peter's description of believers as living stones joined together into a spiritual living house (1 Pet 2:4-10). The pyramid is also a familiar Middle Eastern structure that resists the pressures and stresses of its environment in order to endure and stand strong for generations. This combination of the central outcomes of our study of the nature of discipleship is displayed in figure 8.5, called the Living Pyramid Model of relational communal BMB discipling. Though no diagram can ever adequately depict the living spiritual dynamics of BMB discipleship, my hope is that this image of a living pyramid set solidly at the heart of Muslim society will inspire us to strive toward implementation of sounder discipleship that adapts appropriately into Islamic contexts. Discipling BMBs from within the conceptual framework provided by this model can help BMBs grow and endure amid all of the pressures and opposition encountered inside their families and communities.

Our discussion of the spiritual formation process in chapter seven concluded by identifying five vital elements in the discipleship and spiritual growth processes that appear to be of vital significance. It is now time to complete the Living Pyramid by adding these five indispensable elements in spiritual transformation. In doing so, we now add the pyramid to the circles and spheres of the model, which are the missiological and biblical foundations of the discipleship vision developed in earlier chapters. We will see how these elements create the pyramid that rests in the center of figure 8.5.

Developing personal intimacy with God in prayer and obedience as individuals. The first element is the base of the pyramid—this is the central importance of each individual BMB developing a meaningful personal walk with God. Vital to New Testament Christian experience is individual faith and experience of God gained through obedience to

Christ that is empowered by the Holy Spirit. Clearly, this individual faith must be expressed in the corporate context of the local church. Many BMBs come to Christ within societies and cultures that are influenced significantly by a sense of corporate identity and responsibility. Though all other faces of the pyramid stress the corporate nature of discipleship

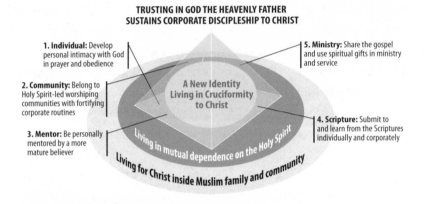

Figure 8.5. The Living Pyramid Model of relational communal BMB discipling

to Christ, it is vital to begin by stressing that in a profound way, New Testament faith in God is also personal and individual. Unless believers from Muslim backgrounds learn to nurture their personal faith in Christ, to become sensitive to the working of the Spirit in their own hearts and learn to live in personal obedience to God, the corporate experience of their faith will be insufficient to sustain perseverance over the long haul. Thus, the personal walk of faith is the foundational spiritual transformation process on which the four corners of the Living Pyramid rest. In the diagram, this base is labeled "Individual: Develop personal intimacy with God in prayer and obedience."

Belonging to a worshiping community led by the Holy Spirit with fortifying corporate routines. The first face of the Living Pyramid is community. It is crucial that BMBs learn to live together with others as committed members of a local, believing community that functions with appropriate fortifying corporate routines. One of the strengths of the monastic traditions, and of some of the Orthodox and Benedictine traditions examined in chapter six, is that they recognize the power of good community habits and the role of corporate spiritual disciplines in bringing about spiritual transformation of individuals. As BMBs gather together regularly, it is important that they develop patterns of corporate worship that include vital elements such as corporate prayer, worship in song, engagement with the Scriptures, baptism and the Lord's Supper in order to strengthen their understanding and practice of faith. Regular corporate disciplines play a huge role in keeping believers' hearts and minds focused on Christ and obedient and open to the leading of the Spirit.

As noted above, these ancient traditions often called these church-based patterns of corporate and individual life and devotion a rule. My phrase "fortifying corporate routines" seeks to express the idea that the pattern of local church life together needs to be consciously shaped so that it empowers our obedience and renews our faith. How to accomplish this is rightly something to be shaped by each local church. The important thing is that it be done together in sensitively shaped rhythms of community life under the guiding and empowering of the Spirit. In the Living Pyramid Model this critical role of community in empowering spiritual growth is the first face of the pyramid: Community: Belonging to Holy Spirit–led worshiping communities with fortifying corporate routines.

Being personally mentored by a more mature believer. In contexts in which believers often have few or no human models of what it looks like to live as Christians, we can readily understand the importance of the second face of the Living Pyramid—having a personal mentor or discipler. This point was emphasized repeatedly in the books I read on ministering to Muslims, and it was stressed with even greater regularity by those I interviewed. The consensus of the disciplers interviewed was that effective one-on-one discipling of BMBs happens when there are strong and intimate personal relationships between new believers and more mature believers. Disciplers must walk alongside disciples, caring for them and teaching, mentoring and modeling authentic Christian discipleship. They often need to do life-on-life mentoring that can often be quite intense, especially at the beginning. This personal

mentoring is the second face of the pyramid: Mentor: Be personally
mentored by a more mature believer.

Submitting to and learning from the Scriptures individually and corporately. As was pointed out in chapter seven, the fourth essential element in fruitful discipling is that believers must learn individually and corporately to obey Christ, the living Word, through study of and submission to the written Word. It might seem natural that former Muslims would instinctively understand the importance of coming to know and understand the Scriptures given the prominence of the Qur'an in Islam. However, as those who live among Muslims know, for most Muslims it is far more important that the Qur'an be honored and that the correct ritual forms of prayer and devotional practice be followed than that the Qur'an be understood. Understanding truth is secondary to conformity to ritual practice and community norms. Often, new believers want to be told what to do. They want to know what is the Christian way of praying, of fasting and of pilgrimage. They expect that being a Christian will consist largely in a new set of practices to follow.

This is one of the reasons why experienced disciplers, and especially those who had themselves been Muslims, stressed the importance of learning and understanding the Bible. Because all Muslim cultures with which I am familiar are much more oral than literate cultures, it is no simple task for a new believer to learn to live based on understanding and obeying the truth found in the Scriptures. Even literate BMBs seldom have habits of reading and learning through individual reading. Whether one engages the Scripture through reading or through a variety of oral methods, it is nevertheless true that permanent change in behavior is closely tied to changed understanding. Bill Hull ties changed behavior to a changed mind that comes from learning to know the Scriptures:

> There is no other path to Christian spiritual formation than *through meaningful interaction with the Word of God.* . . . Spiritual formation begins within, and its primary tool is to take a God-given desire to change and work to *reform a person's mind* with God's thoughts. *A renewed mind fueled by a Holy Spirit-birthed desire creates new actions, which become habits, and habits make our character.* (Hull 2010, 117, 118, emphasis added)

In the interviews, three of the most often mentioned keys to growth focused on the importance of understanding the truth through personal and corporate study and obedience to the Word of God (see chap. 7, table 7. 2, responses 3, 5 and 7). It is only as BMBs live in submission to the Scriptures both individually and in community that a biblical worldview can replace the Qur'anic or Muslim worldview of their past. This vital principle is the third face of the pyramid: Scripture: Submit to and learn from the Scriptures individually and corporately.

Sharing the gospel and using spiritual gifts in ministry and service. It has often been stated that the best way to learn something is to teach it to others. Jesus himself said that if anyone wanted to know whether his teaching was from God or not, that person had to want to obey God (Jn 7:17) and the truth of his message would be made clear. I often find that every new attempt to explain the amazing truth of the gospel to a non-Christian gives me fresh insights. Paula Fuller stresses that it is as we are engaged with God on his mission of proclamation and kingdom service that we grow to maturity.

> When we live with an illusion that we don't have to be engaged in God's mission to grow to maturity, we believe that we can get everything we need for our spiritual development from our personal relationship with God and other Christians. . . . *Jesus never gave the idea that we could walk in fellowship with Him and not be engaged with Him in mission. . . . If we want to walk with Jesus and have fellowship with Him, we must go with Him,* and He is bringing the good news of the kingdom to those who are outside. (Fuller 2010, 216-17, emphasis added)

This important spiritual principle came out in the interviews as well. My sense is that those who stressed this the most were those who had the most effectiveness in discipling BMBs who persevered in the faith. As soon as someone comes to faith, he or she is encouraged to go and share the new discovery with someone the person knows or meets. This principle is also central in a number of the principles being taught by those seeing church planting movements launched. They call it "obedience-based discipleship." In their discovery Bible studies, enquirers are taught to obey whatever they find to be true in the Bible, right from the start.

They are to apply what they learn. Furthermore, they are exhorted to share what they have learned with someone else the same week, and then to come back to the group and share what happened when they told someone else about the truth they had just learned. In obedience-based discipleship, people are taught to learn spiritual truth in order to obey it. Jerry Trousdale describes obedience-based discipleship:

> Jesus didn't tell us to teach all the things that He has commanded us; He commanded us to teach others to obey these things. There is a big difference between teaching knowledge and teaching obedience. A disciple is taught to obey what Jesus commanded.
>
> Knowledge without obedience creates a spiritual dichotomy between knowledge and obedience. This, tragically, is a toxic brew. . . . However, knowledge combined with obedience disciples and draws them closer to God. . . . Knowledge alone never produces spiritual growth and maturity because it doesn't transform life. Obedient discipleship does. (2012, 100-101)

In the interviews, an emphasis was made on the importance of BMBs learning what their spiritual gifts were and exercising them as much as possible from the beginning. The principle is clear, and it is vital to effective discipleship. If we want to see BMBs grow to maturity and flourish in their faith, we must both model and teach obedience to all that is learned, as it is learned. This is the fourth and final face of the pyramid: Ministry: Share the gospel and use spiritual gifts in ministry and service.

THE LIVING PYRAMID MODEL PORTRAYS A ROBUST VISION FOR DISCIPLESHIP

This dynamic, ongoing, spiritual, individual and community reality which I have sought to represent in the Living Pyramid Model is meant to be lived in authentic cultural and social expression in the midst of Muslim families and communities for the glory of God. Fitting in culturally, this living pyramid, like the mature BMB community, is accepted as belonging in its setting, while at the same time raising above the limitations of its cultural and religious environment so as to, through the power of the Spirit, transform and transcend its Muslim community. I hope that this living pyramid effectively captures some of the central dynamics involved in fruitful discipling of believers as they follow Christ in Muslim communities.

A robust vision of discipleship that is biblically, psychologically and socially compelling leads to effective discipling practices. Much of the reason for our failure in discipling BMBs has been due to an inadequate understanding of what we are trying to accomplish and invalid perceptions of the processes that lead to spiritual transformation. For example, starting with the goal of simply discipling individual BMBs is bound to fail because such an inadequate objective inherently undermines success. In his PhD dissertation studying Muslim convert groups in France, John Leonard argues that individualized approaches to ministry are ineffectual for both evangelism and discipleship. Leonard's stress on working with community is crucial, especially for those of us from cultures that idealize the individual:

> You cannot reach a communal people using individual methods of evangelism. We must demonstrate that becoming a Christian is to become a member of a community that is closer than the family. . . . To have a group you need to start with a group. This does not mean that there is not a lot of individual attention given to each person in the group—that is a necessity. It means, for communal people, you do things together. (2006, 300)

Having a biblical understanding of discipleship objectives and processes that is spiritually, socially and psychologically valid, and then seeking to adapt it to the culture of the people with and to whom we minister, will go a long way toward helping us see fruitful discipling. The Living Pyramid Model of Relational Communal BMB Discipling attempts to provide a biblically rooted and experimentally valid vision of the discipling objectives and processes.

PART TWO

Seasoned Practices in Discipling Believers from Muslim Backgrounds

Having explored the nature of discipleship and processes of spiritual transformation, and having presented a comprehensive model for discipling BMBs, we move on to explore some of the most vexing challenges facing BMBs in many societies around the world. The next seven chapters will present practical insights and wisdom that have been gleaned from the rich experiences of mature disciplers working among Muslims. Drawing on published writing and interviews conducted with seventy-five disciplers across the Arab world, this part of the book will tackle several of the biggest challenges facing BMBs and those seeking to come alongside and disciple them. These seasoned practices have the potential to move practitioners toward greater fruitfulness.

9

The Biggest Obstacles to Effective BMB Discipleship

Who shall separate us from the love of Christ?
Shall tribulation, or distress, or persecution, or famine,
or nakedness, or danger, or sword?

ROMANS 8:35

What bothers them more are dilemmas of identity such as:
How can I grow strong in Christ
while still relating to my Muslim family?
How will I find a believing spouse?
What will be written on the "religion"
section of my children's birth certificate?
At school, will they be known as
Muslims or Christians or what?
Will I be buried in a Muslim or
Christian graveyard?
Such questions reveal a search for identity solutions
at all three levels: core, social and collective.

TIM GREEN, "IDENTITY CHOICES AT THE BORDER ZONE,"
LONGING FOR COMMUNITY

A FEW YEARS AGO I WAS INVITED to give several days of seminars on discipling BMBs to a group of workers ministering among a variety of Muslim communities throughout China. Having had no experience of discipling Chinese BMBs, I was not confident that my Arab-world experience would transfer well into Muslim contexts in China. As I described the major challenges that BMBs encounter in the Arab world I was told that the challenges for BMBS in China were very similar. As I worked through the practical advice presented in this section of the book, on wise ways of dealing with several major issues encountered by disciplers in the Arab world, I was told that almost everything that I presented had direct application to Muslim contexts in China. This experience, since repeated in other non-Arab contexts, has confirmed to me that seasoned practices learned in the Arab world apply across many Muslim contexts because the influence of Islam in diverse settings creates similar obstacles for BMBs seeking to live for Christ.

Many have commented that Islam is as much a culture as it is religion. And the culture that Islam carries with it is an ideologically and religiously shaped version of seventh-century Arabian tribal culture. Of course there are major cultural difference between, say, a Chinese Muslim and a French Muslim, yet people who belong to Muslim communities anywhere in the world evidence important identity-shaping similarities coming from Arab Islamic culture. This is why the challenges typical of Arab cultural contexts provide a particularly valuable basis for understanding and responding to the challenges faced by BMBs even in many non-Arab cultural contexts.

In this chapter we examine the nature and variety of challenges that BMBs encounter in the Arab world. Then, in the following chapters we will discuss several of the main challenges and how seasoned disciplers have learned to deal with them. The fundamental nature of discipleship to Christ is the same in all Muslim and non-Muslim contexts and throughout history. The principles gathered together in the Living Pyramid Model can be applied to discipling in any context. However, what makes the task of discipling seem so different in Muslim contexts, compared with how it manifests in non-Muslim contexts, has to do with the specific challenges that the psychological, social, cultural and religious influence of Islam bring to bear on people who come to Christ in Muslim communities.

THE WIDE VARIETY OF CHALLENGES IN ARAB-WORLD CONTEXTS

Before I undertook this study, I believed that the unique challenges facing BMBs arise mostly from Islamic influences. However, I did not expect a lot of variety in the challenges BMBs face. Thus, I was initially surprised that disciplers mentioned such a wide variety of challenges. I heard forty-one different kinds of answers from the sixty people whom I questioned, when I asked them to identify the biggest obstacles to BMB maturity in their contexts.

THE NATURE OF THE CHALLENGES FACING BMBs

Analysis of these challenges led to grouping them into five categories: family and community, spiritual, Islamic ideology and doctrine, sociopolitical and psychological. This classification is of necessity personal and subjective. For example, fear was often cited as a major obstacle to growth. Is fear best understood as an Islamic, sociopolitical, psychological or spiritual obstacle to growth? The way BMBs have been raised in Muslim families and communities, where authorities often use fear to intimidate and control, is often the primary source of their fear. Yet, even though Muslim society accounts for their fear and the solution for fear is largely spiritual, classifying fear as psychological made sense, because it is something that people wrestle with internally at a personal level.

THE MOST FREQUENTLY MENTIONED OBSTACLES TO DISCIPLESHIP

Which were the most commonly mentioned obstacles to spiritual growth among BMBs? As can be seen in table 9.1, the top three, each mentioned by about half of the sixty interviewees, were pressures from family, pressures from the local Muslim community and pressures from being a

Table 9.1. The Eighteen Most Frequently Mentioned Obstacles to Growth

	Obstacles to Growth	Total	Category	Regional Background		Religious Background		Gender	
				Global South	West	BMB	Other	M /50	F /25
1	Pressures from Muslim family; family control especially while single	35	F&C	16	19	7	28	23	12
2	Local Muslim community's hostility, rejection and/or expulsion	29	F&C	14	15	8	21	18	11
3	Vulnerability due to youthfulness, low social status, weak economic state	28	Soc	12	16	6	22	20	8
4	Fear of all kinds: of problems, suffering, persecution and oppression	24	Psych	11	13	5	19	17	7
5	Lack of trust between and among BMBs and BMB groups; lack of commitment to one group	22	Spir	7	15	3	19	16	6
6	Challenges for BMB families: child rearing, education, marriage	19	F&C	10	9	8	11	12	7
7	Spiritual nature of Christian faith; it is about Holy Spirit prayer, faith, not deeds	14	Spir	4	10	2	12	9	5
8	BMB lack of confidence, complexes, victimization, emotional pain	13	Psych	6	7	1	12	7	6
9	Satanic hold of Islam, demonic and occult bondages, hate, anger, lust	12	Spir	8	4	6	6	7	5
10	Local Christians, churches and communities do not accept BMBs	11	Soc	7	4	5	6	8	3
11	The love of money; BMBs need to learn to give and be generous	10	Soc	5	5	2	8	6	4
12	Living in a police state where change of religion is not officially possible	10	F&C	4	6	4	6	9	1
13	The discipler's ineffectiveness, poor response and wrong motives	9	Spir	3	6	2	7	8	1
14	Illiteracy and/or low levels of literacy; oral learners	9	Soc	2	7	0	9	3	6

Key: F&C - Family and Community, **Isl** - Islamic Ideology, **Soc** - Sociopolitical, **Psych** - Psychological, **Spir** - Spiritual

	Obstacles to Growth	Total	Category	Regional Background		Religious Background		Gender	
				Global South	West	BMB	Other	M /50	F /25
15	Poor ethics and lack of integrity; must learn new ethics before a holy God	9	Isl	3	6	2	7	5	4
16	Muslim ideology, doctrine, traditions, and so on, all requiring re-education	9	Isl	5	4	4	5	9	0
17	God is distant and unknowable; difficult to bring God close to BMBs	8	Isl	2	6	0	8	5	3
18	Men especially struggle with sexual issues and lust	8	Spir	3	5	1	7	6	2
	Total in Eighteen Most Mentioned Obstacles	**279**		**122**	**157**	**66**	**213**	**188**	**91**
	Total Responses from Sixty Interviewees	*354*		*163*	*191*	*91*	*263*	*242*	*112*

Key: F&C - Family and Community, **Isl** - Islamic Ideology, **Soc** - Sociopolitical, **Psych** - Psychological, **Spir** - Spiritual

socially and economically vulnerable member of one's family and community.[1] The next three most frequently mentioned challenges, each mentioned by roughly a third of the interviewees, were fear of all kinds, lack of trust among BMBs and the challenges that believers face in having Christian marriages and raising children as believers. All three of these challenges are closely related to the fact that BMBs come to faith in the midst of Muslim societies and communities. The fear of problems, persecution, suffering and oppression are fears related to what one's family and community may do because one is no longer a Muslim. The lack of

---

[1] In this table, as well as in all other tables, it is important to understand my method of analysis. Most questions were open-ended, and when people gave three or four distinct responses, they were all carefully noted. In analyzing the responses and arranging them in tables for presentation here, the full range of answers given were analyzed and categorized. This means, for example, here in table 9.1, that 354 responses were given in response to the question about the most challenging obstacles, even though only sixty of the seventy-five people were asked this question. Further, the discussion in this chapter focuses on the eighteen most frequently mentioned obstacles and does not take into account the further twenty-three obstacles that were mentioned less often (see appendix C, table A.4). The total number of answers analyzed is different in each table because the number of answers given varied from question to question and person to person. The purpose of the analysis is understanding the nature and ranges of obstacles facing BMBs. There was no need to do statistical analysis of the range of responses.

trust that is a major obstacle to individual and corporate growth stems from the social realities of Muslim communities, in which widespread lack of integrity and stress on saving face makes it hard for new believers to trust each other. They have had little or no exposure to families and communities operating on the basis of trust.

Further, the sixth most mentioned challenge—that of sustaining a Christian marriage and family—arises directly from living in Muslim communities where only Muslim families have rights and protection under the law. It is true that people in every context have challenges in getting married and in raising their children as believers, yet for BMBs to be able to marry other BMBs, and to raise their children as followers of Christ when they are legally Muslims, are challenges that are especially hard in Muslim contexts. Thus, the top six challenges that BMBs face, mentioned by one-half to one-third of all interviewees, are explicitly or implicitly the result of believers seeking to live faithful to Christ in Muslim families and societies.

The next six most frequently mentioned challenges fall into every category *except* Islamic ideology and teaching. And yet, when we look at what these obstacles are, once again we notice the pervasive negative influence of Islam. The impact of Islam on Muslim people and society explicitly accounts for every challenge but the eleventh. Let us look at them in turn.

A third of these experienced disciplers describe how difficult it is for BMBs to grasp the spiritual nature of the Christian life. The reason that this is so hard is that in most Muslim communities, pleasing God is tied to religious rituals performed and conforming to community honor, expectations and rules. In contrast, the Christian life is about relationships—with God and with people—not about religious deeds. It is precisely because this is so different from Islamic thinking and practice that new believers often have such a hard time understanding the practice of the Christian faith and learning to develop loving relationships with people and with God.

The second most frequently mentioned psychological challenge to growth is the emotional scars and trauma that many BMBs have to learn to deal with as they follow Christ and grow to maturity (8 in table 9.1). Sarwat, a BMB leader with twenty years of experience in discipling, expressed his deep shame at the extent to which so many BMBs had been physically, sexually and emotionally abused by family members and neighbors. For Sarwat, this was the second biggest challenge (after their need to leave behind their Muslim view of God) to their growth in Christ. So many brothers and sisters whom he has discipled and helped through the years were suffering from huge amounts of emotional pain from the extensive levels of abuse they had experienced. With tears in his eyes, Sarwat described the need that so many BMBs have to be loved and healed emotionally. Of course, high levels of abuse of children is not unique to Muslim families and society. Yet, my experience living in North Africa suggests that it is quite uncommon, even rare, for a Muslim family to be emotionally healthy. The Islam-influenced and sometimes prescribed way that men mistreat women, and the widespread use of shame and fear to discipline and control children, appear to be a common sad tale throughout Muslim communities. Thus, even though believers in most societies, and even increasingly in Western societies, need emotional healings from the scars of abuse, there is a widespread problem of abuse in Muslim societies that is specifically tied to Islamic teachings that shape Muslim social mores. For example, in the Qur'an, Muhammad instructed men to withhold sex from their wives and beat them if they feared that their wives were not being submissive (Surah 4:34). Is it surprising to find wife beating a common practice in Muslim society? Much of the emotional damage that BMBs must work through as they grow in their faith comes as a result of living in Qur'an-influenced families and societies.

Three of the next four most-mentioned challenges (see table 9.1, items 9–12) are tied directly to Islam: the satanic hold of Islam, demonic and occult bondages; the struggle that local non-Muslim background Christians and churches have in trusting and accepting former Muslims; and the challenges involved in living in a Muslim police state where it is illegal to leave Islam. Among the top twelve challenges, the eleventh is the struggle around money and dependency that many BMBs face when they lack decent employment and opportunities to become established. This is a problem faced across much of the developing world, and not particularly caused by Islam. In fact, in wealthier countries like those of the Arabian Peninsula, this is less of a problem.

In looking at the final third of the items in table 9.1 (13–18), it is striking to note that items 15 through 17 are challenges that are a direct result of Islam and Islamic teaching. The struggle with lack of integrity (15) is a direct result of dishonesty and deceit being such pervasive problems in Muslim societies. And, although it appears as only the sixteenth item on this list, the actual content of Muslim teaching, doctrine and religious practices often require specific teaching of truth to counter their persistent, often subconscious influence on BMBs' attitudes and behavior. It is also interesting to note that a higher percentage of BMBs mentioned this challenge than others did. And, interestingly, no women mentioned Islamic teaching among the biggest challenges facing BMB women. A possible explanation for this is the widespread reality that men are educated in orthodox Islam far more than women, and thus women have less doctrinal commitment and understanding to undo following their conversion. For women, the affective (emotional) ties to Islam and the Muslim community play an equal and possibly more significant role than the doctrinal content of Islam as a religious system.[2] Very few of these issues would be central concerns for someone being discipled in non-Muslim contexts.

Among the remaining twenty-three obstacles mentioned but not included in table 9.1, 87 percent (twenty) are challenges found commonly in Muslim contexts. In all, thirty-four out of the forty-one cited obstacles to growth are typical of the Muslim world and not as common elsewhere (refer to those that are shaded gray in table 9.1).[3] Though a wider variety

---

[2]For further information on this see Shaw (2008) and the seven-part series in *SEEDBED* by Tahira (2008–2011), entitled "A Sunni Woman's Heart," which explored ways in which Muslim women are attached to Islam.

[3]For example, the challenge of living in a police state is typical of Muslim contexts. However, believers being discipled in China, for example, the world's largest police state, would face very similar pressures as a result. Yet, the reasons why so many Muslim nations are run as police states, rather than with a form of government allowing greater individual liberty, are closely tied to the influence of Islamic teaching and ideology.

of obstacles were identified than expected, it was still true that about 83 percent can be tied directly to factors typical in Muslim contexts.[4]

Remembering that male interviewees outnumbered females two to one, it is interesting to see that most obstacles were mentioned in similar ratios by men and women. However, there are a few significant differences in the obstacles reported by women. For example, as already mentioned, no women mentioned that Muslim ideology and doctrines were a strong obstacle to women's growth in faith, whereas a quarter of the men talked about this challenge. In contrast, women mentioned the challenge of illiteracy more often than men. Women also mentioned that women BMBs have problems of access to fellowship, of feeling alone, and sometimes having a passive attitude about their lives and of not feeling like they have any control over their own lives. In contrast, men more often mentioned than women the challenge of living in a police state, the dangers of financial dependency and the struggle with lust and sexual perversions.

Interestingly, BMBs noted the challenge of demonic and occult bondages more often than others did. And in the context of the Middle East, they also mentioned the challenge of BMBs not feeling accepted by believers from Christian backgrounds more often than non-BMBs did. Apart from these two exceptions, there was not much difference between what BMBs themselves identified as common obstacles compared with those identified by non-BMBs.

GROUPING THE OBSTACLES ACCORDING TO CATEGORY

Anticipating the kinds of challenges one is going to encounter helps one be more effective in discipling people through these obstacles. Table 9.2 groups the challenges into the five categories. What is amazingly consistent is that regardless of whether the problem is intellectual, spiritual, political, psychological or more directly a family, community or sociopolitical issue, all but two of the most mentioned challenges facing BMBs are found throughout most Muslim contexts. Not surprisingly, the

---

[4]To see all forty-one challenges refer to appendix C, table A.4. There is a lot of rich information collected in one place in this table. It bears reflection.

Table 9.2. The Eighteen Most Frequently Mentioned Obstacles Grouped by Category

Rank	Obstacles to Growth	Total	Category	Gender M /50	F /25
1	Pressures from Muslim family, family control, especially while single	35	F&C	23	12
2	Local Muslim community's hostility, rejection and/or expulsion	29	F&C	18	11
6	Challenges for BMB families: child rearing, education, marriage	19	F&C	12	7
12	Living in a police state where change of religion is not officially possible	10	F&C	9	1
Total Family and Community		**93**		**62**	**31**
5	Lack of trust among BMBs and groups; lack of commitment to one group	22	Spir	16	6
7	Spiritual nature of Christian faith; it is about Holy Spirit, prayer, faith, not deeds	14	Spir	9	5
9	Satanic hold of Islam, demonic and occult bondages, hate, anger, lust	12	Spir	7	5
13	The discipler's ineffectiveness, poor response and wrong motives	9	Spir	8	1
18	Men especially struggle with sexual issues and lust	8	Spir	6	2
Total Spiritual		**65**		**46**	**19**
3	Vulnerability due to youthfulness, low social status, weak economic state	28	Soc	20	8
10	Local Christians, churches and communities do not accept BMBs	11	Soc	8	3
11	The love of money; BMBs need to learn to give	10	Soc	6	4
14	Illiteracy and/or low levels of literacy; oral learners	9	Soc	3	6
Total Sociopolitical		**58**		**37**	**21**
4	Fear of all kinds: of problems, suffering, persecution and oppression	24	Psych	17	7
8	BMB lack of confidence, complexes, victimization, emotional pain	13	Psych	7	6
Total Psychological		**37**		**24**	**13**
15	Poor ethics and lack of integrity; must learn new ethics before a holy God	9	Isl	5	4
16	Muslim ideology, doctrine, traditions, and so on, all requiring re-education	9	Isl	9	0
17	God is distant and unknowable; difficult to bring God close to BMBs	8	Isl	5	3
Total Islamic Ideology and Doctrine		**26**		**19**	**7**
Total in Eighteen Most Mentioned Obstacles		*279*		*188*	*91*
Key: F&C - Family and Community, **Isl** - Islamic Ideology, **Soc** - Sociopolitical, **Psych** - Psychological, **Spir** - Spiritual					

biggest set of obstacles to the growth in faith of BMBs relate to the rejection, ongoing control and hostility that come from their families and their Muslim community. And the top psychological challenges— vulnerability and fear of persecution and oppression—are problems that arise because BMBs were raised in and are still living as believers in Muslim communities. The challenges that relate to their Muslim faith, to Islamic doctrine and ideology, are theological and spiritual in nature. It takes time for a former Muslim to learn to live by faith and trust in a loving and gracious God, rather than living in obedience to an unknown and feared God. In addition, the spiritual (sometimes demonic) and psychological bondages (for examples, fear, sexual temptations and addictions) that BMBs often struggle with are closely linked to Muslim influences. In addition to the huge Islam-related challenges that BMBs face, the socioeconomic challenges that they face can themselves be overwhelming: unemployment, illiteracy, poverty, and so on. The size of the challenges that BMBs face as they press forward in obedience to Christ in their new faith within their new believing community are indeed daunting. Perhaps it should not be surprising that so many struggle and eventually fail to persevere through them all.

IDENTITY TENSIONS FOR BMBs LIVING WITHIN MUSLIM AND CHRISTIAN COMMUNITIES

Before concluding this look at the nature and extent of the challenges that BMBs face, it is helpful to bring two new dimensions to the discussion. When a person raised as a Muslim and still living in a Muslim family and maintaining a Muslim identity confesses faith and begins to follow Christ, he or she soon encounters tensions in life never previously experienced. Following conversion to Christ, a new identity begins to emerge that is often in tension with what had previously been one's identity. One has now joined a new community, the Christian community—whether this is simply a small group of BMBs meeting in secret or the local church made up of Christians from various religious backgrounds. BMBs have begun to develop new personal, social and spiritual identities. In the next chapter we will discuss how to help BMBs navigate these multidimensional identities effectively, but it is helpful now to examine these identity issues and see how they create new challenges.

It is no surprise, given our observations about how many of the

Table 9.3. Top Eighteen Obstacles Facing BMBs from Their Muslim and Christian Identities

Rank	Obstacles to Growth	Total	Category	Gender M /50	F /25
1	Pressures from Muslim family, family control, especially while single	35	Islamic	23	12
2	Local Muslim community's hostility, rejection and/or expulsion	29	Islamic	18	11
3	Vulnerability due to youthfulness, low social status, weak economic state	28	Islamic	20	8
4	Fear of all kinds: of problems, suffering, persecution and oppression	24	Islamic	17	7
6	Challenges for BMB families: child rearing, education, marriage	19	Islamic	12	7
8	Lack of confidence, inherited complexes, victimization, emotional pain	13	Islamic	7	6
9	Satanic hold of Islam, demonic and occult bondages, hate, anger, lust	12	Islamic	7	5
11	The love of money; BMBs need to learn to give and be generous	10	Islamic	6	4
12	Living in a police state where change of religion is not officially possible	10	Islamic	9	1
14	Illiteracy and/or low levels of literacy; oral learners	9	Islamic	3	6
15	Poor ethics, lack of integrity; BMBs must learn new ethics before a holy God	9	Islamic	5	4
16	Learned Muslim ideology, doctrine, traditions, requiring re-education	9	Islamic	9	0
17	God is distant and unknowable; difficult to bring God close to BMBs	8	Islamic	5	3
18	Men especially struggle with sexual issues and lust	8	Islamic	6	2
Total Mentions of Obstacles from Islamic Community and Identity		*223*		*147*	*76*
5	Lack of trust among BMBs and groups; lack of commitment to one group	22	Christian	16	6
7	Spiritual nature of Christian faith: about Holy Spirit, prayer, faith, rather than deeds	14	Christian	9	5
10	Local Christians, churches and communities do not accept BMBs	11	Christian	8	3
13	The discipler's ineffectiveness, poor response and wrong motives	9	Christian	8	1
Total Mentions of Obstacles from Christian Community and Identity		*56*		*41*	*15*
Total in Eighteen Most Mentioned Obstacles		*279*		*188*	*91*

challenges relate specifically to Muslim contexts, to see that fourteen of the eighteen most-mentioned challenges relate to BMBs' Muslim identity and to their still needing to belong and relate to a Muslim community. Roland Muller (2006, 108-9) has aptly described this tension as the tension of having two identities, or faces—a Muslim face, as well as a new Christian face. It is important for BMBs to integrate their sense of personal identity, from what was their former Muslim face to their new Christian face. The tension experienced while transitioning between faces (or identities) can be intolerable. A simple glance at table 9.3 illustrates that the overwhelming majority of the challenges arise as they try to transition from their Muslim personal and community face to their new face in Christ. Appendix D contains Muller's helpful description of what these tensions entail and the goal to which one works as a discipler in helping BMBs unite their two faces into one new, integrated and stable identity.

Another perspective on the challenges of integrating the two faces was recently provided by Kathryn Kraft is her 2007 doctoral study of BMB community and identity issues in the Arab world. Kraft applies theories on identity formation and identity development to better understand the lived experience of BMBs as they develop new identities after their conversion and learn to negotiate their changing identities in their Muslim contexts. In her eighth chapter, "Identity Formation" (Kraft 2007, 152-67), she helpfully discusses the tensions that arise as BMBs seek to work out their new identity, or their new sets of identities, following their conversion to Christ. In *Searching for Heaven in the Real World* (2012), which is based on her doctoral study, Kraft explores the challenges facing BMBs as they seek to develop their new, postconversion identities. She found that many of the BMBs whom she interviewed adopted a strategy called "adhesive integration" in which they sought to add identities to the identities they already had without necessarily leaving behind their original identities. Kraft observed that in regions that do not have a pre-existing Christian community (such as North Africa), BMBs found a strategy of "adhesive identity integration" workable. They were able to successfully "glue on" a new

Christian faith identity to their national and cultural identity—they were able, for example, to learn to see themselves as Moroccan Christians or as North African Christians (2012, 103).

However, in the Middle East this adhesive identity strategy is far more difficult to make work due to the added complexity of the existence of pre-existing minority Christian communities. Kraft describes how difficult it can often be for BMBs to successfully add on a new identity to their existing identity.

> While the theory of adhesive identities helps to conceptualise the process and experience of adapting to a new sense of self within a new faith, the road to adaptation is full of complications and challenges. *Many MBBs state that the most difficult challenge they face is that of redefining their identity*. . . . It is made even more difficult by the hope, even expectation, that they will develop a perfect and unified new identity. . . .
>
> In fact, serious emotional and psychological concerns emerge. Anomie, *the yearning for something better but a perpetual inability to achieve it, is possibly the most common and troubling expression of these difficulties.* (Kraft 2012, 110, emphasis added)

This struggle with adhesive identity formation is similar to the struggles that Muller describes in terms of BMBs needing to bring their two faces together into one integrated new face or identity. Kraft notes that few of the BMBs whom she interviewed were aware that there were alternative options for them as they forged their new identities as Christians. Though the missiological literature is full of discussions of different ways of tackling the identity formation of new believers (discussed in chap. 6), and most readers of this book will be aware of these discussions, the BMBs whom Kraft interviewed were unaware of such options:

> However, most converts I met had never been exposed to any variation in approaches to becoming a "Christian" from a "Muslim" background. Many of them had assumed they had no option but to abandon their Muslim background and fully assume a Christian identity, and they were somewhat frustrated that they had not succeeded in doing so. Often, they expressed surprise and hopefulness when they learned of other models for convert identity. (Kraft 2012, 111-12)

The responses to my question, about the biggest challenges that BMBs have to deal with in their pilgrimage with Christ toward maturity help make clear why BMBs struggle so much in establishing their new identities. Seventy-five percent of the eighteen most often mentioned obstacles have to do with believers wrestling with their Muslim personal and community identity. And that percentage moves up to 79 percent when we include all of the obstacles cited in my interviews (see appendix C, table 9.5, for the list and classification of all obstacles mentioned).

BMBs Navigating Their Core, Social and Collective Identities

Tim Green, who recently completed his doctoral study on BMB identity issues in Pakistan (Green 2014), offers yet another lens through which to better understand the nature of the challenges facing BMBs. Green suggests a three-layered grid as a helpful way of portraying the complexity of the identity challenges facing BMBs. Adapting a categorization proposed by Beit-Hallahmi, Green depicts his identity analysis in the following diagram (2013a, 44). I will explain the model briefly since it is very helpful in understanding the complexities of BMB identity changes.

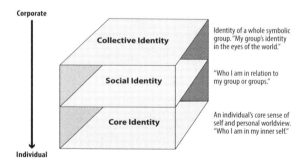

Figure 9.1. Identity at three levels (adapted from Green 2013a, 44)

We all operate with multiple layers of identity. At the upper, most global level, we are identified by the collective to which we belong. BMBs, as part of Muslim societies, are known as Muslims, or Sunnis, or Lebanese Shiites, and so on. Everyone growing up and living in a particular community, within a state or a nation, takes on some fundamental symbolic identity markers that are ascribed to him or her through his or her collective belonging. For example, I am a white Westerner and a Canadian. Underneath our broad collective identity are layers of social identity that are ascribed or adopted as a result of belonging to groups and families, and through our association with the people with whom we live our day-to-day lives. These individual social identities overlap and change. After one completes university, for example, one moves from being identified as a student to being a part of the work force. For example, I am now socially identified as being a member of a college faculty and as a member of my particular mission agency. These are all overlapping and multifaceted parts of my social identity. Under or within the social identity is the inner core identity. This core identity, according to Green, "is the inner heart of a person's self-awareness and worldview, first formed as young children subconsciously internalize their parents' values and outlook" (2013a, 46). This core identity goes through stages of development as a person matures until he or she arrives at a point where the core identity becomes an achieved identity, something chosen deliberately for oneself (2013a, 46).

When Muslims convert to faith in Christ they inevitably go through a radical form of identity transformation that has massive implications for them at all three levels of identity. However, the transformation is not instantaneous. For example, at the core level of their "identity house," though BMBs have a new identity in Christ, this does not mean that their old core Muslim identity immediately disappears. It is often experienced as if a new, in Christ identity is "overwritten" on top of the old core identity—and this means that there is much potential for everything to get confused and mixed up. Green describes some of the complexities of BMB core identity transformation following conversion:

> That is where life gets complicated, for it takes a prolonged internal struggle to change one's worldview—to value humility above honor for example, or forgiveness above revenge. The "voices" of old and new value systems compete to be heard and obeyed, as they argue with each other on the "core identity" layer of the house. . . .

We find the same ambivalence in New Testament descriptions of conversion. At times the apostle Paul stresses discontinuity, for "the old has gone, the new has come" (2 Cor 5:17). But elsewhere, or even in the same passages, he exhorts converts to keep waging war on the old self which still stubbornly exerts its influence, or to put off old habits and take old thoughts captive, or to keep on being transformed by the renewing of their minds. To internalize and prioritize new values is a kind of ongoing spiritual *jihad*. Whether viewed through secular or theological lenses, there is both continuity and discontinuity in the core identity of converts. (2013a, 48-49)

This three-layered "identity house" gives us another lens with which to view the challenges that BMBs face in their pilgrimage from their pre-conversion identity to a mature, stable and healthy new identity in Christ.

When we apply this analysis to the top eighteen most mentioned challenges, we uncover a number of new insights (see table 9.4). The obstacles to growth coming from the outer, collective identity are perhaps the most well-known and can be very substantial. However, in the interviews, they paled in comparison with the challenges faced at the social and the core levels of identity. The two collective obstacles appear sixth and twelfth in the chart and are mentioned by only 10 percent of those interviewed: struggles to do with living as a believing family in a Muslim context and living in an Islamic police state where one is unable to change one's official identity. These can often be significant obstacles, but the challenges are strongest from the social level, with four of the top five challenges being at the social level (32 percent of all the obstacles mentioned). These social identity issues are pressures from family, from the Muslim community, from poor social status and from inability of BMBs to trust one another— a huge challenge that arises from their Muslim social identity. In addition, the challenges that strike at the core identity of BMBs make up fully half of the most frequently mentioned top eighteen challenges. Though the relative frequency of mention of an obstacle is not an objective measure of which are the toughest things that BMBs face, it is clear that they hit every dimension of BMB identity. Yet the biggest pressure is at the social level (187 mentions—53 percent) with challenges to the core identity of BMBS a close second in frequency of mention (132 mentions—37 percent).

This strong weighting of the challenges BMBs face on the level of social and core identity accounts for the fact that BMBs living for Christ in the midst of Muslim minorities in which the collective identity chal-

Table 9.4. Top Eighteen Obstacles Facing BMBs in Their Collective, Social and Core Identities

Rank	Obstacles BMBs Face in Collective, Social and Core Identities	Total	Collective Social Core	Gender	
				M /50	F /25
6	Challenges for BMB families: child rearing, education, marriage	19	Collective	12	7
12	Living in a police state where change of religion is not officially possible	10	Collective	9	1
Challenges at the Level of Collective Identity		**29**			
1	Pressures from Muslim family; family control, especially while single	35	Social	23	12
2	Local Muslim community's hostility, rejection and/or expulsion	29	Social	18	11
3	Vulnerability due to youthfulness, low social status, weak economic state	28	Social	20	8
5	Lack of trust among BMBs and groups; lack of commitment to one group	22	Social	16	6
10	Local Christians, churches and communities do not accept BMBs	11	Social	8	3
14	Illiteracy and/or low levels of literacy; oral learners.	9	Social	3	6
13	The discipler's ineffectiveness, poor response and wrong motives	9	Social	8	1
Challenges at the Level of Social Identity		**143**			
4	Fear of all kinds: of problems, suffering, persecution and oppression	24	Core	17	7
7	Spiritual nature of Christian faith: about Holy Spirit, prayer, faith, rather than deeds	14	Core	9	5
8	BMB lack of confidence, inherited complexes, victimization, emotional pain	13	Core	7	6
9	Satanic hold of Islam, demonic and occult bondages, hate, anger, lust	12	Core	7	5
11	The love of money; BMBs need to learn to give	10	Core	6	4
15	Poor ethics, lack of integrity; BMBs must learn new ethics before a holy God	9	Core	5	4
16	Learned Muslim ideology, doctrine, traditions, requiring re-education	9	Core	9	0
17	God is distant and unknowable; difficult to bring God close to BMBs	8	Core	5	3
18	Men especially struggle with sexual issues and lust	8	Core	6	2
Challenges at the Level of Core Identity		**107**			
Total in Eighteen Most Mentioned Obstacles		***279***		***188***	***91***

lenges of an Islamic state are absent (such as, for example, in parts of India or in the West) nevertheless face much the same kinds of challenges. The core and social identity issues are present similarly in most Muslim social environments. I have heard a number of BMBs say that even when they meet a BMB from a totally different part of the world, it takes only a few minutes for them to realize that they understand each other instinctively. They recognize that the challenges they face, as BMBs, are only rarely understood by believers who have not come out of Islam. The way that Islam shapes an individual's identity at the core, and the way that it molds a person's social mediated sense of identity, appears to be remarkably consistent throughout the Muslim world. Thus, insight into how to handle the big challenges learned in the Arab world will also be valuable for BMBs in most Muslim contexts. Given the size, number and multidimensional nature of the challenges that BMBs encounter at every level of their identity, how can we be surprised that disciples of Christ across the Muslim world need much support as they persevere "through many tribulations" as they "enter the kingdom of God" (Acts 14:22).

10

NEGOTIATING A NEW IDENTITY IN CHRIST WITHIN MUSLIM COMMUNITIES

You are the light of the world. A city set on a hill cannot be hidden.
Nor do people light a lamp and put it under a basket, but on a
stand, and it gives light to all in the house. In the same way,
let your light shine before others, so that they may see
your good works and give glory to your
Father who is in heaven.

MATTHEW 5:14-16

In some ways, this gets to the heart of the identity crisis facing
converts from Islam into a Christian faith. Most of them make a
decision to change after a long and careful investigation of doctrine,
choosing to reject Muslim doctrine and adopt Christian doctrine.
They and their Muslim relations associate Christian doctrine with
Christian religion, and thus with a collective Christian identity.
Many participants told me that they themselves do not immedi-
ately make this association, but that their families assume it.
However, because of their new sense of community honour and
their commitment to their families, they do not want to give up
their Muslim identity.

KATHRYN KRAFT, *SEARCHING FOR HEAVEN IN THE REAL WORLD*

THIRTY-YEAR-OLD NORTH AFRICAN, KAREEM, had been a believer for a few years but had endeavored to keep his Christian activities and identity hidden from his family, with whom he still lived because he was unemployed. The husband of one of his sisters belonged to an underground Islamist group known to resort to violence, and he feared what would happen if his sister's husband learned of his conversion. Finally, things appeared to be looking up when he got a low-paying job through a friend of the family. He worked hard and sought to do his best, hoping that this, his first real job after a decade of unemployment, might eventually lead to a better job.

Then disaster struck. When a local police officer intercepted unsolicited mail from a foreign media ministry, he immediately showed it to Kareem's mother. She confronted him when he arrived home from work, and he denied its implications. He told them that years before he had been curious about Christianity and had written and asked some questions but had not had any contact with that group for years (true). Under pressure, when confronted directly, he told his family that he was not a Christian and that his interest in Christianity had long ago ended. It was simply a part of his naive teen years. Because they had nothing else to go on, his family eventually accepted his denial. However, Kareem's employer immediately fired him when he learned of the incident. He could not risk the viability of his business enterprise by having an employee that he suspected of being an apostate.

Kareem was devastated—he had been accused of being a Christian and had lost his first job only weeks after having started. He also felt horrible for having denied Christ before his family. He stayed home and plunged into a deep, soul-threatening depression. Kareem stopped showing up for weekly Bible studies, and initially none of us knew what had happened. One of his close friends, who was known to the family and also a member of the house church, went to his home to visit him and find out what had happened. Kareem told him only the bare minimum of what had happened and said that he would not ever again meet with the believers. The group prayed earnestly for Kareem. Then, we put together a plan by which his friend managed to get him to come out from his home and meet with his believing friends in our home, making sure that he could not have been followed and no one could know where Kareem had gone. That first meeting was very hard. Kareem would not talk, and he left nearly as depressed as when he came. But the spell of the attack had been broken, and Kareem gradually resumed regular fellowship.

In time, he recovered and became again one of the regular and most committed members of our little discipleship group. Some months later, Kareem began to ask us to pray that God would open up an opportunity for him to be able to let his family know that he *was* a follower of Christ. Some months later, through a conversation he had with an aunt, the family learned of his identity as a Christian. None of what he had feared materialized. His fundamentalist brother-in-law left him alone, and the sister married to the fundamentalist was the most interested in his Christian faith. His family became acquainted with a number of the believers in the Christian group, both locals and expats, and his family accepted his identity as a Christian fairly quickly. Kareem's changed behavior following his conversion, and his years of living before his family had won their respect, even though they had not initially known that the changes were a result of his Christian faith. As of this writing, Kareem has been married to a believing local woman, and they have been in full-time ministry for more than a decade. Kareem's struggles and eventual bold witness to his family illustrate the complex issues involved in forming one's identity as a Christian within one's Muslim family and community.

COMMUNITY AND IDENTITY ISSUES IN DISCIPLING BMBs

This chapter brings us to possibly the most complex issue in the discipleship of BMBs—how they relate to and continue to live within their Muslim families and communities following their new birth and entry into the new community in Christ. The desire to find workable and creative solutions for this challenge is one of the primary drivers for the more radical approaches to contextualization discussed above in chapter six. For many BMBs, the hardest and longest struggle is figuring out who they are with respect to their family and community after they have become disciples of Christ. Many difficult questions come to the surface. Are BMBs still Muslims in some way? Must one reject everything one has been raised to believe? Can one continue to celebrate Muslim religious holidays with one's family? Is Islam unremittingly evil and to be utterly shunned, or are there elements in one's previous Muslim spirituality and spiritual practices that can be retained and adapted as a follower of Christ? All of these questions swirl around the core issue: Who am I now? What does my new identity really mean and how does this affect the way I understand and relate to my Muslim family, friends and community?[1]

Interviewees were asked three different questions that grappled with this vital issue of individual identity as a follower of Christ within a community-oriented culture in which one is considered a traitor to family, community and nation when one no longer believes in Muhammad and the Qur'an. Analysis of the responses to the three questions covers the next three sections.

DISCIPLING INDIVIDUALS IN COLLECTIVE CULTURAL CONTEXTS

The first question sought to elucidate how our Western, more individualistic approaches to discipleship need to be adjusted when discipling within Eastern contexts that place much greater stress on community identity. What needs to be done to ensure that BMB discipleship can be effective and not stumble over typical Western individualistic perspectives and approaches? There were four answers to the question of how to disciple in collective cultures that were cited quite frequently (see responses 1-4). These four responses fall naturally into two complimentary groups: those focusing on the nature of the Christian group people are discipled into (responses 2 and 4) and those dealing with how to relate

---

[1]For a book-length case study of how this issue has played out over the lifespan of a single convert, it is helpful to read Chandler's portrayal of Mazhar Mallouhi as a Muslim pilgrim of Christ in the Muslim world of the Middle East (Chandler 2007). There is also a helpful discussion of Mallouhi and this book in *SEEDBED* 22 (1): 5-31. This issue has several articles responding to Chandler's book and reflecting on the kind of man Mallouhi is and how he wrestled with these identity and contextualization issues throughout his life.

Table 10.1. Ways to Disciple Effectively in Communal Contexts

Discipling in Communal Contexts	Total	Regional Background		Religious Background		Gender	
		Global South	West	BMB	Other	M /50	F /25
1. Disciple BMBs, whenever possible, without breaking relationships with family or community	43	23	20	13	30	29	14
2. Use small groups for discipleship and building trust between BMBs	31	17	14	11	20	22	9
3. Know and be part of the whole family, before and after the first person believes	26	14	12	7	19	18	8
4. Workers and body need to be a trusting new community	23	15	8	10	13	12	11
5. Do a lot of one-on-one discipleship to strengthen faith of BMBs	14	8	6	3	11	8	6
6. Work with and honor the male head of the household	13	10	3	5	8	10	3
7. Introduce BMBs to other local BMBs who are doing well and are good models	12	6	6	5	7	9	3
8. BMBs reach out to their own families only when they are ready	12	8	4	2	10	9	3
9. Be realistic about expectations: some cannot avoid being extracted or expelled	11	3	8	2	9	9	2
10. Be very sensitive to differences in culture and work within their culture	11	5	6	3	8	7	4
11. As much as possible, disciple BMBs within their own Muslim contexts	10	6	4	2	8	7	3
12. Individuals convert, but they must be in community to grow—do everything in groups	5	3	2	2	3	2	3
13. Much harder for women; family opposed to their faith and they have few options	5	5	0	4	1	1	4
14. Be gender sensitive: men with men, women with women	4	3	1	1	3	1	3
Totals	**220**	**126**	**94**	**70**	**150**	**144**	**76**

to believers' Muslim communities (responses 1 and 3). Of the next most frequently cited ten answers, most fell into the same two categories, but three offered additional insights (responses 5, 9 and 13).

The responses to this question point to two complementary top priorities in discipling BMBs that are crucial in adapting our often default individualistic approaches to discipleship to collective Islamic cultures. First, we must do everything possible, without compromise, to help BMBs remain closely connected to their families and communities (see responses 1, 3, 6, 8, 10, 11 and 14) throughout the discipleship process. The second priority is that we must strive to create a strong, intimate, caring and transparent new family and community for the new believer to join upon confessing faith in Christ (responses 2, 4, 7 and 12).

It is intriguing that there seems to be very little difference in the kinds of answers to this question given by people, regardless of their gender, religious or cultural background. Most responses reflected the demographic makeup of the interviewee group quite closely. Perhaps the only exception worth noting is that the fourth point—that the BMB needs to be welcomed into a caring community—appears to have been emphasized more by women, by BMBs and by non-Westerners.

A number of practical and helpful suggestions were given that help BMBs minimize the threat of being expelled from their families and rejected by their communities for following Christ. Perhaps the most frequently emphasized strategy is to train new believers right from the start in appropriate ways of communicating their new faith. It was regularly recommended that the new believer be encouraged to say nothing to his or her family immediately. Rather, the believer should give sufficient time so that the power of a transformed life could lead family members to ask about why he or she has changed. Giving close family members an opportunity to observe life change makes the eventual explanation for it more palatable. Further, many said that the discipler must teach the new believer how to speak of the new faith in ways that are inoffensive and communicate clearly to a Muslim while minimizing the shock. Disciplers are thus encouraged to instruct believers in how to avoid talking about their faith too soon or in an abrasive manner, and they are to be taught how to describe their conversion in ways that are winsome and less likely to cause a strong reaction.

One North African church leader's experience is illustrative of how this dual strategy sometimes plays out. Rashid was in his thirties when he finally came to faith in Christ through several years of faithful witness and friendship from a local believer. Rashid had been an army officer who had earlier treated his mother and sister terribly, abusing them and holding them in contempt. He did not tell his family of his conversion for many months. Finally, one day, his sister followed him into his room, locked the door and told him she would not let him out until he told her the reason for his character transformation. She was astonished that Rashid had been treating her and their mother with gentleness, respect and love for months. She absolutely loved her "new" brother and insisted on having an explanation. In response, he took out a Bible, laid it on the coffee table in front of her and said, "This book has changed my life. Read it and you'll understand." He then left the room and did not talk to her about his faith for quite a long time, until she had read in the Bible and had questions for him.

The other main set of advice repeatedly given, with the goal of lessening the likelihood of BMBs' families expelling them following their conversion, was that the evangelist/discipler must make every effort possible to get to know the whole family of the interested seeker long before the person comes to faith. Then, when an individual in the family does come to faith, the family will know the source of the "contagion" and will have learned to like and trust the people through whom the message of Christ came to a member of their family. This will further decrease the strength of the reaction and/or rejection by the believer's family. In several cases BMB disciplers stressed that it is vital that even the foreigner insists on getting to know the family of the seeker, even when the seeker is reluctant to invite the expatriate to meet the family.

Another strong recommendation was that we work with the family authority structure and honor the role of the head of the family. One Middle Eastern BMB church leader gave examples of how he regularly intervened when a family expelled a new believer for his or her new faith. He would take the believer (usually a young man) with him and speak face to face with the angry father. He would reassure the father that his son's new faith was not a rejection of the father's authority or done in rebellion against the family. He would offer to mediate any disputes between the new believer and family members. Frequently such intervention with the head of the family prevented a rupture and enabled the believer to remain with his or her family and learn to live his or her new faith without the added burden of having to live in the streets. This BMB leader did all he could to directly intervene when the shame-induced response to a conversion happened. This would make it possible for the shamed family to accept the dishonored one and continue to accept him or her in the family, in spite of the seemingly shameful betrayal committed through conversion to Christ.

The other side of this need to be sensitive to the collective nature of Islamic societies in our discipling was the often-repeated advice that the community of believers, the local church, must warmly welcome BMBs into a local church group that includes BMBs. Even if BMBs' families have not rejected them for their new faith, the spiritual change that has taken place in the BMB needs the strong support of a loving and caring Christian family to nurture and sustain the new identity. A new believer has indeed entered into a new spiritual family, and it helps strengthen the new identity when the believer is genuinely welcomed into a truly caring family of believers. The nearly universal default assumption made by BMBs as they come to Christ is that they are the only Muslim who has ever chosen to follow Christ. It is therefore crucial, especially when someone comes to faith through the witness of an expatriate, that new believers meet other local BMBs as soon as possible to help them know that they have entered a new family that includes plenty of others like themselves. Knowing that they are not alone in having taken such a tough decision is tremendously encouraging and reassuring.

In addition to these two top priorities, some other helpful counsel was frequently given. The fifth frequently-given counsel was that the discipler needs to give a lot of time to one-on-one discipleship of the new believer. This ensures that the believers will feel not only that they belong to their new community but also that they are growing in their understanding of what it means to be in Christ. Discipleship needs to be both intensely communal *and* individual.

Even though this very idealistic counsel were repeatedly stressed, it must also be noted that a number of interviewees argued for solid realism on this topic of helping believers stay connected to their families. In points 8 and 9 in table 10.1, interviewees stressed that disciplers must give believers the right and freedom to decide how to interact with their family. Sometimes the best short-term solution is for believers to run from their families to avoid harm and even death. They reminded me that if the believers come from fundamentalist families, they may well have little choice in the matter and will be forced to abandon their family in order to survive and to prevent the family being torn apart over their apostasy. Even the most frequently repeated advice, to disciple BMBs without breaking relationships with their family, was normally expressed using the qualifying phrase "as much as possible." The believers need to stay within their family and community whenever possible. Tragically, far too often it is not possible.

Let me share one sobering example of this. In an interview with an Egyptian Coptic priest, I was told that the best policy for BMBs in Egypt is that they leave their homes and move to another city. The pressures are too great on the believers for them to remain in their families. Often even mothers will report the conversion of their children to the police in order to have their own children arrested and tortured. This sobering assessment needs to be kept in mind, even while we all strive to do everything possible to keep the believers from being rejected by their Muslim family on confession of faith. After all, the root reason for the family rupture is not the sometimes immature behavior of the new believer but the ideological rejection of Christ within Islam. Jesus himself warned that his coming into a family would tear families apart.

THE VALUE OF "COMING OUT" TO ONE'S FAMILY AND COMMUNITY

While interviewing, in order to set the stage for the next question, I usually told the perspective on BMB identity given by Roland Muller

(2006, 108-9), where he explains that BMBs need to unite their two faces. As mentioned in the last chapter, Muller suggests that to grow in a healthy way the BMB needs to integrate his or her Muslim self with his or her new Christian self into a new whole identity. Failure to do this leads to a number of unacceptable solutions to the identity struggle. Muller further argues that a BMB cannot be fully healthy without "coming out" and confessing his or her faith to his or her family and close friends.[2]

After thus setting the stage by recounting Muller's perspective, I asked whether interviewees agreed with Muller that BMBs need to "come out." The overwhelming majority agreed that it was essential that BMBs eventually declare their faith in Christ to their families (see table 10.2, items 1, 2 and 5). In talking with a very experienced female BMB leader and discipler who has been involved in house church leadership and national ministry in North Africa for decades, I pressed her to give some sort of indication of how long it was acceptable to wait before coming out. She said, "The longer I minister, the more I am convinced that the sooner the BMB 'comes out,' the better it is for everyone. Do not let much time pass. Certainly, it is not good for a believer not to confess faith for several years."

Almost everyone stressed that it was very important that the "coming out" be handled effectively. One-third of the interviewees suggested that the key question is not whether new believers should "come out" (that was to be assumed), but rather that they be taught how to "come out" with their family to have minimal rejection and social rupture. Several very experienced BMB disciplers stressed that this was a vital area for discipleship at the beginning—teaching new believers how to communicate their new faith to those close to them. Also, though pretty much everyone agreed that BMBs must eventually let their new identity in Christ be known, a number of interviewees, BMBs especially, stressed that it is not the role of the discipler to tell the BMBs when to come out. That decision must stay with the BMBs. Certainly one can encourage them to be ready, and one can pray with them for the right opportunity, but one must not insist that any particular time is *the* time. It is always

---

[2]Please refer to appendix D to read the quotation from Muller which was the basis for the background context I normally set before asking the question discussed in this section.

wrong to pressure a BMB to declare his or her faith to the family. The discipler must walk a fine line of encouraging openness and transparency while giving their disciple freedom to choose the right time following the prompting of the Holy Spirit.

Even those whose ministry approach was much more "insider" stressed that believers need to let their family know that they are followers of Christ. These disciplers suggested that BMBs could identify themselves as Muslim followers of Christ—they did not need to say that they were Christians. Yet, even they stressed that believers have to tell their families that they are now loyal to Christ. My point here is not to endorse such an approach but rather to note that "high" approaches to contextualization and the less "insider" approaches are not as far apart in their objectives as some would have us believe. Almost everyone is seeking to keep new believers rooted in their community whenever possible, and they all agree that Christians should not hide their faith any longer than necessary. In practice, I have observed that, though the terminology used sometimes varies considerably, the practical solutions that are found to be truly viable in walking alongside believers who are learning to live as Christ's disciples are very similar right across the contextualization continuum.

Much is at stake for the BMBs in this issue. My experience is that if a BMB chooses to never reveal his or her faith to close family members, or explicitly denies his or her faith, the normal outcome is that the BMB will eventually go back into the Muslim family and community as a Muslim, abandon faith in Christ, forsake public identification with Christ and often even walk away from faith in Christ entirely. Because this is such a crucial and very difficult step of obedience, disciplers need to be much in prayer for new believers, that God will cause everything to work for good for the BMB and his or her family when the coming out time comes.

Finding a Suitable BMB Identity Within One's Muslim Family and Community

In her sociological study of the conversion experiences of thirty-three Muslims in the Arab world, Kathryn Kraft (2012) explored the complexities that converts faced in negotiating their new identity as Chris-

tians. The dynamics of their identity journey were often very difficult
and complex, and it was a long journey for them to settle into any sort
of stable new identity as disciples of Christ. To say that BMBs must immediately identify themselves as Christians is to assert something that
is virtually impossible for most BMBs to do while remaining within
their social networks—especially in the Middle East. Kraft sheds light
on some of the personal challenges that BMBs deal with in sorting out
their new identity:

Table 10.2. BMBs' Self-Identity in Their Muslim Family and Community

BMB Ideal Self-Identity in Their Muslim Family and Community	Total	Years Discipling			Religious Background		Gender	
		0-3	4-10	11+	BMB	Other	M	F
1. BMBs cannot live a healthy life without declaring identity with Christ	51	3	21	27	13	38	35	16
2. BMBs must eventually "come out" with family and friends as a Christ follower	46	7	17	22	11	35	30	16
3. Known by being honest, loving, stable and a resource for others	41	3	17	21	10	31	29	12
4. Goal is to live in and reach out to members of their own communities through their lives and witness	25	6	10	9	6	19	18	7
5. Key question is not whether to come out, but how to do so with minimal social rupture	21	2	7	12	9	12	16	5
6. Ideal identity is as "believer" and proud of national and/or cultural identity	15	2	6	7	4	11	9	6
7. The BMB must find new identity in Christ and leave old Muslim identity	13	0	8	5	2	11	9	4
8. Persecution is a likely part of following Christ in Muslim honor communities	11	1	5	5	5	6	10	1
9. Should or can be known and self-identified as a "Muslim follower of Christ"	10	6	2	2	0	10	7	3
10. Their ideal identity depends on how extreme their community is	8	3	1	4	2	6	5	3
11. BMBs do not need to identify themselves as Christians	7	4	1	2	1	6	5	2
12. BMBs must be known in and accountable to a local body of believers	5	1	2	2	3	2	4	1
Totals	**253**	**38**	**97**	**118**	**66**	**187**	**177**	**76**

Although members of their society may see their faith change as an abandonment of the community, that is not usually their wish. To them, their
change is a change in beliefs, not a change in culture or society. . . . [They]
are actively seeking ways to remain in their communities without needing
to abide by the faith of those around them. (Kraft 2012, 101)

BMBs generally do not wish to leave their Muslim community, and so
they struggle to find ways of being known as different in their beliefs yet
still loyal to and united with their Muslim family and community.

When interviewing, our discussion of "coming out" was immediately
followed up by my asking, "What is the BMBs' ideal identity in their
family and community?" The range of answers given is presented in
table 10.2. So, how was this question about the ideal identity for a BMB
answered? Everyone agreed that the ideal was that BMBs should remain
within their communities and become known as followers of Christ
who are respected for the quality of their lives and their contribution to
their families. Everyone seeks to work toward the scenario in which
BMBs are able to witness to their families and communities as respected
community members even though they are known as believers. Some
suggested that BMBs should be proud to be Algerians or Moroccans (or
whatever the case may be) who love their country and its good traditions but who also are known as dedicated and bold followers of Christ.
As mentioned in the last chapter, Kraft suggests that such people are
adding a new identity (Christian) to their old identity (their nationality)
and are thus seeking to create a unique new identity that has not previously been known in the context. Here is how Kraft describes such "adhesive" identity strategies:

> Wanting to live a unified life, many are able to root themselves in a
> national-cultural identification by finding an ethnic identity to match their
> new religious identities, calling themselves, for example, Arab Christians
> or Moroccan Christians. . . . It is a way for them to stay committed to the
> cohesiveness of the *umma*, maintaining their commitment to their Muslim
> community while distancing themselves from the faith-based aspects of
> that affiliation. (2012, 103)

One North African church planter serves as an unusual but compelling example of this attempt to forge a new adhesive identity. He and
his wife are doing everything they can to convince people in their city
that there can be Christian nationals who are loyal to their country even
though they are no longer Muslims. He lives with his family in a city of
several hundred thousand, and they are doing everything possible to let
their whole neighborhood, and the whole city if possible, know that they
are Christians. Through his family's life and example, he wants to re-
educate his neighbors so that they will come to understand what
Christian nationals are like. He is praying and believing that by being
widely known as Christians, many will come to his family for explanations of their loving and compassionate lifestyle and be drawn to Christ.
He believes that they will eventually be able to share the gospel with large
numbers of people as the powerful testimony of transformed Christian
lives is seen firsthand and known for what it is. This stance initially
earned him considerable attention from the local police. Then, after a
few months of frequent lengthy interrogations of him and his wife, he
became friends with the police, and they no longer harass him.

In discussing the ideal BMB identity within their Muslim communities, two-thirds of the interviewees stressed that it is the living of transformed lives, combined with persevering through sometimes very intense persecution, that earns the BMBs the right to be heard, and often,
after some years, the grudging respect of most community and family
members. Further, most agreed that it was generally not appropriate for
BMBs to use the term "Christian" to describe themselves. Various terms
in the local language were suggested, but very few agreed that it was acceptable for BMBs to identify themselves as Muslims without some sort
of qualification or explanation. There was little variation in people's approach to this issue of what to call themselves, regardless of the gender,
religious background and amount of experience as a discipler. Interestingly, however, although ten of the disciplers interviewed believed that
it was acceptable for BMBs to call themselves "Muslim followers of
Christ," none were themselves former Muslims. There was not a single
BMB who was comfortable using such a label (see item 9 in table 10.2).

Furthermore, most of those who were comfortable with BMBs calling themselves Muslims were the least experienced disciplers.

The consensus among those interviewed was that it was desirable, and usually possible, for BMBs to persevere through persecution and opposition. True, sometimes one had to flee one's home for a time in order to survive and later become known by one's family and social circle, and sometimes even by the community at large, as a follower of Christ who is known, trusted and respected for the quality of the life one lives. Thus, even though they may not be accepted fully into the Muslim community, they are respected as people of religious integrity who are willing to suffer for their faith and who treat everyone around them with integrity and kindness.

Several mature BMB leaders tell similar stories of how their Muslim families grew to respect them, after sometimes quite strong and even violent initial rejection. When one female BMB from North Africa returned home from the West to tell her family of her faith, her father wanted to kill her in his rage, but her brothers restrained him. However, within a few years relations improved, and now she is like the sole rock in the family on whom many in the immediate and extended family depend. They all know she is a Christian, and they therefore can trust her with their secrets. She has ongoing opportunities to serve and love her family in Christ's name, and she is highly respected by her family and many in her home town. Many other such accounts could be told that illustrate the central conviction of most of those interviewed that the goal for BMBs and their families is to be known as Christ's and know for the quality of their character and the respect with which they treat their families.

THINKING THROUGH BMBs' RELATIONSHIP TO EXISTING CHURCHES

The final question related to the BMBs' identity in their community had to do with the connection that BMBs should have, or do have, with the local Christian community. I asked people what they saw as their goal for the integration of new believers with existing believers and churches. Across North Africa and the Arabian Peninsula the answer was virtually identical—their goal was to have them integrated into the existing BMB church fellowship, or if none existed locally, to seek to plant a new church of BMBs (see table 10.3, item 1). Because there is no historic church remaining in these regions of the Arab world, the question of how BMBs ought to relate to existing churches made up of believers from Christian backgrounds (BCBs) never came up. This issue is pretty much a nonissue in North Africa and the Arabian Peninsula. One exception to this was in Tunis, where the government, prior to the 2010 revolution, had encouraged the Tunisian believers to meet openly in the few church buildings that are owned and operated by and for expatriate Christians. Additionally, in the Arabian Peninsula, there are increasing numbers of

Table 10.3. BMB Integration in Existing Churches

BMB Church Integration Goal	Total	Ministry Region				Religious Background		Gender	
		NA 26	ME 31	AP 5	FR 11	BMB 23	Other 52	M 50	F 25
1. BMBs in their own loving church groups of mostly BMBs	56	26	20	4	6	13	43	38	18
2. Help people to live as believers within own families and society	21	6	14	1	0	5	16	16	5
3. BMBs and BMB groups need links with non-BMB leaders and churches to be part of something bigger than themselves	18	2	12	3	0	6	12	13	5
4. One-on-one discipleship of the BMBs and their families	17	6	8	1	2	4	13	13	4
5. Network BMBs with other BMBs in the country, and beyond, in order to have peer mentors	10	6	0	0	4	2	8	7	3
6. BMBs in their own church of fellow BMBs, in close association with local non-BMB churches	7	1	6	0	0	5	2	4	3
7. In France, the BMBs need to be integrated into a French church and their contributions valued	7	0	0	0	7	3	4	4	3
8. BMBs need identity as BMBs in non-BMB churches and to be valued for their contribution to them	6	0	5	0	1	5	1	3	3
9. Integrate into non-BMB churches and do not create BMB groups	5	0	4	0	1	1	4	4	1
Totals	**147**	**47**	**69**	**9**	**21**	**44**	**103**	**102**	**45**

churches of Arab Christians from Egypt and the Levant, and so these issues of integration of BMBs into Arab BCB churches are not entirely absent in the region. I will not comment here on how these issues play out in Muslim regions outside of the Arab world. I expect that readers familiar with such contexts will be able to readily apply whatever is most helpful in this discussion to their own contexts.

However, in Muslim immigrant communities, and in the parts of the Arab world such as Sudan, Egypt, Jordan, Lebanon, Syria and Iraq that have local evangelical churches whose members are almost exclusively from among the indigenous Christian communities, this is a thorny question indeed. Should BMBs form their own BMB churches? If so, how should these churches relate to the BCB churches? If one advocates integrating all BMBs into existing churches, how does one overcome the normal fear and prejudice that is felt both ways? Two-thirds of interviewees working in the Middle East stressed the need for BMBs to be integrated into churches made up of all or mostly BMBs. In addition, more than half (eighteen of thirty-one; see items 3 and 6 in table 10.3) suggested that the BMB churches should have association and positive connection with the BCB churches and their leaders. Only four suggested that BMBs should not create their own churches, but three of those four were BMBs. Five BMBs in the Middle East felt that BMBs should normally be a part of BCB churches and that they should be valued for the rich heritage that they bring to those churches as BMBs.

In France, the situation was somewhat different. About half of the interviewees suggested that BMBs should form their own groups, at least fellowship groups, if not separate churches, and the other half felt that BMBs should not form their own churches but rather integrate into French churches. On closer examination, it turns out that people in France who suggested that there should be BMB churches were referring to the ministry situation in Algeria. They all thought that in France it was not appropriate to form BMB fellowships or local churches. Thus, there is a contrast between the situations in France, where the BMBs are immigrants seeking to fit into the majority host culture, and in the Middle East, where BMBs are part of the majority-Muslim community prior to conversion.

In Egypt, Jordan and Lebanon this was often felt to be a contentious issue, and it elicited strong feelings in both directions. I met with several BMBs who have had relationships with local Arab evangelical churches that are very positively reaching out to Muslims. However, the majority of even these BMBs felt that it was better for BMBs to form their own churches rather than integrate into existing evangelical churches. Moreover, even those who advocated some level of BMB integration in BCB churches argued that these same BMBs must also have their own BMB churches, or at least semi-autonomous fellowships.

There was one notable exception to this BMB stress on the value of BMB churches. I interviewed one BMB woman who is part of the staff of a large local Arab church in her nation's capital. She was adamant that BMBs must integrate into local churches and should never form their own churches. However, she was unique among the BMBs that I interviewed in the Middle East (there were ten) in opposing the formation of any kind of BMB fellowship groups. She insisted that the body of Christ is one and must not be divided because of religious or ethnic background.

Interestingly, the strongest advocates of the necessity of forming BMB churches that kept apart from the BCB Arab churches were Arab Christians who were doing fruitful ministry among Muslims using a more socioreligious insider approach to contextualization. They stressed that when BMBs have contact with local non-BMB Christians and their churches there are usually negative consequences for the BMBs. These Arab missionaries, in different Middle Eastern countries, were also very security-conscious and did not tell anyone in the local Arab churches about the ministries they were doing for fear that their socioreligious insider ministry would be damaged by exposure to such churches and their leaders. Fortunately, in a June 2014 visit back to this country, I learned that the situation has improved and those Arab missionaries who used to keep separate from the local Christians have developed trust in the local leaders and have adjusted their ministry approach away from a more radical insider approach so that now, seven years later, they work together with local Christian leaders much more extensively.

Where does this leave us in terms of recommended integration strategies for ministry in areas where existing BCB evangelical churches are located? Clearly, this is a complex matter without easy solutions. Because there are two very clearly distinguished communities in these countries (one is either a Christian or a Muslim on one's identity card, and in one's very name), it is proving very difficult to successfully integrate BMBs into the local minority Christian communities. It seems that the best approach may be for BMBs to be integrated into BMB house churches and house fellowships that largely remain organizationally apart from the Christian communities and their churches. Crucially, however, such distinct sister-church networks (BMB and BCB) should be significantly linked to each other through strong, friendly relationships between their leaders. In this way, many of the considerable resources in books, media resources and digital materials, teachers and leadership training, and so on, that are available in the Christian communities can be adapted to assist the growth in maturity and size of the BMB church networks. In addition, this relational connection can mean that the BCBs and their churches can benefit from the tremendous resource that BMBs provide in helping their BCB brothers and sisters understand and reach out to Muslims.

Although many expatriate workers and increasing numbers of BMBs are seeking to establish BMB churches and launch movements, at the time of writing I am aware of only one or two church planting movements being launched in the Middle East. There are still very few situations in the Middle East where there are significant numbers of Muslims coming to faith through the witness of BMBs. In most Middle Eastern contexts, Muslims are still coming to faith mostly through the presence and the witness of BCBs, their churches and expatriate workers.

However, this is beginning to change. In Cairo in June 2013, I met a local BCB leader who is leading a very fruitful church planting ministry across the Middle East (with some six thousand new believers in the past decade, most of whom are BMBs). Increasingly this church planting movement is being led by BMBs and the BCBs are serving as trainers of BMB trainers and church planters. In addition, with the tragic meltdown taking place in Syria and Iraq, reports are increasingly coming out of God using BCB churches as they reach out in compassion to help Muslim refugees, both in Iraq and in Syria and in neighboring Lebanon and Jordan. Hundreds of Muslims are coming to Christ as the Spirit of God is helping them see the contrast between the violence carried out in the name of Islam and the compassion they experience in the name of Christ. God is doing new and marvelous things across the Arab world and in many other regions of the Muslim world.

In light of the rapidly changing social, political and religious dynamics across the Muslim world, we must continue to seek creative, Spirit-guided solutions that will help growing movements of BMBs to work in cooperation and synergy with existing national church networks. When we shift our attention beyond the Middle East, we find similar challenges, and some creative new solutions being attempted in other regions of the Muslim world that also face the challenge of a Christian minority national church engaging with growing movements of BMBs. At the moment, some laboratories for such creative synergy include countries such as Ethiopia, Bangladesh, Pakistan and Indonesia. Garrison's recent study of movements to Christ across the Muslim world documents movements occurring to Christ among Muslims in every major region of the Muslim world (2014). May God grant us all grace to find God-honoring, creative solutions that help empower growing BMB movements and that also strengthen and nourish the churches within the often beleaguered Christian minorities in Muslim-majority nations.

11

DISCIPLING BMBs IN AND
THROUGH PERSECUTION

But recall the former days when, after you were enlightened, you
endured a hard struggle with sufferings, sometimes being publicly
exposed to reproach and affliction, and sometimes being partners
with those so treated. For you had compassion on those in prison,
and you joyfully accepted the plundering of your property, since you
knew that you yourselves had a better possession and an abiding
one. Therefore do not throw away your confidence, which has a
great reward. For you have need of endurance, so that when you
have done the will of God you may receive what is promised.

HEBREWS 10:32-36

Redemption through a suffering theophany is the only truly
Christian response to the problem of evil. . . . The theology of the
cross, which is also a theology of suffering, is the basis of trans-
forming and transcending the problem of suffering and evil without
being destroyed by it. . . .

Scripture has always insisted that the cross we bear precedes the
crown we wear and that being a Christian involves taking up one's
cross, with all the sufferings and the difficulties that go with it, and
carrying it until it leaves its marks on oneself and redeems one to
that more excellent way, which comes only through suffering.

ISAIAH M. DAU, "FACING HUMAN SUFFERING,"
SUFFERING, PERSECUTION AND MARTYRDOM

ONE DAY, NOT LONG AFTER WE SETTLED BACK in North
Africa following three months in Canada, an expatriate friend
called and asked whether I could come and talk to a local man who had
shown up at the expatriate church and was looking to meet local believers. I went and met this young man, and over dinner in our home
that evening he told us his story. Several years earlier, Abdelkader, who
was from a neighborhood near where we lived, had first encountered
Jesus through dreams. While in his early twenties, he had become a very
committed Muslim and a young leader with growing influence in a local
branch of an international Islamist organization. But curiosity about Isa
in the Qur'an led to him being told, in a dream, to read the Injil, and so
he obtained an Arabic New Testament from the local expatriate church.
After several months of reading it on his own, in response to the leading
of the Holy Spirit, he came to a robust faith in Christ. Then, during
months of endless discussions and arguments with his fellow Islamists,
Abdelkader made every effort to persuade his friends that Muhammad
was a false prophet and that Jesus was the Messiah, Son of God and
Savior. Eventually, he just managed to escape an attempt on his life (his
Islamist friends had come to execute him for apostasy) by driving directly to the international airport and getting on the first plane out of the
country that had an available seat.

After several years of adventure in the Middle East, during which
time the Holy Spirit led him to an evangelical church where he was
discipled for several years, Abdelkader returned to his home country on
hearing that there was an underground church there. He had assumed
he was the only believer from his country, and when he heard that there
was an underground church, he immediately wanted to meet people like
himself. He was arrested at the airport on arrival (his witnessing to of-
ficials in his country's embassy did not help) and sent to prison in his
home city, where he was tortured nightly for two weeks. Once his prison
guards realized that they could not torture him into recanting his
Christian faith, and after extorting money from him, they quietly released him (giving him two weeks to get out of the country with the

threat that if he ever returned he would not live). Shortly after his release from prison, he went back to the expatriate church where he had
procured that first New Testament in order to try to meet local believers,
and he was sent to me.

After confirming his story through a mutual friend in Europe who
knew him the Middle East, I introduced him to a few local BMB leaders.
He was deeply moved to meet them, though as he talked to them he was
quite disappointed and puzzled by their lack of boldness in proclaiming
Christ. Of all of the sufferings he had undergone for the sake of Christ,
the one that was the most painful was his father's rejection. His father, a
prominent and upstanding businessman and proud and devout Muslim,
had disowned him as his son, gone to the law courts and legally removed
all record of his birth and disinherited him. And the last time he had
called his mother from abroad, she had terrifyingly begged him to no
longer call, because his father had threatened her with instant divorce
should she ever speak with their disinherited son again. So, even though
he was then near his family home, for the sake of his mother he did not
attempt to contact them. Before the expiration of the two-week police
deadline, I bought him a ticket and he flew to Europe. Abdelkader was
subsequently accepted as a religious refugee in Europe and was able to
build a new life for himself there.

We who are disciplers from the developed world initially have a
twofold disadvantage in our efforts to help BMBs who face persecution.
First, we have rarely faced persecution personally. Second, because we
have not been forced to think deeply about such matters, we tend to have
an inadequate theology of suffering and persecution. In this chapter we
will begin by considering biblical and theological perspectives on persecution in order to lay a foundation that can lead us in the direction of
developing a more adequate biblical theology of suffering and persecution. Once these theological foundations have been laid, we will explore the helpful array of counsel I received on how to walk wisely
alongside our BMB brothers and sisters and help them face the nearly
inevitable suffering and persecution that their lives as disciples in Muslim
communities entail.

TOWARD A THEOLOGY OF SUFFERING AND PERSECUTION

Though most of the authors of books on ministering to Muslims usually have the experience-shaped conviction that the Bible teaches that persecution and suffering will be the normal experience of believers in every culture and in every situation, this is not the understanding that most people from the West normally have. It is not surprising that we Westerners have thought little about suffering and persecution prior to arriving in the Muslim world. Western theologians and biblical scholars have generally not focused much attention on biblical and particularly New Testament teaching on persecution.[1]

Some recent works by New Testament scholars, however, have begun to explore and develop a biblical theology of suffering, and particularly of persecution. For example, I found Cunningham's 1997 presentation of the theology of persecution in Luke-Acts to be particularly helpful for this study of discipleship in Islamic contexts. After doing a careful exegesis of Luke's teaching on persecution, Cunningham concludes with several statements that express Luke's understanding of persecution. Five of these affirmations serve us: Persecution is part of the plan of God; persecution is the rejection of God's agents by those who are supposedly God's people; persecution is an integral consequence of following Jesus; persecution is both the occasion of the Christian's perseverance and the occasion of divine triumph (Cunningham 1997, 337-38).

In his monograph exploring a theology of religious persecution, Charles Tieszen gives the following definition of the religious persecution of Christians: "Any unjust action of varying levels of hostility perpetrated primarily on the basis of religion and directed at Christians, resulting in varying levels of harm as it is considered from the victim's perspective" (Tieszen 2008, 48). Tieszen goes on to offer the following affirmations as a theological framework for understanding persecution:

---

[1]An examination of a few dozen books of systematic theology, biblical theology and theology of mission in my personal library turn up nothing written on persecution or a theology of persecution. It is somewhat understandable, I suppose, that theologians and scholars who are not personally experiencing persecution do not consider that the topic must be treated systematically and theologically in their works. This is merely one of the context-influenced flaws inherent in our theologizing from within exclusively developed-world contexts.

(1) The presence of persecution is universal. (2) Though Satan is the ultimate persecutor, who wishes to use it as a rejection of God's people, God nevertheless sovereignly allows and appoints persecution for believers. (3) God uses persecution to sanctify his people, glorify his name and extend evangelism and mission. (4) Christians are called to endure persecution, though an appropriate response may at times seek to avoid it or resist it. (5) The church is called to stand with persecuted believers in prayer and action (79-80).

The late Glenn Penner, a tireless advocate on behalf of the persecuted church, was one of the first contemporary Westerners to think carefully about the close tie in the Scriptures between persecution and discipleship. In *In the Shadow of the Cross: A Biblical Theology of Persecution and Discipleship* (2004), he presented a comprehensive examination of biblical perspectives on persecution. Penner observes that because most Western Christians do not deal with persecution as a matter of course, there is a tendency for pastors and teachers to misapply Scriptures so that "the typical Bible student in the West never even suspect[s] that the biblical texts that deal with pain and suffering might be dealing with suffering for righteousness' sake rather than suffering because of sin" (Penner 2012, 72). Penner stresses the vital role that persecution and suffering for the sake of righteousness play in discipleship to Christ. We do well to ponder his insights:

> We fail to recognize that *persecution is normative for the follower of Christ* historically, missiologically, and (most importantly) scripturally. . . . There is a clear scriptural link between persecution and discipleship. Indeed, *there can be no discipleship without persecution*; to follow Christ is to join him in a cross-carrying journey of reconciling the world to the Father. . . . Weakness, suffering and sacrifice are God's modus operandi. This is how God accomplishes his work, not through strength or compulsion but through love and invitation. As . . . the Servant of God suffers and dies . . . [so] do those who follow him. . . . *A cross-centered gospel requires cross-carrying messengers.*
>
> The demand of Jesus on his followers is to tread the path of martyrdom. . . . Without Christ's death there is no redeemed community. But just as Christ's cross was needed to establish his church, our crosses are needed to

build his church (Matt 16:24). Both are needed. As Josef Ton observes, *"Christ's cross was for propitiation. Our cross is for propagation." To be called to follow Christ is to receive a call to suffer.* (Penner 2012, 72, 73, emphasis added)

In 2012 the World Evangelical Alliance's Mission Commission published *Sorrow and Blood: Christian Mission in Contexts of Suffering Persecution and Martyrdom* (Taylor et al. 2012), a comprehensive compendium of Christian perspectives on persecution and suffering from around the globe.[2] In a profound essay on the problem of evil and suffering, in *Sorrow and Blood*, Isaiah M. Dau, Sudanese Archbishop of the Sudan Pentecostal Church of the new Republic of South Sudan, compares African and Western perspectives on evil and suffering and concludes that a biblical theology of the cross can transform and transcend evil and suffering. The cross reminds believers that their suffering is part of what it means to follow Christ (Dau 2012, 126-27).

Let me bring in one final perspective on religious persecution as we conclude our theological reflections on persecution and suffering. Nik Ripken carried out an extensive multiyear study of persecution in Muslim contexts (interviewing more than three hundred BMBs), and he offers perspectives on persecution similar to those of Cunningham, Tieszen and Dau. He defines persecution as "a negative reaction by government, ideologies, society and family to the presence of Christ, incarnated through a positive witness by believing individuals and communities" (Ripken 2004, 11).[3] Ripken goes on to give what he calls a biblically sound missiology of suffering:

> Persecution is biblically and historically normative for the emerging Church; it cannot be avoided or eliminated. The task is to reduce persecution for secondary reasons. Believers in the midst of persecution, victorious in their walk with Christ, share many commonalities. Two of the

---

[2] I highly recommend this collection of thoughtful Christian reflection on persecution and suffering by sixty-eight theologians and missionaries from twenty-two nations around the world (Taylor et al. 2012, xvii).
[3] Ripken also published a helpful discussion of issues in discipling BMBs during persecution. He concludes that short discussion of suffering and discipleship with a list of ten words of counsel, which if followed, would help foreign disciplers do a better job of discipling in contexts of violence (see Ripken 2008, 355-65).

most important issues are that they have claimed their freedom and they have lost their fear, as was noted earlier. Such components of faith are foundational to incarnating Christ within environments of persecution. (2004, 85)

What then are the primary truths that we have uncovered in our attempt to develop a biblical theology of suffering and persecution that can inform our approaches to preparing BMBs for persecution and helping them through it? Religious persecution of Christians by Muslims is (1) Satan-inspired rejection and unjust actions against (2) the presence of Christ in his servants incarnated through a positive witness by Christian individuals and communities, (3) carried out by people, families, societies and governments who think they are God's people acting on God's behalf. Thinking biblically and theologically, what would be an appropriate way of understanding the persecution and suffering that BMBs and all Christians living in Muslim communities undergo?

The first fundamental understanding that we must embrace is that persecution is the normal, universal experience of following Christ. It is part of the cost of following Christ—his call is a call to suffer with and for him. God allows and appoints the suffering of persecution for believers and uses it for our sanctification. There is no discipleship without persecution. Following Christ involves carrying his cross until it leaves its marks. The second core biblical understanding of persecution is that our perseverance in the midst of persecution is used by God to extend evangelism because it demonstrates the triumph of God. As we imitate our Lord in his suffering and dying, God uses this suffering to help build his church. It is in this painful taking up of the cross of Christ and taking on his suffering that human suffering and evil is redeemed. Our persevering response to suffering and persecution brings glory to God and is a core part of his mission to redeem a suffering world.

PERSPECTIVES ON PERSECUTION FROM OTHER EXPERIENCED DISCIPLERS

A good place to begin is Linda Smith's description of how she helps women BMBs through the inevitable suffering they must endure when they decide to follow Christ (2000, 123-37). She speaks of women who are abused, kicked out of their homes, divorced, beaten and abandoned because of their decision to follow Christ. Smith describes an uncomplicated but sacrificial process of opening her home to these sisters and walking alongside them as they go through intense suffering and trials. She encourages them with strong teaching that suffering is the expected lot of those who choose to follow Christ. Some of her friends have persevered and others have given up and chosen to walk away from Christ rather than continue to suffer for his name. No special formula is offered: love them, care for them, pray for them and help them understand the role of suffering in the Christian life. Smith assumes that this level of persecution is a normal Muslim reaction against the truth and against those who choose to embrace Christ.[4]

Most of the authors who mention persecution have a similarly seasoned perspective. In his book on discipling BMBs, Pietzsch devotes a chapter to helping BMBs learn to appreciate and cope with the privilege of suffering and persecution. "In this world there is always going to be suffering and we cannot avoid it. The Lord is there to carry us through" (Pietzsch 2004, 86). He matter-of-factly reports that many BMBs die because of their faith and that Islam naturally persecutes those who embrace Christ and apostatize from Islam. In spite of this severe Islamic reaction against apostates, he counsels against believers keeping their faith hidden from their families and communities for very long.

This straightforward approach to dealing with persecution and suffering, similar to what we see in the New Testament, is echoed by many. Canadian Mennonite missionary Gordon Nickel stresses that within Islam the law of apostasy has been a major source of severe persecution, and so disciplers must be ready to suffer for Christ along with the BMBs they are helping to disciple (Nickel 1999, 51-53). He recounts the observation of a Muslim convert from Ghana who has pastored BMB churches, saying, "The Muslim convert churches he knows which are strong and growing are the ones in which the leaders are willing to suffer along with

---

[4]This is a summary of her excellent chapter (2000, 123-37) which is full of stories of compassionate ministry and of women BMBs' perseverance through persecution and trials.

the members" (52). Writing from within the Anabaptist tradition, Nickel links this common BMB experience of persecution to the early Anabaptist experience of persecution and, echoing the theology of persecution discussed above, suggests that standing strong in the face of violent opposition is the normal expectation of a disciple of Christ.

One exception to this approach to helping BMBs through suffering is that taken by Phil Parshall. In *Beyond the Mosque* (1985) Parshall focuses on what he sees as a large amount of unnecessary persecution, which takes place because of extraction evangelism.[5] Earlier, in *New Paths in Muslim Evangelism*, he told the "typical" story of Halim Ali's conversion and of the almost immediate persecution and rejection by his Muslim community that followed. Parshall's point was that most of the persecution in that case was a result of inappropriate methods of evangelism and discipleship (Parshall 1980, 181-82). It also led, in such cases, to the total extraction of the new believer from his Muslim community. More recently, however, in *Lifting the Veil*, Phil and Julie Parshall deal with the persecution of BMBs in ways similar to that of the other writers. They discuss how difficult it is for women BMBs in particular, because they seldom have the option of fleeing persecution. They acknowledge that it is a humbling task to disciple BMBs and that BMBs must be helped through the frequent, if not inevitable, persecution that follows their decision to follow Christ (Parshall and Parshall 2002, 259-63).

Writing from an Asian ministry context similar to that of the Parshalls, Greeson claims that though severe persecution, including torture and killing, has been normal within the more contextualized church planting movements birthed using the Camel Method,[6] this persecution has not

---

[5]Finding ways to prevent unnecessary persecution could even be seen as the focus of this whole book.

[6]What Greeson calls the Camel Method is an evangelism strategy that he and others developed in unnamed Asian Muslim countries. It is a combination of a number of methods advocated by people before Greeson: seeking the man of peace; house church multiplication; Henry Blackaby's experiencing God approach of finding where God is already at work and joining him; church planting movements approach (Garrison and Watson); significant contextualization; and using Qur'anic passages as bridges to talk about the gospel with Muslims. A practitioner of the Camel Method learns how to talk about the Qur'anic passages that instruct Muslims to go to Christians for explanations about anything they do not understand in the Qur'an, and then they go to a few key passages in the Qur'an that describe Jesus and his virgin birth and invite Muslims to learn

led to very many cases of BMBs reconverting to Islam. Among these movements in South Asia, reconversion has been minimal. It is worth citing his explanation for this:

> The reason for this may be found in the indigenous nature of the movement associated with the Camel Method. This is a sharp contrast to the history of Muslim conversions to Christianity which typically meant a conversion from Muslim culture into some form of Western culture. That type of cultural conversion has a very high rate of reconversion. . . . In the kinds of churches associated with the Camel Method, there is much less cultural conversion and consequently much less foreignness in the resulting Isahi [Jesus-ian] Muslim community. (Greeson 2007, 168)[7]

Greeson's claim that there are higher levels of reconversion to Islam when the Christian faith is viewed as a foreign phenomenon by both the BMB and the Muslim community needs to be explored further. However, the suggestion that falling away from Christ is rare in these South Asian contextualized movements, in spite of harsh and often severe persecution, is indeed a very different experience from the Arab-world experience, where such falling away is a very common experience. According to Greeson, in these Asian movements, BMBs are often severely persecuted for leaving Islam, but they are not persecuted for rejecting their communities, because their expression of Christian community (their local church group) has little resemblance to anything foreign or Western.

There is no doubt that persecution normally arises when people come to faith in Christ from within Muslim communities. However, in my North African experience, it is also true that how much the Westerner is visibly connected to the believers, and how new believers handle themselves and are taught by those discipling them, often have a significant impact on the way that persecution unfolds and on the intensity and permanence of the family's and community's opposition. General expe-

---

more about Jesus by looking at the Injil (the New Testament) with them. For a full explanation of this approach to ministry among Muslims, see Greeson 2004, 2007.

[7]Greeson explores aspects of this topic in several places. For example, see his discussion of cultural barriers to faith (2007, 170-72).

rience in North Africa is that when careful attention is given to avoid *unnecessary* offense, many of the extremes of persecution can often be avoided. Most of the BMBs I worked with were eventually able to reconcile with their Muslim families (and some experienced no break at all), and many are seeing members of their families following them into faith in Christ. There does need to be boldness, but that boldness has to be tempered with wisdom and common sense. Permanent hostility and total family rejection tend to occur only in more extreme cases where the BMB has, for example, publicly shamed the family or where the BMB comes from a very devout Islamist family. Persecution is indeed normal in the context of Muslim communities, but BMBs can be supported through this time of rejection and violence.

Having laid a foundation of a sound theology of persecution and heard some of the counsel of writers with experience discipling BMBs, it is now time to explore the range of counsel given by the seasoned disciplers whom I asked about how we can prepare BMBs for persecution and walk with them through the persecution that is virtually inevitable.

Seasoned Practical Advice on Supporting BMBs in and Through Persecution

In the interviews, the advice given by BMBs typically flowed out of their personal experience of persecution, whereas the advice given by Westerners came primarily from their experience helping BMBs through persecution,[8] not from experience of themselves being persecuted. When we look at the responses given in table 11.1, it is interesting to note that the top three pieces of advice, which accounted for more than half of the top twelve items, were all to do with teaching people how to prepare for persecution theologically and spiritually.[9] These inter-

---

[8]This is more valuable than comparing by gender, because gender did not show significant variation. For the comparisons in this table, novices are those have been discipling up to ten years, and the experienced disciplers (Experts) are those with eleven years and more experience.

[9]As with earlier topics, had I given the interviewees a list of twelve different things and asked them to say which ones would be good in helping BMBs through persecution, most would likely have selected all of these responses to my questions. Nevertheless, it has proven to be very insightful to compare the spontaneously mentioned advice offered in response to my open-ended questions, because they are what came to the mind of the disciplers immediately.

viewees recommend that disciplers help BMBs understand that in the New Testament persecution was normal and that Christ has the power to take all believers through it. Many interviewees encouraged BMBs to be familiar with and memorize key passages and stories in the New Testament prior to facing persecution. In effect, their first advice is to provide BMBs as quickly as possible with a solid, biblically based the-

Table 11.1. Advice for Discipling in Persecution

Advice Given to Help BMBs Prepare for and Thrive During Persecution	Total	Regional Background		Religious Background		Experience Discipling	
		AW People	The Rest	BMB 23	Other 52	Novice 28	Expert 47
1. Teach a theology of persecution and suffering from the New Testament early in process	41	15	26	9	32	18	23
2. Encourage them with Christ's power to protect and guide; listen and pray with them	35	14	21	8	27	18	17
3. Know and memorize key passages: Matthew 10, John 16, Acts 7, 1 Corinthians 10:13 and stories from Acts	19	7	12	2	17	10	9
4. Do not let people fall; help them in practical ways (give shelter, etc.)	17	10	7	8	9	6	11
5. Stand alongside them and suffer with them, even as foreigners	13	1	12	0	13	6	7
6. Share advice on how to live life, love family and pray for opponents, in order to decrease opposition	13	9	4	5	8	4	9
7. Share testimonies of BMBs, Chinese Christians, others coming through it well	12	7	5	5	7	3	9
8. Devise practical strategies and options and train in how to be interrogated	9	5	4	4	5	2	7
9. Develop strong, deep relationships among BMBs and maintain unity	6	5	1	4	2	4	2
10. Church needs to provide practical assistance and use advocacy as needed	6	5	1	4	2	1	5
11. Pray together for other persecuted BMBs; this helps BMBs know that believers care and remember	5	2	3	2	3	2	3
12. Teach them to have a personal walk with God so they can stand when opposition comes	5	1	4	1	4	1	4
Totals	181	81	100	52	129	75	106

ology of persecution so that they can make sense of their experience and be equipped spiritually to face persecution when it comes.

However, when I reflected further on the results in table 11.1, I noticed that those with the most experience with persecution—BMBs, others from the Arab world,[10] as well as experienced expatriate disciplers—all concurred in stressing practical support for those undergoing persecution more than they did the value of learning from the Scriptures. This entire group of experienced disciplers stressed that believers should be taught in advance how to speak and act in a way that will considerably decrease the likelihood and the intensity of persecution, and that, when persecution came, believers must be given practical assistance and not be allowed to fall when they are under intense pressure. Although everyone interviewed agreed that the top priority is good teaching about persecution and spiritual preparation, the BMBs and those with more experience with persecution seem to concur that it is also very important to provide practical advice and solutions, such as giving shelter to people thrown out of their homes and a safe place to hide for those whose lives are threatened (see items 4, 6 and 8 in table 11.1).

Everyone placed a similarly high significance on the value of having young believers hear testimonies of other BMBs and other persecuted Christians being sustained by Christ in the midst of severe persecution. One pattern is noteworthy: when comparing inexperienced Western disciplers on the one hand, with BMBs, Arab-world and experienced Western disciplers on the other, we see that solutions that stressed church and community care are stressed more by the experienced group than spiritual solutions involving prayer or individuals having strong personal faith (compare items 8 and 10 with 11 and 12). It is perhaps not surprising that people who have experienced persecution themselves, or who have helped many persecuted friends, would put a greater stress on solid practical solutions and helping people avoid and escape perse-

---

[10]The thirty-four interviewees (45 percent) from the Arab world accounted for all but four of the non-Western interviewees, and in this case, they accounted for eighty-one of the remaining ninety-one people who chose these top twelve responses. I thought this comparison group more interesting for this comparison because most from the Arab world would be more likely to have undergone persecution than those from outside the Arab world.

cution than would those with less direct experience of persecution who tend to spiritualize the solutions.

This reminds me of some of the realism that was highlighted in the earlier discussion about helping people stay in their families and communities as much as possible. When persecution is intense, those who know what it is like advise disciplers to help BMBs escape and get out from under pressure as soon as possible. Providing contingency escape plans are part of the responsibility of anyone discipling BMBs in the Arab world. This is not surprising when one realizes that many of the most experienced BMB disciplers were people who had themselves fled from prison, torture, cruel treatment by their families and threat of death. They thus survived and grew in their faith and have since helped many other disciples through similar persecution. The wisdom of these brothers and sisters must be heeded even as we prayerfully ask God that he will give young believers the grace to stay within their families and endure the opposition and persecution in order to be there for their Muslim families.

It is perhaps valuable, in finishing our treatment of this topic of persecution, to summarize and list the advice given by the interviewees on how disciplers can stand alongside BMBs undergoing persecution and support and care for them during their times of trial. I find that the eighteen different suggestions offered can be boiled down to these four primary recommendations:

1. Teach them a sound theology of suffering and persecution. Teach them the core principles given in the first part of this chapter, that persecution is normal and that God uses their perseverance through persecution to strengthen them in faith, to give him glory and advance the church. Help them be familiar with key scriptural texts, promises and stories. Help them be spiritually strong so that they will be able to stand strong when persecution strikes. Help them to recognize and resist "fear itself," a major tool of oppression in Islam.

2. Encourage them to know that Christ will be with them and will protect and guide them through persecution. Share testimonies of

other BMBs and believers who persevered through intense persecution. Pray for other BMBs so that they will understand that if they are cut off while being persecuted, they will not be forgotten by their believing friends. Remind them of the sustaining grace that God provides during persecution.

3. When they are persecuted, help them in practical ways. Stand with them and suffer with them if need be. Let them know that their suffering is shared by others who have gone before them. Help them devise practical strategies for coping during persecution. The church is to provide support, advocacy and rescue when needed.

4. Give them teaching that will help them to decrease the intensity of likely opposition and persecution. Teach them how to respond under interrogation and give them counsel on strategies for avoiding unwise actions and words that would bring persecution on them unnecessarily. Help them learn to be wise in the way they speak and act among their Muslim friends and families.

12

DISCIPLING IN THE FACE OF DEMONIC OPPRESSION AND ATTACK

*The seventy-two returned with joy, saying,
"Lord, even the demons are subject to us in your name!"
And he said to them, "I saw Satan fall like lightning from heaven.
Behold, I have given you authority to tread on serpents and scorpions,
and over all the power of the enemy, and nothing shall hurt you.
Nevertheless, do not rejoice in this, that the spirits are
subject to you, but rejoice that your
names are written in heaven."*

LUKE 10:17-20

*No greater disservice could a discipler render
to a young believer than to keep him or her in the dark
about the spiritual battles that have raged and will rage over
his or her soul and over his or her tribe, clan, people and nation. . . .
Teach your disciples, by all means, the nature of spiritual warfare,
the reality of the spiritual enemy of all mankind, and how to
exercise authority and power over him in Jesus' name.*

DON MCCURRY,
HEALING THE BROKEN FAMILY OF ABRAHAM

K HADIJAH, A NORTH AFRICAN IMMIGRANT, came to faith
in Christ in a powerful way after dreams of Jesus had led her into
a local evangelical church in Scandinavia. In their ongoing discipling of
Khadijah, our friends there took her into their home to care for her for
a couple of years. Excited about the new freedom she was finding in
Christ, Khadijah became very burdened for her aging and very sick
father, Abdel-Kareem, back home in the city where we lived in North
Africa. A decade or so earlier, Abdel-Kareem, a successful businessman,
had come under strong demonic influence during a visit to a mosque
during Ramadan. As he became steadily worse, he moved away from
home to a nearby city, so as not to be a burden to his family when he was
under the influence of the demons. Every Ramadan he lost his capacity
to work and live a balanced and normal life under the renewed demonic
attack, and the length of time that he was incapacitated grew each year
until, by the time Khadijah came to Christ, he had become a wretched
alcoholic and diabetic who could barely function for much of each year.
Khadijah told her father about how much Jesus had helped her and pled
with him to permit someone to visit him and tell him about Jesus, because she had strong hope that Jesus could heal her desperately ill father.
Abdel-Kareem said that he would be happy to welcome someone to come
and tell him about Jesus.

When our friends contacted me from Scandinavia and asked whether
I could go and visit Abdel-Kareem, I sought the help of an experienced,
godly Egyptian living in our city, and together we visited Abdel-Kareem
in his apartment. When we entered the apartment Abdel-Kareem was
sitting half-naked on a chair with bottles of alcohol littering the floor
around him and his gangrene-ravaged feet soaking in a basin of water.
Over the following six months, the two of us met with and ministered
to Abdel-Kareem regularly. He was initially very open to hearing about
Jesus and to being prayed for. Within a few weeks, his tormenting
demons seemed to have left him alone, he had stopped drinking and
had obtained medical treatment for his diabetes, and he was returning
to health. He was being transformed and, though his business was on

the edge of bankruptcy, he returned to work, seeking to re-establish it and get it growing again, and he resumed spending time with his wife and family. We were very encouraged at the way God had healed, freed and restored him as he prayed with us and welcomed our intercession on his behalf.

Tragically, however, even though he had seen Jesus heal him, deliver him from demonic oppression and restore his life and family to him, he would not abandon his love for his prophet Muhammad. He said he loved both Jesus and Muhammad. Gradually, as he got busy with his restored life, his interest in Jesus waned—Jesus had served him in his time of need and he did not need him anymore. Because he was not interested in being discipled into faith in Christ, we stopped meeting with him. Months later, a few weeks before my departure from the country, I arranged a final visit to say goodbye to Abdel-Kareem. Shockingly, when I opened the door of his apartment, the same sickening smell greeted me that we had encountered on our first visit. Abdel-Kareem was in a pitiful state—he had given in to alcohol again, had come under demonic attack and his diabetes was worse than ever. None of the healing and restoration had been permanent after he rejected the One whom had healed him. This tragic experience evokes Jesus' description of what can happen to someone who has been cleansed of demons:

> "When the unclean spirit has gone out of a person, it passes through waterless places seeking rest, and finding none it says, 'I will return to my house from which I came.' And when it comes, it finds the house swept and put in order. Then it goes and brings seven other spirits more evil than itself, and they enter and dwell there. And the last state of that person is worse than the first." (Lk 11:24-26)

THE NATURE OF SPIRITUAL OPPOSITION AND OPPRESSION IN MUSLIM COMMUNITIES

One cannot discuss the attacks that people and governments carry out on BMBs without also addressing the demonic warfare that Satan so often wages against believers and fledgling churches emerging in Muslim communities. During our ten years of ministry and residence in North Africa, we constantly felt the reality of spiritual opposition and oppression on those we sought to disciple. Along with our colleagues around the country, we were very aware that discipling BMBs and church planting was serious warfare against spiritual powers that were accustomed to controlling and dominating people. Abdel-Kareem's story tragically illustrates how our inability to deal effectively with demonization frequently led to failure in discipleship.

Our experience of ministering in the face of unrelenting spiritual oppression and outright demonic attack is a common experience for those who minister to Muslims. Don McCurry clearly understands the degree to which Satan is at work through Islam: "Islam is virulently anti-Christian at its core. . . . Because of its unusual hostility to the Gospel of Jesus Christ, we have to conclude that behind the system of Islam is a supernatural anti-Christian power" (2001, 152). McCurry insists that all persons working among Muslims must learn how to exercise God's power over the power of Satan operating in Islam if they want to see BMBs grow and mature:

> The gifts and power of God's Spirit are as available today as they were in Jesus' day and were not confined to the apostolic period—they are available for all who believe and appropriate them. This issue becomes especially pointed when we struggle with Folk Islamic practices right where the people live. *No demonstration of God's power on our part over the power of the enemy means no lasting fruit.* Maybe there will be surface "conversions," but in the absence of knowing how to deal with the demonic power that may have affected the would-be believer . . . the potential convert may never learn how to escape the grip of the evil powers that held him. (2001, 159, emphasis added)

McCurry argues that as Western workers we must ensure that we operate from within a biblical supernatural worldview. We must be effective in the spiritual battles that are central to the discipleship process.[1] In the

---

[1]McCurry (2001) deals with these issues in several places. In chapters 21, 26 and 36 he deals with spiritual warfare in ministering to Muslims.

citation that heads the chapter, McCurry stresses the need to teach BMBs about the reality of spiritual warfare and equip them to resist and overcome the enemy.

In a similar way, in his book on discipling BMBs, Pietzsch devotes a whole chapter to the challenge of helping BMBs get free of occult power through Christ. Pietzsch tells the evocative parable of a slave seeking freedom who jumps into a boat to row across a wide, crocodile-infested river to freedom on the other side, only to be caught by a hidden chain attached underneath the boat, which the slave master used to pull the boat back to slave territory and recapture the slave. This is his application to BMBs:

> The story of the slave illustrates BMBs who fail to have all unseen and un-
> derlying controls of their old faith removed. Muslims live under a collective
> bondage. Salvation is experienced, but there needs to be complete deliv-
> erance, otherwise the BMBs "get stuck in the mud" and do not make it to
> "the other side." The invisible chains draw the BMBs back. (2004, 93-94)

UNDERSTANDING THE WARFARE WORLDVIEW OF THE BIBLE

At this point, it is important for us to reflect on the nature of our world as understood from the Bible and the experience of those who have dealt with demonic forces. In the paragraphs above, McCurry speaks of "the reality of the spiritual enemy of all mankind" (2001, 313) and Pietzsch refers to the "unseen and underlying controls of their old faith" (2004, 93). Both authors assume that the worldview of the authors of the New Testament, who believed in the existence of actual evil spirits and in the sobering reality of a powerful enemy of God and of humankind, is in fact the way the world truly is today. In chapter four, I mentioned Gregory Boyd's treatise on the biblical worldview entitled *God at War: The Bible and Spiritual Conflict* (1997) in which he argues that "the atmosphere of the world is diabolical" (279). In order to provide context for the discussion of deliverance and spiritual warfare in discipling BMBs in this chapter, we need to reflect on the nature of our world, as understood from both personal experience and study of the Scriptures.

Growing up in a believing Christian home, I initially assumed that the biblical worldview presented in the Scriptures, populated with angels, evil spirits and miracles, was the way the world was. In contrast, secular public schools, and then university, continually sought to re-educate me that such a religious worldview could perhaps provide some mythic and comforting ways of interpreting our human experience. But no one who really knew the way the world operates continued to believe in such things as a personal Satan, evil spirits, or even angels. Such beings populate only the imagination of premoderns.

Providentially, however, my parents' experience strongly confirmed the validity of their biblical worldview. Both my father and mother told of their own separate encounters with angels who saved them from certain death in an automobile accident (my mother) and, years later, a potentially fatal car accident (my father) averted by an angel. And even more profoundly, as a teenager I was a praying supporter and team player as my parents wrestled with demons in our own living room. For a few months, they helped deliver several young couples from the demons that tormented them years after their involvement in the hippie and drug cultures of the 1960s. It was not hard to believe in the existence of demons when one has heard them speak and felt the shock of momentary terror on hearing their voices, and then witnessed the relief of victory as some of these couples experienced deliverance from the bondage of demons that had afflicted them for years. Thus, long before I arrived in North Africa, I had had a number of worldview-shaping encounters with the demonic, which meant that the concentrated attacks of Satan that we encountered while ministering among Muslims did not come as a surprise.

In the last couple of decades, evangelicals in around the world have begun wrestling with theological and practical issues having to do with the demonic and spiritual warfare. In 2000 the Lausanne Committee for World Evangelism sponsored a small global consultation on spiritual conflict, called "Deliver Us from Evil," that was held in Nairobi, Kenya, August 16-22.[2] In *Deliver Us from Evil*, the book published following the consultation, Wheaton

---

[2]*Deliver Us from Evil: An Uneasy Frontier in Christian Mission* (Moreau 2002) contains many of the papers and case studies from that consultation. I reference a number of those papers in this discussion.

College mission professor Scott Moreau gave a survey and critique of some of the main contemporary North American evangelical writers and teachers on spiritual warfare (2002). In his often perceptive, though highly skeptical, analysis of some of the imagery used in the literature on spiritual warfare, Moreau argues that contemporary spiritual "warfare fads" show significant danger of being held captive to American cultural values rather than to biblical practices and worldview (2002, 120-23).

Charles Kraft, professor emeritus of anthropology and intercultural communication at Fuller Theological Seminary, who has been involved in teaching on spiritual warfare and ministering in "deep-level healing" along with his wife, Marguerite, for thirty years, offered a different perspective. In his contribution to *Deliver Us from Evil*, Kraft surveys "contemporary trends" in spiritual warfare from the perspective of one who has been at the heart of some of those trends (Kraft 2002, 177-99). He discounts many of the critiques because the critics have no experience in deliverance ministry and thus do not really know what they are talking about. Kraft describes what he sees as an unfortunate polarization over differing perspectives on how to deal with the demonic and bring about deliverance and freedom in Christ, and he warns against ignoring the reality of the spiritual conflict (Kraft 2002, 198-99). Few of those who minister among Muslims have the luxury of ignoring the reality of the conflict, because they are often caught up in it whether they are looking for it or not. Where can we turn to arrive at a balanced and biblically sound perspective on spiritual warfare?

Near the beginning of *War on the Saints,* the classic treatise on spiritual warfare written in the aftermath of the Welsh revival in 1904–1905, Jessie Penn-Lewis wrote:

> If all that the Bible contains on the subject of the supernatural powers of evil could be exhaustively dealt with in this book, we should find that more knowledge is given of the workings of Satan, and his principalities and powers, than many have realized. From Genesis to Revelation the work of Satan as deceiver of the whole inhabited earth can be traced, until the climax is reached, and the full results of the deception in the Garden of Eden are unveiled in the Apocalypse. (1912, 3)

American theologian and pastor Gregory A. Boyd writes on similar themes to those of Penn-Lewis. He argues his case with much greater theological and philosophical sophistication. In *Satan and the Problem of Evil: Constructing a Trinitarian Warfare Theodicy*, Boyd seeks to philosophically and theologically elucidate what he calls the Bible's "warfare worldview" (2001, 29):

> There is a dominant motif running throughout Scripture—I have elsewhere argued that it is the *central* motif of Scripture—that depicts God as warring against human and angelic opponents who are able in some measure to thwart his will. . . . God genuinely strives against rebellious creatures. According to Scripture, the head of this rebellion is a powerful fallen angel named Satan. Under him are a myriad of other spiritual beings and humans who refuse to submit to God's rule. Scripture refers to this collective rebellion as a kingdom (Mt 12:26; Col 1:13; Rev 11:15). It is clear that God shall someday vanquish this rebel kingdom, but it is equally clear that in the meantime he genuinely wars against it.
>
> This motif expresses what I call the "warfare worldview" of the Bible. I argue that the narrative of the Bible and all events in world history are best understood against the backdrop of this worldview. The world is literally caught up in a spiritual war between God and Satan. (2001, 15)

All of my experience in life and ministry, and my understanding of the Bible gained through a lifetime of reading and study, cause my heart to resonate with Boyd's thesis and his understanding of the Bible's warfare worldview.[3] When God's servants move into Muslim territory, settle in,

---

[3] Boyd's purpose in writing this book, the second in his series, is to present a cohesive argument for his free-will theology that interprets God's sovereignty as allowing full freedom for human beings and fallen angels to vigorously battle against God's will. Though his thesis lies outside of the scope of this chapter, I find that his theodicy also provides a meaningful answer to a question that I have struggled with for years. In dealing face to face with Islam for a lifetime, one cannot help but ask questions like "Why did God allow the creation of Islam?" and "What was God's purpose in allowing the creation and growth of Islam with its virulent anti-Christian agenda?" If I understand Boyd correctly, his answer would be that it was not God who purposed the founding of Islam; it was Satan and men working under his influence. It is one more of Satan's many attempts to destroy Christian faith, and if failing that, to destroy the lives and flourishing of countless thousands of Christians throughout the past fourteen centuries who have come under the domination of Muslim rulers and empires. However, because he is God, he is well able to work in the hearts and minds of Muslims and draw them to himself, even using truths about Christ buried in the very book that is the basis for Islam's opposition to Christ and his church.

learn the language of the people and love them to Christ, Satan is not happy. My experience working and living in the Muslim world confirms to me the profoundly troubling and often tragic truth that every advance of the gospel is met with fierce opposition. Space does not allow me to take the time to develop many of the implications of what Boyd calls the warfare worldview of the Bible. Yet, I think it is completely reasonable to expect that advancing the gospel in regions of the world dominated by Islam will be a spiritual battle and that there will be many casualties along the way.

Much of the reason for the seeming endless advances followed by defeats in ministering among Muslims is that bringing the God of love to people who have been prevented from knowing him is an act of war against Satan's deceptions in the minds and hearts of Muslims. When we declare war against Satan, he does not sit idly by and let his goods be plundered. When Jesus was accused of casting out demons by the power of Beelzebul (Satan), his explanation of the nature of reality in the spiritual realm was instructive:

> "And if I cast out demons by Beelzebul, by whom do your sons cast them out? Therefore they will be your judges. But if it is by the finger of God that I cast out demons, then the kingdom of God has come upon you. When a strong man, fully armed, guards his own palace, his goods are safe; but when one stronger than he attacks him and overcomes him, he takes away his armor in which he trusted and divides his spoil. Whoever is not with me is against me, and whoever does not gather with me scatters." (Lk 11:19-23)

Jesus knew that his ministry was a frontal assault on the "strong man." Jesus had the power to defeat him "by the finger of God" and take away his spoils—thus liberating people held captive through Satan's deception.

As we engage in discipling BMBs, we are undertaking serious spiritual warfare in that we are seeking to preserve the freedom of those whom Jesus has liberated from satanic deception and bondage. It is for this reason that effective disciplers in Muslim contexts must be spiritually equipped to counter the stratagems of the enemy, and then they will be able to equip BMBs to stand against Satan's wiles. Any approach to BMB discipleship that does not include a way to deal effectively with demonic oppression will be ineffective for the many BMBs who need help to overcome demonic oppression. People who remain in bondage even though they have begun to live as disciples of Christ are unable to develop and grow as believers. Those of us who are called to help disciple BMBs must deal with this unfortunate and pervasive spiritual reality. In this, as in all other matters, as disciplers we are unable to take someone further along the road of discipleship to Christ than we ourselves have traveled. Unless we are learning increasing levels of resistance to and victory over the enemy in our personal lives, we will be powerless to counter the attacks of the enemy in the lives of those whom we love and seek to serve.

SEASONED DISCIPLERS' INSIGHTS INTO DEALING WITH DEMONIC OPPRESSION AND ATTACK

Given the encounters with the demonic that I had while in North Africa, when I began interviewing I expected to find that dealing with demonic oppression and attacks would be a major challenge consistently across the Arab world. However, it was surprising to learn that only about half of the interviewees had personally encountered unmistakable demonic attacks in their ministry. A few more (almost two-thirds) said that demonic problems and attacks were frequent even though some had not dealt with any themselves. More than one BMB suggested to me that they, as BMBs, were more likely to discern demonic activity than were Western workers. Some Western workers suggested that they themselves probably did not see or discern demonic activity because their theological backgrounds prevented them from expecting or seeing what was there.

The accounts collected during research also suggest that Satan appears to attack in different ways in different cities or countries. In some places, as in Morocco, for example, there may be a much higher incidence of demonic manifestation. In other places, Satan may attack through attempting to destroy marriages, or, for example, through strong attacks on men in the area of sexual temptation and illicit sexual activity. As in all situations of demonic opposition, much prayer and spiritual discernment is called for to be able to help BMBs to find victory in whatever area they are under attack.

Counsel on the ministry of deliverance from an experienced BMB church planter. Though only about half of those interviewed had personally encountered the demonic, I did hear some valuable counsel on how to undertake deliverance ministry. Most of the experienced counsel came from people ministering in Morocco or among North Africans in France. One North African church planter, whom we will call Amir, made a number of helpful comments that set the ministry of deliverance in its appropriate context. Though he suggested that the vast majority of families in his country have some form of demonic bondage, he said that deliverance should *never* be the focus of one's ministry. Rather, the need to practice deliverance follows the work of church planting. As you preach the gospel and disciple BMBs, demons will manifest. It is often in the corporate worship of a group of believers that demons manifest.[4] It is not uncommon for him to look around a group during a time of worship and notice someone—usually a visitor or a newcomer to the group—manifesting a demon, sometimes even though the person is not aware of it. Amir notices that for a short time, the person's eyes are controlled by a different person who is very uncomfortable with the manifest presence of God in the corporate worship—demons are clearly *very* uncomfortable in God's presence during worship.[5]

When that happens, he always acts. After the meeting is over, Amir will speak to the person privately, explain what he witnessed and ask if the person would like to be freed. If the person wants to be set free, then

---

[4]British Anglican Michael Green, in *I Believe in Satan's Downfall*, also mentions this tendency for demons to manifest during corporate worship times. "It ought to be added that the demonic powers, like their Master, prefer to remain hidden, and normally manifest themselves most readily in a specifically Christian context—in a meeting for praise and worship, at the Eucharist, in church, or in the presence of a Christian. . . . The person will be drawn both because of the beauty of Christ in the believer and because of the hope of deliverance. But the spirits will be stirred into rebellion and opposition" (Green 1981, 136).

[5]Green also mentions the eyes as the final indication, in a list of eleven indicators, which makes him suspect demonic influence: "Something strange about the eyes. The eyes are the window to the inner man. The eyes of the possessed are often unnaturally bright, glazed, or full of manic hatred" (1981, 135).

he calls in one or more trusted church members and prays with the person in Jesus' name. Typically only one or two demons will manifest, but sometimes there are many more. Usually, the deliverance occurs quite quickly and with little battle, but sometimes it takes much prayer and fasting. He stressed the need to protect the privacy and the dignity of the person in bondage and never to deliver people in public.

Amir also has found that the level of bondage varies according to the degree of the person's personal involvement in past evil. If the person was the victim, the bondage is not as strong as when that person was the one who did the evil act. When blood has been used in ritual occult activities, the bondage is the strongest. When a person has drunk the blood, the bondage is the most severe. In light of the varying degrees of bondage in victims of demonization, he warned that we must not try to pray with everyone who manifests a demon. In some cases, we must be willing to get help. Amir warns that learning to do deliverance can be very dangerous. He stressed that there is a lot of poor teaching found in books. One must follow the counsel of the Scriptures above all.

Generally, those who had experience in deliverance ministry stressed the need for focused prayer and for fasting, and they cautioned that deliverance often does not come easily. Rather than making comparisons among the advice given by various people, I think it is more valuable to pass on their counsel as a whole. Typically, the advice given overlapped considerably and indicated a common experience of effective deliverance ministry. The counsel given fell naturally into two distinct though sometimes overlapping categories. There was advice for those helping deliver others from their demonic oppression. Then there was advice for those who needed deliverance. There are a number of crucial attitudes and perspectives that believers need to have in order to receive and maintain freedom through Christ. First we will note the kinds of attitudes and preparations needed in those who are seeking deliverance from demonic bondage. Then we will discuss the preparation and actions needed for those seeking to help others be freed of demonic oppression.

Counsel for those seeking deliverance. Foundational to effective and permanent deliverance is the yielding of one's life to Christ. People seeking deliverance must believe in Christ, confess and repent of their sins and desire deliverance. It is only in rare, extreme cases that one encounters a person so fully possessed that he or she has lost all capacity for decision or thought.[6] In all other situations one should discuss the person's attitude toward Christ before seeking to help a person be freed from demonic oppression. We need to lay the proper foundation by explaining who Christ is and encouraging the person to yield himself or herself wholly to him and his lordship, in faith. The story that began this chapter illustrates the often-tragic outcome of helping deliver people who do not yield wholeheartedly to Christ.

It is also important to help believers seeking deliverance to understand at least some of the many ways that strongholds of sin and rebellion can permit demonic bondages to take hold of one's life. I do not have space to make the case here for my conviction that true and faithful believers in Christ can be demonized to varying degrees, but allow me to explain why I believe this is true. Christian psychologist Robert

---

[6]In one such extreme case about which I was told by a BMB colleague, a young Moroccan man had been severely oppressed for years. He had no real independent life. He was in a mental hospital and spent much of his time in a straitjacket so that he could not hurt himself or those around him. His mother came to faith in Christ, and after experiencing freedom in Christ, she desperately sought deliverance for her son, whom she believed to be demon possessed. When she heard, one summer, that there was a large gathering of BMBs being held in Europe, she went to great expense and effort to bring her son to the conference and pled with the leaders to do something for her son. Several of the most experienced BMB leaders took the two of them into another room, and while the 400–500 BMBs present interceded and worshiped together, they began what proved to be a lengthy deliverance session. Once the demons had been bound in Christ's name and been ordered to release the man's mind, they explained to him what they were doing and asked him whether he wanted them to continue. When he told them that he did want freedom, then they shared Christ with him and he responded positively. Then, once he had committed himself to Christ, they continued with the deliverance, and eventually the young man was able to go out to the gathered worshipers rejoicing in his dramatic deliverance—after years of life in a mental institution. His mother was ecstatic!

In *Counseling and the Demonic*, Robert Bufford refers to such rare cases: "In demon possession, the individual may be so strongly influenced by demons that he or she is unable to think clearly or make an independent decision. The demon is quite readily able to maintain control, and thus to effectively block the person's efforts to break free. In such extremes, exorcism or the casting out of demons seems appropriate" (1988, 171). Also, Green suggests that in such cases, leaders in the church should step in—it is not the place for novices to tackle such extreme cases of possession. He suggests that in cases like the one mentioned above, we are dealing with exorcism, and not merely a ministry of deliverance (1981, 132).

Bufford asserts his conviction that demon possession occurs only in the unsaved, without giving any justification for his conviction (1998, 111). He discounts the case studies that indicate the opposite that he found cited in the literature as "not compelling" (127). As I read his book dealing with counseling and the demonic, which is in many ways quite helpful, I nevertheless felt much as Kraft expressed—Bufford lacks the direct experience to know what he is talking about. Bufford declares: "I believe that possession of Christians is not possible since they belong to the kingdom of God, and are indwelt by the Holy Spirit. Also, God protects them from the evil one" (127).

There is nothing automatic about the spiritual life—one is not automatically protected from demonic attack because one has entered the kingdom of God. Satan attacks and seeks to oppress everyone he can— especially those who are threatening the security of his kingdom of deception. In working with BMBs, one must understand that it is only once they are believers that they can have their own spiritual resources to resist and overcome demonic influence in their lives. Depending on their family and personal history, new believers in Christ from Muslim background can more or less be expected to be demonized to some extent until they renounce Satan and all his works and deliberately seek freedom in Christ. To suggest that on conversion all BMBs experience instantaneous, complete deliverance strikes me as naïve and rather dangerous, because it gives new believers little help in dealing with the psychological, emotional and spiritual reality of their lives.

Generally, demonic bondage can occur in the thoughts, in the feelings and in the body. Believers must repent of their sins and ask for God's help. They must understand how their decision to obey Christ can lead to ongoing victory over demonic deception and oppression. Furthermore, they must be taught Christ's authority and then claim Christ's authority and power over the enemy whenever he attacks them. Also, BMBs must explicitly renounce Islam, cut ties with the Islamic religion and cease believing its doctrines. So long as new believers still keep loyalty to Islam as a religious ideology, they cannot be permanently protected from or free of demonic attack and the deception that is linked to Islam. More than half of Rick Love's book on ministering to folk Muslims deals with spiritual warfare and countering demonic powers. Love stresses the need for repentance and renunciation: "Repentance in folk Islamic contexts must involve both renunciation of occultic practices and deliverance form the power of these forces" (2000, 69-176).

Pietzsch, the German missionary who worked for decades among Muslims in sub-Saharan Africa, suggests a four-step process in helping BMBs to overcome the power of sin and Satan in their lives. (1) BMBs need to confess by name and renounce all past and present sins of false religion, occult practices, lies, habitual sin and rebellion. (2) They need to confess sins of their ancestors and reject Satan's right over their lives. (3) They must renounce Islam and all of its strongholds with an understanding of their deception. Finally, (4) BMBs need to learn how to maintain their freedom, how to deal with curses and how to live in a demonically hostile environment (Pietzsch 2004, 90-100).

One key element that was particularly stressed by BMBs was that for BMBs to maintain ongoing victory over demonic influence in their personal lives they need to know and understand God's love for them. An encounter with the God of love can overcome the power of the enemy in their lives. BMBs need to be shown from the Scriptures that God is love and taught how to encounter God and his love personally. They need to be prayed for so that they will encounter God in his love in their personal experience.

In the interviews, seven things were emphasized as being vital in maintaining the freedom of those who have been delivered of demonic oppression. First, they need to live in a close-knit community of believers who can hold them accountable and care for them as they learn to live as new creatures in Christ. Writing out of several decades of experience discipling BMBs in North Africa and France, John Haines similarly stressed that a significant factor in victory is the protection and security that comes from being a part of the church community with its extended network of brothers and sisters who can assist, encourage and help protect the new believer from attacks of the enemy (Haines 1998, 89-108).

Second, they themselves must make a profound commitment to try to live, for the rest of their lives, in obedience to Christ as they seek to live holy lives by the grace of the Holy Spirit. Third, it is good if they can occupy themselves in doing good. Idleness tends to lower resistance, and the more focus they have on serving and loving others, the less likely that demons can once again gain access to their inner lives. Fourth, it is helpful to listen to good worship music as much as possible. And fifth, even though it sounds almost intuitive, it still needed to be stressed that those who had been delivered must *not* return to the occult practices that they had relied on prior to their deliverance. It seems that recently delivered BMBs often trip up in this way. When things got difficult for them, following their healing and deliverance, they automatically returned to the places and activities that had provided them with a sense of power or protection in the past. Sixth, everyone stressed that BMBs need to pray continually for the fullness of the Spirit. Michael Green also stressed this as a vital part of helping those who have been delivered: "Above all they need to be filled with the Spirit of God (Eph. 5:18), for an internal spiritual vacuum is a very dangerous thing. I have no hope of anyone maintaining the deliverance with which Christ has set him free unless he is prepared to allow the Lord to fill the place which has been filled by other lords" (1981, 146).

The seventh and final thing that my informants emphasized was that those who had been delivered from bondage need to be ministered to for deep inner healing. Because their years under the influence of demons has done much damage, there is much healing needed and much lost ground that has to be made up. Charles Kraft has written a number of books on the ministry of inner healing.[7] He prefers the term "deep healing" because it expresses more of what is needed. He has spent years ministering and seeing God heal deep-seated emotional, psychological and spiritual problems. He teaches spiritual disciplines that can help people find renewing of their minds and spirits following psychological or spiritual trauma. I first encountered Kraft when he visited the

---

[7]Three of Kraft's books dealing with deliverance and deep inner healing are *Deep Wounds, Deep Healing: Discovering the Vital Link Between Spiritual Warfare and Inner Healing* ([1993] 2004), *I Give You Authority: Practicing the Authority Jesus Gives Us* (1997) and *Defeating Dark Angels: Breaking Demonic Oppressions in the Believer's Life* ([1992] 2011). I commend Kraft's wisdom to help equip you in deliverance and deep healing ministry.

country in which we were serving in North Africa more than twenty years ago. He and his wife, Marguerite, ran a weekend of ministry to many of the workers in the country. They both evidenced significant spiritual discernment, exercised much authority in Christ's name and significantly ministered to a number of colleagues. Regardless of whether one finds the Krafts' style of ministry helpful, I would note again that those who have been victimized by demonic oppression often need deep inner healing following their deliverance from demonic oppression.

Counsel for those undertaking deliverance ministry. Before leaving the topic of deliverance ministry, it is time to pass on advice for those seeking to help deliver BMBs and others from demonic attack and oppression. One Middle Eastern Christian couple, Rashid and Natifa, observed that in their place of ministry (a large Middle Eastern city), the way that demonic attack and oppression most often manifested was in sexual addiction. They said that they were worn out from dealing with this heavy demonic oppression. In their area, the Shiite doctrine of "travel marriages" justifies one-night stands and affairs as being permitted by Islamic law. Young women readily give themselves sexually to any man who asks. They believe that there are strong evil spirits active in their area and that nearly everyone is affected by this demonically empowered sexual perversion and addiction. In this situation Rashid and Natifa *always* minister together as a couple and are very careful in their conduct to make sure that they do not give any impression that they themselves participate in the rampant sexual promiscuity around them. When helping BMBs seeking to recover from such sexual addiction, Rashid and Natifa try to have them meet with other believers as much as possible, and they encourage them never to be alone. If they are single, they encourage marriage. Near tears, Rashid and Natifa said that it was very hard to deal with this kind of continual, demonically empowered, oppressive sexual perversion. It was wearing them down.

In North Africa, I found it interesting to note that the two BMB leaders with whom I spoke about their rather extensive experiences in deliverance ministry had almost identical experiences. They offered almost the same advice, even though the church traditions of the expatriate church planters that they were connected with were quite different (one charismatic, and the other non-charismatic and more conservative). Khalid said that in his experience, about 80 to 90 percent of BMBs come to Christ with some sort of demonic oppression, and Amir said that 97 percent of people have some level of demonic bondage. Yet, in spite of the very high incidence of demonic bondage, both men said that they never speak about it in the church or teach on deliverance ministry. They want to downplay it and not give it any prominence. Both men have found that expatriate workers often do not discern the presence or manifestation of the demonic, even when for them it is glaringly obvious.

What further practical counsel did everyone give for helping those dealing with demonization or oppression? A simple point was most often made, that to bring about full deliverance, much prayer, fasting and spiritual warfare prayer would be needed. Furthermore, most people stressed that the person seeking to help others must have an intimate walk with Jesus and a life of prayer in order to have authority over demons. There is no automatic spiritual authority that comes from "being a Christian"—the spiritual authority comes from a strong relationship with God. A number of people warned about inappropriate motivation and said that our motivation for helping others must be love. Other motives will result in failure and harm. It was also repeatedly emphasized that one must never seek to minister deliverance alone—one must always work as a team in ministering deliverance.

Those with experience offered a few practical instructions on how to handle the deliverance sessions themselves.[8] First, one must find out if

---

[8]Michael Green, in *I Believe in Satan's Downfall* (1981, 140-45), offers a helpful set of practical instructions for how to handle deliverance sessions that are worth summarizing here, for ease of reference as a supplement to that learned through the interviews. This also gives a good idea of the ways that deliverance sessions often unfold. I encourage readers to get Green's book and read all of it, but especially chapter 5, in which he outlines practical counsel for deliverance ministry (I retain Green's use of "he" to refer generically to the person being helped, regardless of gender).
   (1) Get his full cooperation before the demon is activated. (2) He must be willing to be set free and must be totally honest about his condition and any sins that may have led him into the condition. (3) Lead him in a time of confession, including emphatic renunciation of the devil and all his works. He must commit his fear to the Lord and forgive anyone who has hurt him. (4) The power and protection of the name of Jesus Christ needs to be claimed explicitly by all present. (5) The minister then commands "the spirit in the name of Jesus Christ to manifest itself and to depart; to harm nobody; never to return and to go to the Lord of Spirits" (140). The com-

the person truly wants to be delivered. So long as the person wants to keep the demons, those seeking to help have no authority over the demons. Once one is assured that the person truly desires to be free, then one must audibly address the demons in Christ's name and then cast them out in Christ's authority. Though there is much debate in the literature about whether one should engage in conversations with the demons and seek to learn about the sins that are the basis for their presence, those with experience with whom I spoke did not recommend getting into conversations with demons because they are deceivers and there is no way to trust the information given by demons. One person noted that the demons would often try to engage in conversation, hoping to trick and manipulate the deliverer. But one must resist this temptation and cast the demons out in Jesus' name.

Several people warned against seeking out a deliverance ministry. If one is supposed to deliver BMBs, the need to practice deliverance will present itself. But one should never give in to the temptation of making deliverance one's primary ministry. Also, it was stressed repeatedly that deliverance ministry is not for everyone. It is wise to get the assistance of people who have giftedness. A number of expatriate workers mentioned that they had been much helped by the books by Neil T. Anderson, *The Bondage Breaker* (2000), *Victory over the Darkness* (2013) and *The Steps*

---

mand may need to be repeated. The ministry partner can be praying and/or singing quietly. (6) One must be prepared for anything to happen, and pay close attention to what does happen. (7) Demons love to hide so one must be authoritative and persistent—especially using verses of Scripture that God brings to mind. (8) Use a variety of potent symbols such as a cross, holy oil, holy water or, the most powerful of all, the Eucharist (communion). (9) Members of the deliverance team need to remain attentive to what God is saying to them throughout the session, which can be quite lengthy. (10) Other symbolic actions can be helpful, as led by the Spirit. (11) Often during the session one of the team, or the patient, will become aware of an object that needs to be destroyed (a book or talisman, for example)—destroy it! (12) There is danger in such sessions, but only if one is not living close to Christ. Watch for attacks on your own children—and then claim the protection of the blood of Christ over them. (13) Remember that the evil spirit will have to go because Jesus Christ is Lord. (14) The patient will know when the spirit is gone. (15) It is important to challenge any other spirits that might be lurking in the patient, commanding them to manifest and leave. (16) The process is physically and emotionally exhausting for all concerned, but particularly for the patient. Food, drink, rest and love are essential! (17) Sometimes God gives a special indication to the patient that it is all over. Following deliverance, the patient needs much pastoral care. Green goes on here to give a detailed and rich list for postdeliverance care that coves some of the same ground that we just covered above in the main text.

to Freedom in Christ (2004). They found that Anderson's books offered wise insight in the whole area of demonic deception and oppression and how to help both themselves and the BMBs they were seeking to disciple learn to live in ongoing freedom from both demonic oppression and negative thought patterns of all kinds.

In concluding this discussion of ministering to those harassed by demons, I want to make two clarifying comments. First, the vital necessity of accurate diagnosis and appropriate care for those struggling with oppression or other deep-seated problems must be stressed. As our North African brothers have advised, we do not go looking for demons. When we encounter abnormal behavior and addictions we always assume that the cause is sin, or illness and disease or mental disorder, unless there is clear reason to believe that demons *are* involved and the Spirit enables us to discern their presence. All of the above discussions of appropriate approaches to deliverance assume an accurate diagnosis. We do no one any good if we treat psychological disorder as if it were a demonic problem, if it is not. The fact that about half of those interviewed had not knowingly encountered a demonic manifestation suggests that one can spend years in ministry among Muslims without ever having occasion to confront a demon.

The final clarification to make is the reminder that people are complex beings. There are multiple sources for pain and disorder in our beings, and healing care must pay attention to every aspect of our beings. If a psychological disorder is caused by a chemical malfunction in the brain, then by all means, accurate diagnosis and prescription of appropriate drugs can help tremendously. There is abundant need for physicians of the body, the soul (friends, counselors, pastors and so on) and the spirit (deliverance and inner healing ministries, spiritual direction and so on). I have devoted a chapter to the topic of deliverance because this is, in my experience, a vital aspect of ministering to BMBs that Westerners, especially, are often poorly equipped to understand or handle well. Belief in the reality of personal evil beings does *not* mean that ministering deliverance should take precedence over all of the other valuable and essential forms of teaching, healing and counsel with which the Holy Spirit has gifted people in Christ's body.

13

Understanding and Handling Money Well in Discipling BMBs

I know how to be brought low, and I know how to abound.
In any and every circumstance, I have learned the secret of facing
plenty and hunger, abundance and need. I can do all things through him
who strengthens me. . . . And you Philippians yourselves know that in the
beginning of the gospel, when I left Macedonia, no church entered
into partnership with me in giving and receiving, except you
only. . . . And my God will supply every need of yours
according to his riches in glory in Christ Jesus.

Philippians 4:12-13, 15, 19

The most obvious problem is the great difference in access
to resources between the average African and the average Westerner
who is in Africa. To put it simply: the African sees the Westerner as rich
while he is poor. This creates many difficulties in interpersonal relations. . . .
They see you as an okay human being, but of course a rich one.
Your riches cannot for a minute be forgotten or disregarded.
After all, your household income is some thirty
to sixty times greater than theirs.

David Maranz,
African Friends and Money Matters

THE COMPLETE TRANSFORMATION in our financial and social status was almost instantaneous on our arrival in North Africa, but it took us quite a while before we began to understand some of the implications of the transformation. Back home in Canada we had lived the first three years of our married lives in a tiny basement apartment, driven an older model of a very inexpensive car and had managed to survive without debt on my wife's secretarial salary while I completed my education in preparation for ministry in North Africa. Then, when we began living off of support in Europe, we had become even poorer. During our first two years we did not own a car and went everywhere by foot or public transport. Then, in North Africa, during our first two years we lived in a two-bedroom ground-floor apartment in a beautiful house in a middle-class neighborhood. The combined income from my fulltime teaching job and support from Canada was barely enough for us to cover expenses as we struggled to provide for our family with two infant daughters. It was impossible to save any money, and we lived from paycheck to paycheck, sometimes having to avoid eating meat for the last few days of the month.

Yet, in contrast to the thousands of people living in the shantytown a few hundred feet from our house, we were infinitely better off—we had a home, a car, clothes, food, friends, a job, security. Almost every day, while I was away at work, very poor women with babies dressed in rags would ring the doorbell seeking some sort of handout or assistance. My wife, Jeanie, with her still very limited ability in the local language, would have to somehow deal kindly with these needy neighbors who hoped for some generosity from the wealthy Westerners. This overnight transformation in our perceived socio-economic status in a society that put a very high value on generosity was one of the hardest aspects of our early years in the country. At times Jeanie could hardly face going out because of the way strangers viewed and treated her because she was seen as a wealthy Westerner living in their midst.

Some of the stress would have been relieved if we had had the capacity to be more generous, but during the first few years we felt as if we ourselves were barely managing to survive. We wrestled with how to cope with our change in status. We wondered how to relate to the poor in our neighborhood and to the beggars sitting at many main intersections in the center of the city. During those first two years, we had a number of conversations with various friends trying to resolve this deeply troubling struggle. After two years in North Africa, we returned to Canada for a two-year furlough and study leave. Once again, we were again comparatively very poor, living through the generosity of family and friends in an expensive part of Vancouver. And yet the fact that we could travel and I could devote myself to two years of full-time graduate study was a further indication of how much wealthier we were than our North African friends.

On our return to North Africa, with master's degree in hand, to the same job and neighborhood, with our financial circumstances somewhat improved, we were able to rent a whole house to accommodate our growing family. Over the course of the previous four years, we had wrestled through to some sort of peace with our status as people perceived locally to be among the wealthy. We sought to have generous hearts and to give whenever we could and, with growing understanding of the culture, we developed a strategy for dealing with the neighbors who once again were ringing our doorbell daily. With a somewhat improved income, we had more capacity to give small gifts of food and clothing to those who came to our door.

Nine months after our return, our retired elderly neighbor asked for and received from me enough money to buy prescription medicine for his ailing wife, which he promptly returned to me when his next pension check came. The next time we talked, he complimented Jeanie and me on the gracious and generous way he had seen us engaging with the poor neighbors who came asking for help. That comment led to first his son, and then he himself a few years later, confessing their faith in Christ. Our deep struggle to understand our status as "wealthy Westerners" led to our developing new habits in responding to the poor who came to our door. In time, by God's grace, we wealthy Westerners were learning to exemplify Christ's generosity toward the poor in our adopted homeland and new culture.

Even though issues of identity, persecution and the demonic are some of the most challenging issues that disciplers of BMBs encounter, perhaps the one that Western disciplers have the hardest time understanding and handling well has to do with our attitudes toward material wealth. Understanding and finding fruitful ways of living our lives of comparative wealth that bless our BMB friends repeatedly proves to be a major challenge for many would-be disciplers.

THE COMPLEXITIES THAT AFFLUENT WESTERNERS MUST OVERCOME TO HANDLE MONEY WELL

We were not alone in struggling to learn how to be "wealthy missionaries" with Christian humility and integrity and to know how to disciple BMBs in matters of money, possessions, wealth and poverty. As I have taught this material on discipling BMBs in various parts of the Muslim world, this topic always stimulates keen interest among church planters. Several helpful recent books suggest that such questions continue to challenge those serving cross-culturally: *African Friends and Money Matters* (Maranz 2001), *When Charity Destroys Dignity* (Schwartz 2007), *Cross-Cultural Partnerships: Navigating the Complexities of Money and Mission* (Lederleitner 2010) and *Complexities of Money and Missions in Asia* (de Neui 2012). For many people living in countries across the Muslim world, the discrepancy between their daily economic realities and the affluence of the Western world continues to expand exponentially. With the exception of some wealthy countries in the Arabian Peninsula, most Westerners seeking to incarnate Christ among Muslims globally face the challenge of learning to love humbly and care for their less affluent neighbors and BMB friends in ways that promote dignity, respect and mutual friendship. As the subtitle of Jonathan Bonk's *Missions and Money: Affluence as a Western Missionary Problem* (1991) puts it so disturbingly well, affluence is a Western missionary problem. Local non-Western disciplers who are living and working without outside money have not encountered so many challenges with money, to put it mildly.

Tentmakers living and working locally, employed by nationally owned local companies, encounter this issue differently than do non-tentmaking missionaries. Because we tentmakers earn some or all of our living in the local economy, we are not forced to deal with the added dimensions of this subject that come for those working in Christian institutions established and run through funds from outside the country. Nor have many colleagues faced the unique challenges that come from working in socio-economic development projects. In *When Charity Destroys Dignity*, Schwartz (2007) mentions several times that some missionaries he had met had told him that they had no personal experience with the century-old kinds of dependency issues that Schwartz faced in Africa. Clearly, Schwartz found it a bit hard to believe that not everyone faced the same kinds of dependency issues. Yet, in many of the places where readers of *this* book likely minister, Christian mission is either unknown in recent centuries or is carried out unofficially in countries with high levels of security concern. Yet, despite the very significant differences in economic and social-political contexts, when we live among people who are significantly poorer than ourselves, we must learn to grapple with these issues as they arise.

An additional dimension for those working in Muslim-majority communities is that the common Muslim understanding is that Christian missionaries always use the offer of money or jobs to entice people to convert to Christianity. This makes it doubly difficult for ministries doing development work in Muslim contexts because local Muslims automatically expect that the Christian motivation for such work is proselytism. It is natural that they think this way because this is generally the way that Muslims are expanding their presence in Africa and elsewhere. Very often with the help of money from the Saudis, they build a mosque in a town or village and then provide jobs for everyone who attaches himself to the new Muslim "community." Muslim "humanitarian" work, when it is occasionally undertaken, is almost exclusively done to help Muslims. Muslims know very well that Christian humanitarian and relief agencies help whoever is in need, regardless of their religious identification. Yet this Muslim belief that Christians use money to gain converts is pervasive. Even in contexts where there is no Christian aid work, when someone comes to Christ, everyone around him or her immediately assumes that there must have been some financial incentive proffered by Christians. Muslims cannot imagine anyone ever leaving Islam as a result of conviction or conscience.

The interviews with experienced disciplers confirmed that money is a significant discipleship challenge across the Arab world, and an important issue (explicitly affirmed by twenty-two people). During the interviews, I raised the topic and then asked them to give their advice on how to handle money so that it would be a blessing to all. There were two tracks to the discussion of money: dealing with money in the discipleship relationship and handling support from outside the country for local ministry projects and BMBs in ministry.

PRACTICAL WISDOM ON HOW TO HANDLE MONEY WELL IN MINISTRY RELATIONSHIPS

A wide variety of counsel was offered in response to my query (some thirty distinct suggestions were made), but a few common themes emerged (refer to table 13.1). Five of the top six most frequently given guidelines expressed much caution about giving money to BMBs who need or request help. The most mentioned advice was to keep money out of the relationship entirely. One very experienced Christian Arab discipler put it quite graphically: "Ninety-nine percent of the time, do not give *money*. Receiving money distorts the relationship. They become 'slaves' and a slave will accept everything you say." Yet, despite this strong sentiment, *most* did encourage displaying generosity wisely when appropriate. Even those who initially advised that one should not give at all eventually qualified their earlier statements as we continued our discussion. Nevertheless, even those who would not say that we should never give still urged restraint.

Once the strong encouragement to be cautious about giving money was made, the interviewees went on to offer some helpful counsel. First, a full third said that it was acceptable to give small amounts when there was a genuine emergency. We must help when there is urgent need for medical care, or when help is needed to enable BMBs to escape or survive under severe persecution. The concern was always to try to avoid developing a pattern where the BMB becomes financially dependent on the expat or local worker. Everyone encouraged generosity and mentioned a number of significant ways that more affluent expatriates can help without directly giving money. We can purchase or give clothes or med-

Table 13.1. Advice on Handling Money While Discipling

Dealing with Money and Discipleship	Total	Regional Background		Religious Background		Experience Discipling	
		AW People	The Rest	BMB /23	Other /52	Expert /47	Novice /28
1. In discipleship, avoid all money as it distorts the relationship	31	9	23	4	27	14	17
2. It is acceptable to help in medical emergencies and in small ways that avoid dependence	23	8	15	5	18	16	7
3. Avoid giving money, but if you do, give only through the local church	21	11	10	9	12	16	5
4. Present biblical teaching on money, tithing and generosity to BMBs	13	7	6	3	10	9	4
5. Avoid giving money, but give clothes, medication, school fees	11	3	8	2	9	4	7
6. Encourage BMBs to put trust in God, not in the worker or discipler	11	6	5	6	5	7	4
7. Build a sense of community in local church so that needs are met through it	8	3	5	2	6	5	3
8. Open your home; share meals and housing and model Christian living	8	7	1	3	5	4	4
9. Can help BMBs find work so they do not need outside help	7	4	3	4	3	4	3
10. Provide training so that BMBs can start their own real businesses	5	0	5	2	3	2	3
11. In a city with several workers, agree on a coordinated approach	5	1	4	0	5	2	3
12. Send those who ask for help to their families: Who helped before believing?	5	0	5	1	4	3	2
Totals	**148**	**50**	**98**	**41**	**107**	**86**	**62**

ication. We can help pay school fees for BMBs' children and help in other ways that may involve quite a high level of expenditure without giving money directly.

A number of experienced disciplers stressed that most problems with money can be circumvented by teaching new believers that generosity and giving is the norm for believers. The common charge, mentioned earlier, that Muslims make against converts is that people convert in order to get money or for other personal advantage. When we teach new believers, from the beginning, to give generously and sacrificially to the local church and to others in need, we also help BMBs avoid developing a habit of asking for money. Karim, one of the most experienced Arab disciplers I talked with, put this rather humorously. He painted a scenario in which a new believer was immediately taught New Testament principles of generous giving and giving to the ministry and needs in the local church. Then, only a few weeks after his conversion a Muslim friend or relative confronts him about his conversion and accuses him of being in it for the money. He would be able to respond, naturally and emphatically, "On the contrary, these Christians expect me to give! I don't get anything out of this. I am supposed to give my money away, even if I have nothing." Karim, like a number of other experienced disciplers, stressed that early and thorough teaching on New Testament perspectives on possessions, generosity and stewardship goes a long way toward preventing money problems, both for the new believer's relationship with Westerners and with other believes. Such teaching also helps prevent misperceptions related to money, and the BMBs' relationships with foreigners, in the eyes of their suspicious Muslim family.

One way to teach and model Christian attitudes toward money was mentioned eleven times. When a believer comes to you with a need, encourage her to trust God to meet her need. A number of people suggested that expats should frankly tell the believer that they are unable to help with a need, but they will fast and pray, asking God to meet the need. Then when God supplies in answer to their prayer, the BMB is encouraged to trust God to provide what her or she needs. Giving help when it is asked (unless one senses a clear nudging from the Spirit to help in a particular case) tends to teach people to trust in the human agent, rather than directly in God, their loving Father.

A few other good recommendations (see items 7 and 8 in table 13.1) merit mention. As the local BMB church develops, strive to create a strong sense of community and mutual care so that the genuine needs of all believers can be met through their own local believing community. Interestingly and significantly, eight people—seven from the Arab world—stressed that it was important for the foreign workers to open their homes, share meals, host people and model generous Christian living for BMBs. Someone else added that birthdays, weddings and such celebrations are good opportunities to show generosity in culturally appropriate gift giving. One valuable suggestion had more to do with strategy: several workers stressed that it is important that all the workers or evangelists in a given city communicate regularly and work out an agreed approach to this issue, so that BMBs are not tempted to go from worker to worker until they find someone willing to give them what they want.

A few years ago, I heard a somewhat humorous illustration of the need for such coordination. I visited a mature couple with adult children, who were experienced in ministry in the West but new to the Middle East and doing language study. They told how, some months earlier, they had been invited for a meal to the home of a poor refugee family, who were new believers struggling to survive without real jobs. While there, the wife had occasion to go into their little kitchen, and after the visit the expat couple felt very sorry for them because they had a small, battered, old fridge, whereas the expatriate couple owned a nice, large fridge. So, acting generously, they purchased a new, considerably larger fridge, and brought it and gave it to the refugee family. The refugee couple expressed much gratitude.

Then, some six to eight months later, the expatriate couple were once again in the home of the refugee family and were surprised to find that the new fridge that they had given them was gone, and the original old fridge was where it had always been. When asked, the believers were somewhat embarrassed as they came clean. When they had received the new fridge they did not particularly feel the need for such a large fridge, and they had so many other urgent needs that they accepted that the fridge was God's way of providing for their most urgent needs. So they sold the new fridge and spent the windfall on other more urgent needs.

As the expat couple told their story to other colleagues, it turned out that two or three other expat couples had done the same thing for this couple. Without fully understanding what was happening, God had been providing for a number of the refugee family's needs through a series of new fridges given to them, partly as a result of the guilt feelings of expatriate workers embarrassed by their own relative affluence. When I heard the story, I laughed with them at their own inexperience and at the resourcefulness of this couple who turned several unsolicited and unneeded generous gifts into something that could meet their pressing needs.

Were there any significant variations in the advice given according to people's experience and backgrounds? Reflecting on the most common advice given—that money should not be part of the relationship—it is interesting to note that a much lower percentage of BMBs, Arab-world people and experienced disciplers gave this recommendation (see table 13.1, item 1). In other words, even though it was the most mentioned advice, it was *not* the strongest counsel that Middle Eastern and experienced expat disciplers gave. In fact, as we examine the responses more closely, it is illuminating to notice that the top advice given by BMB, Arab-world and experienced expat disciplers was that one should always give through the local church, or, if there is no church, through a local believer who understands the culture (see the third item in table 13.1).

Likewise, a higher percentage of the same three categories of disciplers advised that BMBs should be taught to trust God for the supply of their needs (see item 6). Though it is a small number, more BMB disciplers mentioned the importance of teaching BMBs to trust God for their needs over saying that one should not give money or that it was acceptable to give in emergencies. They said that it was good to tell the new believers that they would pray, and sometimes fast, for their need, and then when God supplied, everyone's faith would be bolstered. A plausible interpretation of this "small" statistic might be that the BMBs, among all those interviewed, had the most balanced and biblical understanding of the best way to teach younger BMBs to handle money. I suppose this is not too surprising, because they have had to learn such lessons themselves.

A couple of other good pieces of counsel should be noted before moving on. Several people mentioned that one should try to help unemployed BMBs to find work so that they could care for their own needs. A few suggested that it would be good to help train BMBs to that they could start their own businesses, and five also strongly recommended that one should send BMBs who come asking for help back to their families. They want them to continue to rely on the social network that they relied on before they believed. This would also help keep them strongly and naturally connected to their families.

To conclude this review of advice received through the interviews, it is helpful to mention in some detail the solution to this money challenge that one American worker shared with me. Stan, an experienced discipler in North Africa, agreed that the issue of money is one of the biggest problems that Westerners face when they disciple people from a significantly lower economic level. At one point, he was so distressed by all of the problems that he and others were encountering that he undertook a fresh study of the Scriptures in search of better understanding of how to handle money and how to teach disciples and leaders of emerging house churches. After that, he was consistent in his teaching and approach as he applied what he had learned from his reflection on scriptural principles for dealing with the poor, and he found that far fewer problems developed.

Here is a short summary of what he learned. First, he believes that in the New Testament, the poor are normally understood to be people who do not have food, clothing or shelter. As Christians, and as a church, we are obligated to help such people. Furthermore, the local church collection is to be used to help the poor among them and to support other ministries of the church. Now, whenever someone asks for help, he always says, "I'll talk to the church and its leaders about your request." He never gives to anyone secretly but rather brings any urgent requests for help with food, clothing or shelter to the local (BMB) church. He keeps all of his own giving accountable to the leaders of the local church (a small group of perhaps fifteen to twenty believers). Furthermore, in the church, they teach everyone the importance of tithing and giving generously to the church so that the church always has some money available to help the poor in their midst and so that believers have a vision for the ministry of the church and the kingdom of God. Once he understood these things clearly and began implementing them consistently, far fewer money problems developed.

PRACTICAL COUNSEL ON PARTNERING WITH BMBs AND THEIR MINISTRIES

The other aspect of handling money discussed was the issue of money coming from outside the country for projects run by national BMBs and for the support of the ministries of some key BMBs and churches. This is increasingly proving to be a thorny issue. I know of situations in several Arab countries where complications of this issue caused by overly eager outside agencies and churches are causing broken relationships, destroying new churches and undermining years of faithful work by nationals and expat workers. As we now begin to see a maturing BMB church in parts of the Muslim world, many of the long-standing issues surrounding the use of money in missions undertaken by affluent Westerners elsewhere have come to trouble church planting ministry among Muslims as well. Growing numbers of American and Korean megachurches are acting independently and bringing significant amounts of money to field situations without much understanding of the kinds of unhealthy dependencies that have plagued such use of foreign funds in missions for more than a century. It is easy to see why Pocock, Van Rheenen and McConnell issued this strong caution:

> The sad reality is that many mission-sending churches and some agencies operate with no model for the use of money in missions. Their decisions about money and mission are, therefore, likely to be inconsistent, haphazard, and paternalistic. Mission history indicates that providing finances without a model for ministry and accountability often means that the mission endeavour will face corruption, controversy, and paternalism. It is imperative, therefore, that agencies and churches carefully consider the implications of their relative wealth if they truly want to support local churches that are healthy and vibrant. (2005, 297)

One North African evangelist and leader living in France spoke with grief and bitterness as he described the annual partnership meetings for the region as a circus in which local church leaders showed up with open hands eagerly vying for the increasingly large amounts of money on offer from a potpourri of Western agencies, megachurches and foundations. It grieved him deeply that this generous offering of money was corrupting people who used to be strong leaders. He was convinced that money was destroying what had been a major move of God in his home country. In his experience-born cynicism, he saw all the Western funding groups wanting to "get in on" the big things that God was doing in the region so they could tell their shareholders about the amazing work of God they were a part of through their donations. Furthermore, it looked like these Western churches and agencies wanted to find their own North Africans to implement their own Western ministry plans and programs.

How then can the funding of national ministries in the Muslim world be handled wisely? Should we shut down the whole circus? This issue was beginning to crescendo into a big problem about the time that we left North Africa in 1998. In the underground church of a few hundred believers in small groups in a dozen cities across the country, there were perhaps a dozen or so young, maturing national leaders. Dozens of American and European churches and funding agencies were making trips directly into the countries seeking to find a national leader to "partner with." They often came in without taking any time to ask around and find out who might already be working in the region and how those on site might advise that these matters be handled. Instead, they too often came in confident that *their* new program or leadership training program (which had usually never been done cross-culturally before) was *the* answer to the training needs of the national church. Leader after leader has been corrupted, new factions have developed, and now most young leaders expect that they can be supported from outside the country to do all kinds of ministry, provided they can meet the right benefactor organization. The result is that the growth in the church has slowed to a crawl.

In a chapter entitled "Are We Nourishing or Choking Young Plants with Funds?" Meydan and Harris paint a sober picture that is deeply disturbing because of its accuracy in describing what has been happening for fifteen years or more in regions familiar to me:

> Unwise use of foreign funds can of course damage the work of God in any context. But certain specific realities in the Muslim world present particularly acute challenges—perhaps unique challenges—for the use of external funds.
>
> First, God is using world events and the media to give many Christians a burden and a passion to reach out to Muslims. . . . One consequence is that unprecedentedly large numbers of Christian organizations and donors are interested in "having a ministry" in some Muslim context, while security concerns mean that relatively few of these wish to place resident workers in Muslim countries where they might develop a deep understanding of local culture values and deep relationships with local believers. At the same time, the number of MBBs . . . in most Muslim contexts is tiny, and most are new in the faith. So, relative to non-Muslim contexts, the Muslim world has a disproportionately large number of donors seeking partnership with a disproportionately tiny number of mature local believers. This imbalance between the number of eager donors and the number of recipients means that unwise use of money may have a more profound and distorting effect on church-planting ministry, unintentionally "choking" the faith of young believers. (2008, 248-49)

Colleagues on the ground had initially hoped that they could keep low to the ground and the circus would pass by and leave them unscathed. This is no longer an option. Throughout the Muslim world we must learn some of the hard lessons that missions in other parts of the world have been struggling to master over the past century and more. This reality is here to stay. I have been told that in a certain Middle Eastern country, something approaching 80 percent of the salaries of all the pastors of evangelical churches (and there are dozens) in the country are funded from the West. No contemporary evangelical church in the country believes that it can afford to pay its pastors without Western financial assistance. Brothers and sisters, there is something seriously wrong with this picture.

Though I ended up discussing this issue of the funding of BMBs and of national ministries in Muslim countries with only a few people, the responses I received on this question communicated a unified message. As can be seen in table 13.2, the top recommendation was that outside ministry organizations should channel funding only through national organizations or in-country local churches, rather than giving money directly to individuals in those churches. Yet, even though that was the advice on how to channel such assistance, the next three points all strongly recommended against any form of partnership model. Though two people did believe that ongoing funding of some BMBs' ministries in country is sometimes necessary and beneficial to the growth of the indigenous church, the majority of people who commented on this issue stressed that funding people or ministries from outside is rarely a good approach. It is better to have BMBs ministering using a tentmaking or

Table 13.2. The Fruitful Channeling of Foreign Money into National Ministries

Foreign Support for BMBs and Their Ministries	Total	Regional Background		Religious Background		Experience Discipling	
		AW People	The Rest	BMB /23	Other /52	Expert /47	Novice /28
1. When funding from outside, give through national bodies and churches but not to individuals directly	8	4	4	3	5	7	1
2. Use relationships to help BMBs find work so they do not need outside help	7	5	2	4	3	4	3
3. Bi-vocational model provides the best model for BMBs; effective Arabs are bi-vocational and self-supporting	6	3	3	3	3	3	3
4. It is normally better for people to minister without foreign support; foreign support raises red flags	6	2	4	2	4	2	4
5. There are now tasks that need to be done by full-time national workers, and they need outside support (North Africa)	2	2	0	2	0	2	0
6. Funding from outside needs to have a time limit; help especially with special events and projects	2	1	1	1	1	1	1
7. Best model is national church funding its own ministries; outside help is never a good model	2	1	1	1	1	1	1
Totals	**33**	**18**	**15**	**16**	**17**	**20**	**13**

bi-vocational model, or to have local churches supporting their own local and national ministries.

Strong caution was urged against setting up ongoing local ministry funded primarily by foreign money. One worker with long experience in the Middle East put it like this: "Foreign support is not good. It is a simple matter of integrity. Support from outside raises red flags all over the place. The most effective Arab BMBs are bi-vocational and fully self-supporting. This is the best model for BMBs ministering inside the Arab world." A veteran worker in North Africa commented, "Foreign support creates a pattern that is unhealthy, especially in such a young and vulnerable national church." Even a BMB in Europe, who is actively funding BMB projects within the Arab world, stressed that it is better to help fund special short-term projects and events, rather than provide ongoing support. He stressed that any funding of a BMB's ministry in country should have a specific time limit.[1]

However, it needs to be noted that not all agree with this consensus sentiment. I interviewed a few BMBs who are ministering full-time in effective ministries in their own countries (church planting, theological education and follow-up work) who are almost entirely funded from outside. They did not see this as being a problem for themselves or others. They did offer the counsel that such support is best handled through a national church or organization rather than direct to the individual, but they felt that some such outside-supported ministries are necessary, and when handled appropriately are effective and are no different from foreign missionaries being funded from outside the country. The only consistent advice that can be drawn from this research is that foreign funding of ongoing ministry of BMBs within their own countries ought to be the exception rather than the rule. And when it is done, it is vital that proper mechanisms are set up to handle the management of this kind of ongoing support. Doubtless, this will continue to be a contentious issue across the Muslim world for the foreseeable future.

---

[1] There is a widely acknowledged change in the recommendation when it comes to fully funding BMBs in media and training ministries that are based outside of the Muslim world and focused on their own people back home. Many such BMBs are funded full-time and are doing outstanding work in media and training ministries that are based outside the Muslim world in order to serve people living and ministering in Muslim countries.

Before leaving this topic of the use of money in discipling BMBs and partnering with the emerging national church, let me draw on a couple of people who have recently proposed some positive models for partnership. These suggested models are a big improvement on those that have been the main options in other parts of the world. Because the amount of advice I received in my field research was rather limited, passing on some of the counsel of current authorities on cross-cultural partnerships that involve the exchange of funds can be of help, for these matters are increasingly of vital concern to everyone working among Muslims.

In the concluding chapter of *Cross-Cultural Partnerships: Navigating the Complexities of Money and Mission* (2010), Mary Lederleitner suggests that there are seven ways that you can tell if "Christ Is Lord of Your Partnership." She draws her seven points from a reflection on Philippians 2:1-16, in which Paul holds up Jesus as a model for how we are to live with others. Here are the seven questions that she suggests that we use in assessing the quality of our partnerships:

1. Are you intensely and actively looking for the good in your cross-cultural partner?

2. Are you focusing on the bigger issues of modeling unity and love?

3. Are you making sure that your partner's needs as well as your own are being met?

4. Are you setting aside legitimate power to be a servant in the partnership?

5. Are you walking humbly, trusting that God will reward your obedience?

6. Are you doing the hard work to ensure your partnership is effective and fruitful?

7. Are you speaking in respectful ways and turning away from the sin of grumbling? (Lederleitner 2010, 182-87)

Lederleitner expresses an inspiring vision for God-honoring cross-cultural partnerships in missions. Echoing the style and format of Martin Luther King's "I have a dream" speech, Lederleitner calls us to dream

God-sized dreams for the way that partnership may one day function:

> I dream of a day when Philippians 2:1-16 is not the exception but rather
> the norm for cross-cultural ministry partnerships. I dream of the day
> when we choose not to compartmentalize our theology and how we do
> ministry, but rather, our theology informs and transforms how we work
> with one another. I dream of a day, and I can see it in my heart, when the
> world stops and takes notice of what is happening in our cross-cultural
> ministry partnerships. I dream of the day when world leaders come to
> Christians to see how they can get along better because the global church
> is modeling this so very powerfully. (2010, 187-88)

In the final chapter of a 2012 collection of papers on effective partnerships for missions in Asia, Chinese Filipino theologian and mission
strategist David S. Lim proposes measures that we can all strive after as
we seek to create a positive climate for mutuality and spiritual synergy
in kingdom partnerships. These three key core principles offer a possible
way forward for those of us serving the cause of Christ among Muslims
globally: Key Relationship: friendship of equals; Key Objective: empow-
erment of locals/nationals; and Key Attitude: servanthood of expatriates.
Lim challenges churches from the Global North to name and celebrate
what they received through partnership with churches from the Global
South. Echoing the kind of visionary application of Philippians 2 that
Lederleitner outlines, Lim challenges all participants in the partnerships
to "empty ourselves of autonomy and independence" (Lim 2012, 137).

Missionaries must embrace the inequalities in the partnership and
receive from our partners even as we share money, resources, education,
land, technology, ownership and power; while receiving stories, traditions, ancient knowledge and customs, inheritances, joy, kindness,
goodness, beauty, sustainability and difference in order to maintain even
power dynamics within the partnership (Lim 2012, 138). As we move into
the time ahead of us of increasing turmoil and unprecedented opportunity across the Muslim world, my prayer is that we will find ways to
make the too-often dysfunctional partnerships into sources of renewal
and blessing for BMBs and all in the global church.

14

DISCIPLING BELIEVING FAMILIES
IN MUSLIM COMMUNITIES

"Do not think that I have come to bring peace to the earth. I have not come to bring peace, but a sword. For I have come to set a man against his father, and a daughter against her mother, and a daughter-in-law against her mother-in-law. And a person's enemies will be those of his own household. Whoever loves father or mother more than me is not worthy of me, and whoever loves son or daughter more than me is not worthy of me. And whoever does not take his cross and follow me is not worthy of me. Whoever finds his life will lose it, and whoever loses his life for my sake will find it."

MATTHEW 10:34-39

Experience indicates that only Christian families can provide the necessary stability, maturity, and ability to understand and minister to all the members. The Christian home is an indispensable place for fellowship, prayer, study of the Word, and counselling. Single believers, many of whom are isolated islands in the hostile sea of their Muslim environment, need a haven in the atmosphere of a home away from home. The missionary family, being a foreign element, cannot fill the gap. Only national families can provide the atmosphere necessary for a church to develop properly.

WENDELL P. EVANS,
CHURCH PLANTING IN THE ARAB-MUSLIM WORLD

As we sat together in a colleague's apartment in the Middle East, Halima shared some of the struggles of being a BMB and how BMBs need support and encouragement from those seeking to disciple them. My heart went out to Halima as she described her life as a mother of two girls who was still trying to appear as a Muslim in order to keep her Christian faith hidden from her Muslim family, even though she had been married to a non-BMB Christian man for many years. Halima had been a believer for sixteen years and was increasingly embittered as her life as a secretive BMB became more and more difficult to endure.

As a result of a series of negative experiences, she had stopped her involvement in a well-known evangelical church in the city. Then, for a few years she had been part of a small group of BMBs led by a colleague, but when that group disbanded following her departure from the country, Halima was left with no regular fellowship. She had found some support and friendship with one or two expatriate women and was still holding on to her Christian faith. She felt very much alone as she tried to live her life as a Christian and raise her two daughters. Her husband's income fluctuated, and so she had to work long hours as a private translator in order to afford to send her daughters to a small private international school so that they would not have to be indoctrinated with Islamic teaching in school.

She described marriage for BMBs as a huge social issue. Muslim women are unable to marry Christian men because that would complicate their identity far too much. Were it to become known that they had left Islam, they would be shunned by their Muslim family. Her own life exemplified the struggle that she said was normal for BMB women in her country. Though she had married a Christian man, she could not let her family know that he was a Christian. This meant that they had to remain quite distant from her Muslim family.

The thing that troubled me most was her conviction that it was wrong for her to raise her own children as Christians—she felt that they must discover the Christian faith and choose it for themselves when they became adults, as she had. It would compromise their rights as Muslim children to be taught Christianity by their mother, and it could get her in trouble and expose her identity as a Christian. One of the sad outcomes of this attempt to raise her daughters with no clear religious identity was that her young teenage daughter was apparently becoming schizophrenic. She was deeply confused about her identity and was not coping with daily life. She had begun to receive psychiatric care. Halima was very burdened for her mentally ill daughter, yet could not see a way for her to change the way she lived without exposing her own Christian identity to her Muslim family and social circles. She wondered whether her attempt to live with two identities was driving her daughter toward insanity.

My four-hour visit with Halima was personally disturbing. As the father of two girls, in their late teens at the time of that conversation, I could not help but see the stark contract between the healthy self-esteem and identity of my own daughters as committed followers of Christ with the uneasy and confusing identity that Halima's daughters were trying to shape for themselves because their mother did not feel that it would be right or safe to nurture them as Christians in their own home. Halima's struggle with her identity, and the choices that she had thus far made to try to keep her faith hidden from her extended family for sixteen years, left their damaging marks on her and appeared to be threatening her children's ability to live normal lives.

This chapter begins to explore some of the issues involved for BMBs, as illustrated in Halima's struggles, as they live in their families and as they marry believers and raise believing families and live as Christians in communities that give little freedom for them to forge new social identities. The longer BMBs continue to live in their birth communities, or in some other part of the Muslim world, the more complicated and stressful their lives as BMBs can become. After BMBs have sorted out their new identity, survived persecution and learned to overcome numerous demonic assaults, they will continue to face challenges that come as they live out their lives in their families and as believing families in Muslim society. The discussion in this chapter is only a beginning because the issues introduced here warrant a book-length treatment on their own.

WISDOM ON DISCIPLESHIP AND FAMILY RELATIONS FROM EXPERIENCED AUTHORS

The nature of family relations in Islamic societies presents at least two distinct and significant challenges to discipleship. The first reality is that traditional Muslim families are typically patriarchal and hierarchical. It is very difficult for individual members, especially women and younger members of extended family networks, to break away from the religious heritage of the family without encountering much opposition and hostility. Typically, the severest persecution that BMBs face is from the father and other family authority figures. This creates a major challenge to both evangelism and discipleship in Muslim communities.

The second significant obstacle is that despite the strong family authority structures typical of Muslim families, very few families evidence anything like healthy and warm domestic relationships. The experience of someone growing up in a typical North African Muslim family, for example, is that of being a part of a complex network of manipulative relationships in which each member of the family is vying for power and control over other members of the family. Because of the widespread dysfunctional nature of Muslim families and paucity of good models, the discipling of BMBs has an additional challenge in helping individual disciples, couples and church communities learn how to create and nurture healthy and loving family relationships.

A number of books reference these two major family-related challenges. Perhaps most optimistic is the perspective of David Garrison, in his 2004 survey of church planting movements (CPMs). Garrison reports that in CPMs the web of conversions normally happens through family networks and relationships. New believers take the gospel to their family first, even in the face of severe persecution. Family-based conversions are the norm in CPMs. He illustrates this with a story from Afghanistan where the patriarch embraced Christ subsequent to a dream that came to him after he had heard from a younger member of his family about his own dream. Then, within a week, all thirteen members of the clan had given their lives to Christ (Garrison 2004, 229). Garrison portrays the family mostly as a potentially positive conduit of the gospel and as a means of rapid multiplication of churches.

More recently, in his survey of movements to Christ among Muslims, *A Wind in the House of Islam* (2014), Garrison's discussion is much more nuanced. In his description, in chapter eleven, of a movement in "Western South Asia" (which encompasses Afghanistan, Pakistan and western India), Garrison tells pieces of the story of the founding of a movement, under the leadership of one Ahmed, that consisted entirely of men in the beginning. Because men were so culturally separated from women, it had not occurred to the men that their women would have any interest in their new faith in Christ. Garrison explains a culture that is perhaps difficult for many readers to even begin to relate to:

> An American Christian who has spent many years among these people explained that the gap between men and women is even greater than any ethnic divide or tribal separation. Up to this point, he said, this Muslim movement had been almost entirely a men's movement. So even after these men came to faith in Christ and are born again, they still have little to say to their wives. All of his married life a man may have never had a meaningful conversation with his wife. Now suddenly he has this tremendous spiritual change, he's been born again, but if he goes home and tries to speak to his wife about it, she will think him crazy. He has no meaningful relationship with her. If she discovers his faith in Isa, she would likely leave him, or report him to the imam.
>
> Ahmed explained, "In our culture, women are like shoes. We just wear them, and then when they are old we throw them out." (2014, 198)

Garrison then tells how some of the male leaders in this movement of thousands of male Christ followers discovered that women could also come to know and love Christ, as they had. He recounted how the missionary couple had brought in a young American woman educational consultant to teach some of the tribal women how to be teachers in areas where there were no schools. God used this event in a bizarre way to help some of the men to understand that women could also be touched by Christ.

It all started when Ahmed asked the American woman, over lunch, "Should we not be beating our wives?" Her shocked response was, "No, of course you should not be beating your wife!" Ahmed's innocent response was, "Well, what does the Bible say about this?" (200). This question led to the woman missionary texting him a series of Scripture passages that evening that gave the men new insight into a biblical perspective on how men should treat their wives. After the men stayed up all night talking about this amazing new insight and what it could mean for them, the next day all the men present pledged to stop beating their wives. Garrison recounts Ahmed's story:

> "It has not been easy," Ahmed admitted. "It has not been easy for me. That was a big change for us. Since we had begun studying the word of God, we didn't think about what it meant to the women. We were reading it, but focusing on what was happening in our culture as men, how could we change it? We knew it would be very difficult for us to change it. But we were not thinking that God might also be calling women. We were just happy in *our* life. Men, men, men, men's jamaat; men's training; men's ministry."
>
> With the close of the teacher conference, a women's movement was launched. The male leaders of the movement requesting more training that would encourage reaching the women. They didn't have to look far. . . .
>
> Ahmed said, "We learned [through a missionary's book, *The Insanity of God*] that when the persecution becomes severe, and the men are killed or put in prison, our wives would be given over to the mosque or to the tribal leaders. Our children would have no one to teach them the way of Jesus. Within a short time, our movement would cease to exist. . . ."
>
> This made sense, even to the most hardened men. "Things are changing," Ahmed said. "Last year, more than 100 jamaat leaders said to me, 'I no longer beat my wife.'" Today, though it remains smaller than the men's movement, the women's movement has started hundreds of women's jamaats, and is growing at the same pace as the men's movement. (202)

I find this story both disturbing and heartening. It very well illustrates the need for effective discipleship in these often very culturally sensitive issues. It also illustrates that the gospel transformation of people in movements takes time—just as it does with individual believers. The changes that are needed can be massive. But this story is also encouraging in that it illustrates the power of the Word of God. Those men were eager to do whatever the Word of God told them to do. Yet, it was not easy for them to be transformed at such a basic level of cultural conditioning. The story of Ahmed's conversion (which I have not recounted here) begins with Ahmed almost murdering the missionary friend of his brother simply because he was an infidel. The challenges to effective discipling of BMBs are closely related to the pressures and realities of family life in Muslim cultures.

Similar to the way that Garrison speaks about the positive potential of families when he describes Muslim people movements to Christ, Greeson reported that in one indigenous movement of BMB churches in Southeast Asia, which has surpassed one hundred thousand believers, the gospel is spread primarily through family and village community networks.

> As I continued to interview church members, I soon realized that three of the church members were leading churches of their own in nearby villages. Each of these churches had been started through relatives or close friends. One particular jump of the Gospel struck me. The pastor of the church I was visiting told how the Gospel had jumped from his church to his sister's village some 40 miles away. He told me that his sister's village now had 100 Muslims who have become followers of Jesus. (Greeson 2007, 36)

In a parallel way, so much of what Phil Parshall advocates in terms of sensitivity to cultural realities is in order to make it possible for faith in Christ to spread along family lines. The goal is to avoid making faith in Christ be seen as rejection of the family and its values. For example, Parshall urges us to approach women and children through the men and to approach students and young men through the fathers. We are encouraged to work within the family social structure, not in opposition to it (Parshall 1985, 187-88).

However, a number of people mention the negative side of family social structure when they talk about the family rejection and persecution that flows from families. For example, Linda Smith, in discussing how to help women BMBs through trials and persecution, tells a number of stories that illustrate the powerfully negative impact the family often has on women believers. Their families react and exert huge pressure on the female BMBs to return to their families and to Islam. One of the primary methods of attack is through the Muslim nuclear and extended family. Here is one cameo that illustrates the danger and the hope for women in Muslim families:

> Unbelieving husbands can be a dangerous threat to a new believer. When Julia became a Christian, she was afraid to tell her husband. But one day he came home and found her reading her Bible. His fury was so great that he beat her in front of their two young children, then tried to strangle her, leaving her for dead.
>
> Through her painful recovery, she continued to cling to her faith and prayed daily for her husband. God brought a spirit of repentance to him, not only for his shameful cruelty toward her, but for his sinful, hardened heart. He became a believer. (Smith 2000, 127)

Smith comments on the relief of having women BMBs being able to marry believing husbands. She also discusses the suffering that results when single women are forced to stay in their family homes while their families continue to revile them for being Christians and traitors to their family and nations. Most of her article deals with the suffering and persecution of female BMBs, and almost all of her examples are of families persecuting the female members of their family who abandon Islam and follow Christ (Smith 2000, 123-35). Phil and Julie Parshall also refer to the difficulty that female BMBs have in that they are generally less independent than men are, and they must live and grow within their family contexts. Of course, this cuts both ways, in that often a believing husband finds that his Muslim wife chooses to follow Christ as well. In fact, the Parshalls suggest that this is the norm when believing men marry Muslim wives: "Most women who are married have come to Christ following the conversion of their husbands. This opens the door for their discipleship" (Parshall and Parshall 2002, 254).

Given the centrality of the family in Muslim society, I was surprised to notice that few of those writing about ministry to Muslims take time to discuss what is involved in discipling BMBs so that they can develop healthy Christian family life. Of those who do deal with the issue, Pietzsch, as usual, is the most thorough. He devotes his short tenth chapter to the challenges of helping BMBs develop strong, biblically informed families with godly relationships among members of the family (Pietzsch 2004, 101-8). His descriptions of typical Muslim practices and attitudes within families are insightful and demonstrate considerable familiarity with Muslim families. He shows how important it is for appropriate discipleship to take place in terms of roles of husband and wives, treatment and discipline of children, relationship to in-laws, and so on. He also has a good discussion of how to stand alongside of BMBs in situations of severe domestic violence. Pietzsch deals with husbands abusing their wives. He treats other family crises such as divorce, depression, co-dependency, rape, wife abuse and suicide. For example, he discusses scenarios in which a BMB is married to a Muslim spouse and the problems that go with such a situation. He advises the counselor, or discipler, to be brave and decisive in dealing with crises or chronic abuse. Overall, Pietzsch's thoughts on BMB parenting and marriage are helpful but very short and more suggestive than instructive. He does not have the space to deal with some of the more intractable problems BMBs face living as believers in Muslim societies.

Rick Love mentioned that divorce was a major problem among the people where he labored for eight years. He and his wife, Fran, found that they had to spend hours and hours training BMB couples how to have healthy marriages and spouses how to love one another in a biblical way. "Marriage became a central aspect of church life for us. We put on marriage seminars, did pre-marital counseling, and spent hundreds of hours focusing on the family" (Love 2000, 167). In North Africa, the lack of good Muslim models of strong family relationships was one of the primary reasons why it was very difficult to see solid churches established. It was only when a number of single believers married, founded believing families that grew in Christian maturity and had their own homes that the churches were able to begin to mature and reproduce strongly.[1]

---

[1] In early 2008, I had the privilege to be invited to a consultation of about fifty church leaders from across North Africa. The focus of their three-day consultation was the challenge of families in

This leads to one other aspect of the discussion of families. Several writers stress that for BMB house churches to be successfully established in Muslim communities there have to be several believing families who can host the meetings of the BMBs. In discussing the best strategy for church planting in North Africa, Wendell Evans stressed the need for having believing BMB households in order to see churches established:

> Experience indicates that only Christian families can provide the necessary stability, maturity, and ability to understand and minister to all the members. . . . The missionary family, being a foreign element, cannot fill the gap. . . . Experience indicates the wisdom of beginning church meetings in national homes under national leadership. This will both encourage quicker assumption of responsibility by national elders and avoid the necessity of eventual transfer of meeting place(s). . . . The normal elders of the church would then be the heads of the households in which the church meets. (Evans 1985, 2, 12)[2]

To sum up insights from these workers, we can say that foundational elements to effective discipleship in Islamic societies must include working as much as possible within the normal family networks, discipling BMBs so that they can have strong families and building the emerging house churches around the homes of maturing BMBs, some of whom marry and form Christian homes. Western workers especially must learn to work increasingly within and for the strengthening of family networks and of believing cell churches within them.

Nevertheless, it must be stressed that is often far from easy to work effectively within Muslim family networks. We must not be surprised when the fiercest opposition to the work of the gospel comes from people within family networks who are shamed when some of their members choose to align themselves with Christ. Much of the socially cohesive

---

evangelism, discipleship and BMB churches. Everyone present agreed that these are crucial issues that need attention and teaching. They also recognized that very little effective work had been done to address this urgent matter until that point in time.

[2]Schlorff makes the same point (1981, 9-12). This stress on the need for the church fellowship to meet in BMB homes is echoed and agreed to by Livingstone (1993, 173-74), a former colleague of Evans and Schlorff. In the context of Central Asia, Daniels also stresses the need for the local church to be run by local heads of BMB families and hosted in their homes (2005, 183-99).

power of Islamic communities consists in their strong hierarchal families that use fear and intimidation to keep people from leaving Islam. In a passage very familiar to BMBs and their disciplers, Christ himself warned that this would be the case, and he called BMBs to stand strong in obedience in the face of strong family opposition. Matthew 10:34-39, cited at the beginning of this chapter, has been read and memorized and given comfort to countless BMBs as they struggle to understand and stay faithful to Christ in the face of hostility from those nearest and dearest: "And a person's enemies will be those of his own household" (Mt 10:36).

WISDOM FROM EXPERIENCED DISCIPLERS ON DISCIPLING WITHIN FAMILIES

Part of the discussion in the interviews dealt with the challenges that BMBs face related to their families. These challenges were readily iden- tified, and there was generally agreement on how much these factors get in the way of effective discipling. Typically, problems that were identified fell into three main groups. The first kind of problem are those that single BMBs face from their Muslim families, such as mistrust, persecution, rejection or forced marriage to nonbelievers. The second type of problem consist in those that believing couples face seeking to live as believers and raise their children in Muslim communities. These social and psy- chological challenges involve knowing one's religious identity in the community, Islamic education being forced on non-Muslim children, BMBs' children being ostracized and the difficulty in finding a believing wife or husband. The third family-related type of problem that BMBs face occurs in the contexts where they are among BCBs and their churches. In such contexts as the Middle East, BMBs often face a lack of genuine acceptance by non-Muslim-background believers and their churches and a refusal by Christian parents to allow their children to marry BMBs. Together, these kinds of challenges sometimes push BMBs to unhelpful long-term solutions, such as moving outside of the Muslim world or marrying foreign Christians in order to be able to raise their children as believers.

How does one effectively tackle these discipleship challenges? Analysis of this topic draws on just a little less than half of the people interviewed (thirty-four of seventy-five). In examining the top seven types of advice offered, the counsel offered falls into two broad perspectives (refer to table 14.1). The first focuses on how to help believers become good fathers and mothers and how to have good marriages as believers. The second category of counsel is more strategic, in that it stresses the value of seeking to help believers remain connected to their Muslim families so that they are able to share Christ with their family, over time. Fifty-nine

Table 14.1. Advice on Discipling Families

Ways to Disciple in Families	Total	Regional Background		Religious Background		Experience Discipling		Gender	
		AW People	The Rest	BMB /23	Other /52	Expert /47	Novice /28	M 50	F 25
1. It is very important to teach and train on parenting and marriage	19	7	12	6	13	11	8	12	7
2. Disciplers must take the BMBs into their own family and must not separate family from ministry	9	3	6	2	7	8	1	6	3
3. Good to teach on family issues, gender issues, couple issues, and so on, in the church	6	3	3	3	3	5	1	4	2
4. Crucial discipleship issue to deal with is fear of family and community pressure	3	2	1	1	2	2	1	2	1
Section Subtotal	**37**	**15**	**22**	**12**	**25**	**26**	**11**	**24**	**13**
5. Goal is to have BMBs remain with their families in order to model new life in Christ	11	4	7	3	8	5	6	9	2
6. Good when possible for members of one family to come to Christ and meet as a believing family	10	3	7	1	9	3	7	6	4
7. When accepted into the Muslim family as a believer, one has a right to share with whole family	5	0	5	0	5	1	4	4	1
Section Subtotal	**26**	**7**	**19**	**4**	**22**	**9**	**17**	**19**	**7**
Totals	**63**	**22**	**41**	**16**	**47**	**35**	**28**	**43**	**20**

percent of the counsel given falls into the first category—advice for effective family living as believers.

Helping BMBs have strong Christian marriages and families. The most often repeated counsel was that disciplers must teach and train BMBs on parenting and marriage relationships. One cannot leave this to some sort of natural process, hoping that former Muslims will automatically figure out how to be Christian parents and how to have Christ-honoring marriage relationships. Most former Muslims have not been around many godly men and women in order to see their domestic lives up close. Just as Rick and Fran Love found that their ministry was much occupied with marriage counseling and training of couples and parents, several whom I spoke with told of organizing special weekend retreats for couples that dealt with issues of marriage and child rearing. As expatriates, they found that such events were the most helpful when a mature local BMB couple who had done a good job of raising their kids shared from their experience. I know of several Christian and Muslim-background leaders who devote a significant part of their ministry to running conferences and seminars for BMBs that deal with marriage and family training. Most of the international Arab leaders working with BMBs clearly believe that this is a top priority in their ministries.

One expatriate woman who had significant interaction with both single and married women in the local house church mentioned that when they did women's events together, such as painting, cooking events or picnics, much of the conversation naturally focused on topics related to issues with their children and husbands, and she found that she was frequently able to help these women sort through how their new life in Christ applied to their marriages and families. She believed that it was these kinds of informal conversations and informal mentoring situations that were the most effective in helping her women friends develop increasingly Christian marriages and homes. Another effective woman expatriate discipler said that she has taught and discipled women a lot on marriage and family issues. She often used stories of families in the Bible in order to address the family issues.

At the consultation on family issues held by North Africans that I attended in 2008, the entire program was built around an oral approach of telling stories of family life in the Bible. The stores from the Bible often strongly resembled the dysfunction of Muslim and BMB families. The recounting of stories of families in the Bible was followed by discussion in small groups facilitated through carefully designed questions exploring the issues raised in the stories. It was moving to see these Bible stories eliciting frank admissions of the challenges the BMBs were facing daily, which, in many cases, they had never before talked about. It was apparent that when their own family experiences were brought to the surface in the discovery that families in Scripture dealt with many of the same issues, there was permission given to be open and vulnerable with each other about the depth of the challenges they faced. Prior to these few days together with other BMBs from across North Africa, many had never before felt free to talk to anyone about their struggles. Though talking about the challenges with other BMBs did not resolve them, it was a great step on the journey to seeing transformed family relationships.

Of course, we know that simply telling people how they should behave, or can behave now that they are in Christ, is not enough either. So, it is instructive to note that the second most repeated counsel in this first category is that as much as possible disciplers should welcome BMBs into their homes and families, so that they can see and experience Christian family life in real families. As a married man with young children working mostly with single men, I was often unconsciously modeling a different way of being married than any they had seen in their Muslim families. They watched how my wife and I treated each other and how we related to and raised our children. One incident stands out in memory. One night, as I was about to finish an evening visit with a thirty-five-year-old BMB friend, he suggested we get together again the coming Saturday. I responded and said that as far as I knew, that could work, but I would have to check with my wife and see if that worked for her and the children, because Saturdays were important days for our family. He then exclaimed that he was astonished that he had so often seen me defer to Jeanie's needs and schedule. He said that he had *never* seen his father consider what his wife's needs may have been when planning his own schedule.

We found that as we worked and lived with these young men for a number of years, one of the most important contributions we made was modeling Christian marriage and family life. Most of those men have since married believing wives and are raising their children as believers and seeking to model Christian families to their Muslim extended families. The oft-given advice that disciplers must welcome BMBs and their families into their own homes points to a vital element in effective discipling of families.

One team in a very rich city in the Arabian Peninsula deliberately uses their own families as a form of evangelism. They spend entire days and camp out with their families with local Muslim families who have no material needs and evidence no spiritual hunger. In sharing their family life in this way, they find that their Muslim friends comment on the different family relationships that they see among the Christian expatriate families. They are finding that this sometimes opens the door to deep spiritual conversations in rather unique ways. Of course, it is not easy to open our home and families in such vulnerable ways to others. During our time in North Africa, those whose ministries bore the most fruit in discipling BMBs were those who lovingly, deliberately and freely opened their lives and their families to BMBs in multiple ways. Also noteworthy is that eight of the nine who strongly advised that disciplers welcome BMBs into their homes were more experienced disciplers.[3]

The value of BMBs maintaining good relationships with their Muslim families. The second category of counsel given (refer to items 2, 3 and 6 in table 14.1) by those with whom I spoke was that BMBs are to be encouraged to do all they can to keep good relationships with the members of their Muslim families in order to enable ongoing influence for Christ in their family networks. Another aspect of this strategic counsel is that

---

[3]It is intriguing to note that there was no discernable contrast between men and women in the advice given on discipling families. In referring to the Gender column in table 14.1, the advice in the top half of the table were given in almost identical proportion to the number of men and women interviewed. This suggests that men and women substantially agree on the importance of these topics and on how to address these challenges.

when one person comes to faith in Christ, that person needs to pray and work to see more members of his or her family believe so that what was formerly a Muslim family becomes a believing family. One very experienced Christian-background Arab man with whom I spoke said that, in his experience, when a married Muslim man came to Christ and had proper coaching, his wife usually also came to believe not too long after. Following her conversion, the newly believing couple could begin raising their children in increasingly Christian ways.

BMBs staying in healthy relationship with Muslim family members can bring good fruit in multiple ways. A number of the most mature BMBs described their role in their extended Muslim families as being the one person that everyone else in the family leans on in a crisis. It was the Christian member of the family, whether male or female, on whom many in the extended Muslim family had come to rely. This sometimes led to others coming to faith, but even when it did not, there was a clear respect for and trust in the believing member of the family that came about over time as the transformed life of the BMB led to increasingly positive influence over time. Of course, were the BMB to have no ongoing contact with his or her family, such influence would never develop.

There are, however, other aspects of keeping closely tied to one's family that are not so positive or easy to bear. In a recent conversation with a North African BMB woman living in Europe, who has been a believer for some forty years, she described how strong the influence of her Muslim family remains. Even though her mother has known of her Christian faith for forty years now, every time she visits her family in North Africa, her mother appeals to her to return to her family heritage and return to Islam. She struggled to explain to us non-BMBs the powerful pull and burden that one's non-believing family has on believers, even decades after their conversion to Christ. Even though this woman has lived among Christians for her entire adult life, in many deep levels of her being she still feels Muslim and feels the pull of her extended family who do not accept that her conversion to Christ is permanent. Until she dies, they will still hold onto hope that she will one day return to them and once again confess Islam with them. This expectation, and the pressure that it puts on the BMB, is matched by an internal longing to be able to have normal relationships with one's family again. If only one's allegiance to Christ did not have to divide families.

There is another way in which remaining close to one's Muslim extended family creates significant pressure on a believing family. When a believing family who are seeking to create a new Christian home keeps closely tied to their extended Muslim family, the Muslim members of that family continually interfere in the lives of their children and seek to influence their marriages to be more like Muslim marriages. At the above-mentioned seminar of North African BMBs, one of the biggest and most intractable problems that most struggled with were mothers-in-laws. In typical North African Muslim families, the mother of the husband believes she has the right to rule the domestic life of her son's family. Far too often, the wife of the son is treated as a virtual slave in her own household. Muslim husbands generally put up with such treatment of their wives by their mothers, because that is the way their families operate. For believing couples, it sometimes seems that every encounter that they have with the family of the husband brings great tension and conflict into their marriage. The believing husband has to be taught to stand up for his wife and not allow his mother to abuse his wife. Often, the only way that a believing couple can develop a loving marriage where the husband treats his wife with loving respect is for the BMB couple to keep a significant distance between their family life and that of their Muslim in-laws and siblings.

Though I strongly endorse this strategic desire and teaching that BMBs are to make every effort to keep close ties to their unbelieving families, one must also recognize that this is a somewhat unnatural thing to do. When a Muslim woman, for example, comes to Christ, perseveres through persecution from her father and family and is finally able to marry a believer and set up a new family in Christ, the values of this new family unit soon become radically different from the values of her Muslim family. As the years pass, and one raises one's children as believers and remains in close fellowship with other Christians, one gradually finds that one has little in common any longer with the members of one's non-believing family. When one does meet socially, it becomes increasingly hard to have anything to talk about. In my experience, even as a Canadian from a Christian background, I have found that it has been hard to maintain close relationships with my unbelieving brothers and their families, simply because we have almost no common interests or shared values. It is intriguing to me, in looking at the very limited data reflected in table 14.1 that the advice to remain in close contact with one's Muslim family and aim to share one's faith with them is a much higher priority for non-BMBs and for inexperienced disciplers than it was for BMBs and expert disciplers.

I conclude this discussion of the strategic counsel with a word of caution. Might it not be wise for those of us who are passionate about seeing Muslims reached for Christ by BMBs sharing Christ with their extended families, to temper our enthusiasm and listen to the wisdom of experienced BMBs? Life often does not fit our models of ministry. And when it does not, then in our continuing to teach BMBs to make it a top priority to keep closely tied to their Muslim families, we may find ourselves inadvertently putting pressure on our believing friends that could well push them back into Islam. The unrelenting pressure from their Muslim families can become too strong to resist when it is repeatedly encountered, day in and day out.

It is a good thing, after all, that BMB families find their primary source of strength and loving relationships from fellow believers, in their new family the church, rather than from their Muslim friends and family members, with whom they have increasingly less in common. The friendship and fellowship that we usually experience within the church, regardless of our backgrounds before we came to know Christ, far surpasses anything that is available with friends and family outside of Christ. Christ himself said that non-believers will know that Christ is real, not by how we love non-Christian family members, but when they see how we love one another. So, let us keep our priority, in our discipleship, on helping new believers experience and develop strong Christian families that belong to loving Christian fellowships. When this strongly characterizes the believers living in the Muslim world, then the love and quality of relationships in the church and in the Christian families within the church will draw even more Muslims to Christ.

15

SUITABLE ROLES FOR
EXPATRIATE DISCIPLERS

*Therefore, having this ministry by the mercy of God,
we do not lose heart. But we have renounced disgraceful,
underhanded ways. We refuse to practice cunning or to tamper with
God's word, but by the open statement of the truth we would commend
ourselves to everyone's conscience in the sight of God. . . . For
what we proclaim is not ourselves, but Jesus Christ as Lord,
with ourselves as your servants for Jesus' sake.*

2 CORINTHIANS 4:1-2, 5

*As brothers and sisters in Christ our purpose is to walk
alongside a MBB . . . walking the road together, praying, encouraging,
having fellowship, correction, discipling, tutoring and waiting on God's
answer to prayer. In other words, just being a true sister or brother
in the Lord. The MBB needs to see Christ in you and
to observe how to lead a Christian life.*

HORST B. PIETZSCH,
WELCOME HOME: CARING FOR CONVERTS TO CHRIST FROM ISLAM

*More than fifty villages were visible, and hundreds more lay hidden
in the valley and behind the mountains. . . . "These people have never
heard of our Saviour," said my companion. . . . Deep in my heart the
conviction was born, "I am the man to tell them. This is my corner
of the great white field." A deep compassion, and irresistible yearning,*

gripped my soul. During the forty years of service that followed I could never look out over that panorama of mountains without . . . feeling the continual yearning to reach out to those villages to tell of new life through Christ.

CHARLES MARSH,
THE CHALLENGE OF ISLAM

J
UST BEFORE MOVING TO THE ARAB WORLD for the first time, at the age of twenty-two, I sat in a room filled with other young men and women setting out on their journey to love and befriend Muslims. Charles Marsh was in his eighties—a fifty-two-year veteran of ministry in Algeria, Tunisia and Chad and an anointed apostle to Muslims under whose ministry countless Kabyles had come to Christ. That day he spoke to us from his heart. One of his exhortations has remained seared in my heart to this day, thirty-five years later. Having spoken about some of the deep challenges of ministering to Muslims (he saw many of his early converts martyred soon after confessing faith in Christ), Marsh paused and then warned us earnestly with words something like this: "You have no right to even begin to speak to a Muslim about Christ unless you have yourself first settled in your heart that you are prepared to die for the sake of Christ. I challenge every one of you listening to me today, have you settled this with Christ? If you have not surrendered to him completely, then I repeat, you have no moral right to talk to Muslims about Christ, since your proclamation of the gospel of Jesus Christ to a Muslim may result in that person's martyrdom. Only one who is willing to die for Christ has the right to ask someone else to die for him too." Marsh's challenge was formative of my understanding of my role as an expatriate sharing Christ with Muslims. My response to his challenge, in obedience to the call that God had given me some years earlier, helped

shaped a foundational attitude for my ministry as an expatriate—I was prepared to lay down my life that Muslims might come to know the giver of life.

Looking back, I can see another experience that also proved formative of my understanding of my role as an expatriate discipler. Just a few years after we arrived in North Africa, Greg Livingstone, who had recently founded the agency Frontiers, spoke at our annual in-country conference. Drawing on the story in Acts of how Barnabas proved to be an encourager and a mentor for the apostle Paul, Greg challenged us and suggested that if God could lead us to just one BMB, whom we could mentor and help get established in ministry in a way analogous to the way that Barnabas mentored the apostle Paul, then we could look back on our ministry knowing that God would continue to use the fruit of our ministry in ways that far surpassed our own gifting and personal contribution. From then on, I began to be on the lookout for men whom I could disciple and launch into their own faithful and fruitful ministry. I saw my ministry not so much as planting churches myself but rather as discovering and mentoring local men who could become church planters and leaders in movements that they would start and nurture to maturity under the equipping and anointing of the Holy Spirit.

As our journey of exploration into the discipleship task of nurturing the faith of BMBs nears its conclusion, it is fitting for us, as both expatriate and BMB disciplers, to think through the roles that expatriates can and should play in discipling BMBs and in church planting across the Muslim world. It is good to examine carefully our call from God to disciple, and not assume that we automatically have the right to enter a Muslim environment and minister as disciplers and church planters. It is good to scrutinize the significance of expatriate discipling ministry, and in so doing, we need to be willing to frankly acknowledge the harm that such ministry often does despite the best of intentions.

The words of Pietzsch and Marsh cited at the beginning of this chapter express two kinds of roles that expatriates can have. Pietzsch, in talking about discipleship, encourages expatriates and all would-be disciplers of BMBs to walk alongside BMBs, showing through our lives and love what a Christian is like. In contrast, Marsh describes his sense of being called to an apostolic ministry of proclaiming Christ across a vast, mountainous region that was completely unaware of Christ. What kinds of roles are expatriates to play in the launching and strengthening of believers and launching of new churches in such regions? And even in regions without an established, ongoing local witness, when is it appropriate for expatriates to do direct evangelism and church planting and when might it be better to help from the outside by equipping and sending people from neighboring communities into such regions?

One of the last questions posed during the interviews dealt with the various roles that expatriates have in ministry among BMBs. Because we expats come as foreign guests and have to struggle to learn to communicate in new languages and immerse ourselves in cultures very different from those within which we were nurtured spiritually, we need to examine the value of the contributions we bring. There was a wide variety of responses to the simple question that I asked: "What are the expatriates' ideal roles?" As I evaluated the various convictions expressed in the forty-one different responses from the sixty-one people to whom I asked the question, I found that they fell into three broad, somewhat overlapping categories. We will examine these three categories in the order of their most frequent mention: be a church planter, facilitate church planting and serve under BMBs.

SERVE AS PIONEER CHURCH PLANTERS IN PARTNERSHIP WITH BMB LEADERS

The total number of responses in the first and second categories are pretty similar (ninety-six and eighty-six responses—refer to table 15.1). In the larger group, the emphasis is on the expatriates doing the ministry of evangelism, discipling and church planting and thus serving as catalysts and pioneers. Such pioneers raise up, under God, local believers who become the next generation of evangelists, disciplers and church planters. In the second group of responses, a bigger emphasis is placed on expatriates facilitating such ministry rather than primarily doing it themselves.

In the first category, the most common response to the question about the ideal role of expatriate workers was that the expatriates should do what God has called them to do and get on with the work of church planting. It was stressed that to be effective, one has to learn the local language(s) well and persevere over the long haul. There was a strong sense that if God was the one who was calling these men and women to ministry, they should be released and encouraged to exercise the ministry that God has called them to undertake. The people who gave this type of response clearly affirmed the role of pioneer work in regions with few if any believers. Always the hope was that their pioneer work would lead to reproducing movements of churches being planted and led by local BMBs once the initial launch had happened successfully. Some noted that expats should be discipling BMBs because they are trusted by both the BMBs and the local Christians. It was also stressed by some in Europe and in the Middle East that the expatriates must be wise, gentle team players who have a clear experience of salvation and a call from God into ministry. There was an overall sense that mature and godly expatriates could do effective ministry and thereby provide helpful models and inspiration for local disciplers from both Muslim and Christian backgrounds. In thus carrying out Spirit-anointed ministry, expatriates can serve effectively in helping call, empower and inspire the work of local men and women to undertake similar kinds of ministries among their own people.

Yet, even here, among those affirming the importance of such a catalytic role for foreign workers, there was also a strong stress on doing such pioneer work in collaboration with BMB churches and other local churches and their leaders. Those with a strong call to church plant will do so most fruitfully when they do it in full collaboration with local BMBs. Amir, the experienced church planter in North Africa whom we met earlier in the book, was nuanced in his discussion of the roles of expatriate workers. He had come to faith through a local friend and had been discipled and trained by both expatriates and local believers. When I interviewed him in 2007, he and his wife were teamed up with an expatriate couple and together they were planting the first church in their

Table 15.1. Appropriate Expatriate Roles and Attitudes

Roles and Attitudes for Expatriate Disciplers	Total	Gender		Ministry Region				Religious Background		Experience Discipling	
		M 42/50	F 19/25	NA 27/30	ME 23/30	AP 5/5	EU 6/10	BMB 20/23	Other 41/52	Novice 21/28	Expert 40/47
1. Be a Church Planter (Totals)	**96**	**69**	**27**	**47**	**37**	**6**	**6**	**23**	**73**	**39**	**57**
1. Serve as catalysts, modeling, encouraging and doing evangelism, discipleship and church planting	43	29	14	21	18	4	0	7	36	22	21
4. Go with own vision, visit Muslims, evangelize and be fruitful; take initiative; do pioneer work	17	15	2	9	6	2	0	5	12	5	12
5. Serve as tentmaking church planters partnering with BMB churches and training	14	10	4	12	1	0	1	3	11	4	10
12. Should be discipling because they are trusted by all	6	4	2	2	4	0	0	3	3	3	3
13. Have a clear experience of salvation, a clear call and a heart for people	6	4	2	0	2	0	4	2	4	2	4
14. Must have the Holy Spirit and be gentle, wise team players	5	4	1	0	5	0	0	1	4	2	3
16. Room for anyone whom God has called who will persevere and learn language	5	3	2	3	1	0	1	2	3	1	4
2. Facilitate Church Planting (Totals)	**86**	**62**	**24**	**50**	**24**	**6**	**6**	**27**	**59**	**49**	**37**
2. Role changes: move into the background as soon as possible; shadow pastor; train leaders and allow them to fail	24	17	7	16	4	3	1	5	19	14	10
3. Serve the BMB churches and help the BMB leaders take responsibility	22	16	6	15	5	1	1	7	15	13	9
6. Give counselling, teaching, rebuke and spiritual input; suffer with and encourage BMBs to develop and fulfill their dreams	11	7	4	4	6	0	1	5	6	7	4

Roles and Attitudes for Expatriate Disciplers	Total	Gender		Ministry Region				Religious Background		Experience Discipling	
		M 42/50	F 19/25	NA 27/30	ME 23/30	AP 5/5	EU 6/10	BMB 20/23	Other 41/52	Novice 21/28	Expert 40/47
7. Invest in discipling and training a few BMBs and then help them train others	9	7	2	5	2	2	0	1	8	6	3
8. Be mediators and facilitators	7	6	1	2	5	0	0	3	4	3	4
15. BCBs, BMBs, and expatriates all need each other	5	2	3	0	2	0	3	3	2	2	3
20. Plant a church that will reproduce and the BMBs will reach their city	4	3	1	4	0	0	0	1	3	0	4
21. Have excellent communication and cooperation between expats and BMBs	4	4	0	4	0	0	0	2	2	4	0
3. Serve with and Under BMBs (Totals)	**38**	**29**	**9**	**7**	**22**	**0**	**9**	**20**	**18**	**13**	**25**
8. Support BMB ministry, not in charge of it; bring converts to local churches	8	6	2	1	4	0	3	4	4	0	8
9. Provide skills training: integrity, business, micro-enterprise	8	7	1	2	3	0	3	4	4	4	4
10. There are limits to how much an outsider can model discipleship and community	7	4	3	2	3	0	2	1	6	2	5
14. Set aside their own expectations of how to minister and instead learn and serve	6	5	1	0	6	0	0	4	2	2	4
17. Can help with discipleship and curriculum and be consultants	5	5	0	2	2	0	1	3	2	3	2
19. Need to be very careful about lifestyle and conscious of its impact on BMBs	4	2	2	0	4	0	0	4	0	2	2
Totals	**220**	**160**	**60**	**104**	**83**	**12**	**21**	**70**	**150**	**101**	**119**

city. Now, in 2014, Amir is conducting training for local believers from across North Africa on church planting and offering multiple levels of support and encouragement to North African pioneer church planters. Amir's comments are illustrative of the kind of advice given by those who encouraged expatriates to do what they are called to do:

> There is still plenty of work to be done in this country! There is lots of room for more expatriates to come and do pioneer work. But they need to work together with us and submit their ideas to the input of local leaders. They need to have the right attitude to the work and to the local believers. Whenever possible, the expatriates should work behind the local leaders and support the joint church planting project. If God is calling some foreigners to a city with very few believers and no known house church, it will work much better if they can get to know local BMB leaders in neighboring cities and cooperate as much as possible. Their church planting work can be much more effective when they work closely with local partners.
>
> I thank God for Americans! However, they often think that they have the best way, the best strategy to minister in our country, in our culture, using our language. Clearly, when they reach out humbly to local BMB churches and share their strategy ideas with them, the input they receive from local cultural insiders can go a long way toward correcting and improving the strategies that Americans have when they enter the country.

In examining the responses more deeply, some interesting contrasts become apparent. Generally there was little significant difference in the number of responses by men and women, or in the responses of novices and experts. Of more interest was the contrast in responses between BMBs and non-BMBs on a few points. For example, the percentage of BMBs who strongly expressed the conviction that expatriates should do pioneer work was much lower than the number of expatriates who stressed a similar perspective. Consistent with this observation was the fact that a much higher percentage of BMBs than expatriates suggested that expatriates need to serve under BMBs rather than taking their own initiative.

Also intriguing was the fact that twelve of the fourteen who stressed the need for expatriates to work in close partnership with local BMB leaders minister in North Africa. As will be seen below, far fewer of those interviewed in the Middle East and in Europe thought that expatriates should proceed with their own pioneer church planting ministries. Traveling in these regions through the years, a clear contrast in contexts has become apparent, which seems to be reflected in what people believe to be appropriate ministry roles for expatriates. In the North African countries that I have visited (Libya, Tunisia, Morocco and Mauritania), expatriates workers sometimes outnumber local BMBs. In several North African cities I have visited there are dozens of workers (most in their first term of service) in cities with perhaps only twenty or thirty local believers.

One experienced expatriate discipler interviewed in one city expressed frustration that in his city, with more than a hundred expatriate workers (most with limited ability in the local languages), most of them wanted to work with the local church. In that city there were only two or three small house churches. And the expatriate workers were not themselves reaching out and making connections with their Muslim neighbors and seeking to plant churches—they all wanted to work with the local churches. In such contexts it is completely understandable that the most common advice for expatriates is that they should directly evangelize, disciple and plant churches.

In contrast, in the Middle East and Europe, for example, where there are much greater numbers of local Christians, many of those interviewed thought that expatriates should serve the local churches as their top priority, even when those churches are not interested in planting churches among Muslims. In a conference I attended in a large city in the region in 2013, one of the expatriate keynote speakers stated categorically that the *only* valid role for expatriate workers was to serve the local churches in the region, submitting all of their own agendas to those of the local church and its leadership. This Middle Eastern perspective stands in sharp contrast to the consensus perspective in North Africa, where both BMBs and expatriates envision a much wider range of appropriate roles for expatriate workers.

FACILITATE CHURCH PLANTING RATHER THAN
DOING IT THEMSELVES

During the years spent church planting in one North African country, I was surprised and puzzled when, in meeting colleagues in a different North African country, I heard them expressing in no uncertain terms that they were called only to facilitate church planting. They were *not* called to plant churches themselves. Ministering in a national context where almost all of us were involved directly in significant ways in planting churches in most of the major cities, the idea that we should *only* facilitate such church planting and not be involved in it as well came as a surprise. When I visited Indonesia for the first time in 2013, it did not take me long to realize that the standard approach to church planting, among the dozens of colleagues there was to facilitate local Christians to do cross-cultural church planting. To help in this facilitation, expats expected to contribute a major portion of the funding to enable local believers (seldom from Muslim backgrounds) to be able to serve as full-time supported workers to do the church planting. This understanding of the expatriate role in church planting is very different from what had been commonly understood in my initial North African experience.

In interviewing disciplers across the Arab world, the conviction was expressed that the best role for expatriates was facilitating church planting rather than planting churches. This was the second most frequently mentioned perspective (refer to table 15.1). As already indicated, this preferred expatriate role was especially dominant in the Middle East. Kevin, an American who had served nineteen years in a Middle Eastern country when I interviewed him, articulated this clearly:

> Expatriates are here to model and encourage others to do evangelism, discipling and church planting. I cannot model community with BMBs. A white face even just appearing in a Muslim neighborhood causes problems for BMBs and raises concerns from the government and security police. Foreigners in Muslim neighborhoods do not work at all. Even after nineteen years of immersion and fluency in Arabic, I am still several layers back from being an insider in Muslim culture. I have had deep grief over not being able to become an insider. Trust is not given here, it is only

earned. Thus, the best role for us as expatriates is to be a catalyst for locals, both local Christians and local BMBs. We can help train local church planters but cannot do it effectively ourselves.

One idea that was popular among a number of people was that of being a shadow pastor (refer to item 2 in table 15.1). This was the second most often mentioned role for expatriates among those interviewed. This was understood to be someone who quietly discipled a local BMB from the background, without leading any groups, and encouraged and facilitated BMBs so they could launch into their own evangelistic and church planting ministry.[1] Some who sought to work in this way were hopeful that it would avoid some of the common dependency issues, in which the local believers rely on the expatriates to do the teaching and training and ministry. It is intriguing to note, however, that only five BMBs (out of twenty) recommended this role, whereas half of the non-BMBs recommended this approach. Equally interesting is that two-thirds of the inexperienced workers recommended this type of role, whereas only a quarter of experienced workers endorsed this approach. A role very much like shadow pastoring is implicit in most models of church planting movements, because it is believed that rapid multiplication is not going to happen if growth is dependent on an expatriate guiding and steering a movement.

There were also a number of intriguing regional variations within this category of expatriates as facilitators rather than church planters. Generally, this perspective was recommended by about twice as many people in North Africa as in the Middle East, even though the number of people who discussed expatriate roles was pretty much the same in each region. The strategy of serving the BMB church and helping its leaders take responsibility for the church work was stressed much more in North Africa

---

[1] Much of my initial research took place around the same time as the Fruitful Practices conference, held in Thailand in March 2007, where this term "shadow pastor" was much used. Two chapters of *From Seed to Fruit*, the proceedings of the gathering in Thailand, describe this concept. "Many people are choosing the 'shadow pastoring' model. The expatriate leader is not present at the gatherings, but is coaching the local leaders from the beginning. This often seems to be a quicker and better way to see local leaders actually leading and having responsibility for the gathering" (Duran, Schuler and Sy 2008, 235).

than in the Middle East or the Arabian Peninsula. But the regional variation between the Middle East and North Africa becomes perhaps more pronounced as we move to the third category of expatriate role—serving under BMBs and helping them.

SERVE UNDER LOCAL CHRISTIAN AND MUSLIM BACKGROUND LEADERS

As articulated by Kevin above, a number of people clearly believed that the primary role of expatriates was to serve local Christians. As expatriates move into a region and minister, they must fully set aside their own expectations about how to minister and devote themselves to learning and serving as asked and as opportunities arise. Expatriates can provide training in skills that will help BMBs thrive in the workplace. They can help them set up micro-enterprises and small businesses. They can help design curriculum and be consultants to the ministry that the locals are doing. Those expressing this perspective on expatriate roles have sometimes had quite negative experiences with expatriates.

Though many Arab Christians whom I met, both BMBs and those with a Christian upbringing, have had very positive experience with expatriate workers, some expressed serious concerns and even bitterness over their repeatedly negative encounters with workers in their region. Cyprian, a young, North African, full-time evangelist working in a ministry in Europe reaching North Africans, had come to faith in Christ through expatriate-run media outreach while a teenager in his home country. Though he had had extensive contact with Western workers in several countries, he expressed sadness and bitterness over the poor examples they had been:

> The biggest obstacle to effective ministry in our city is the missionaries. They come with high expectations but do very little ministry. There are hundreds of missionaries here with very little fruit in ministry. Some come to love this European city, but they are not involved with North African culture. They have no contact with North Africans; they never open their homes to them or learn their culture. So, they try to use North Africans to fulfill their vision and to do their jobs for them. This is destructive.

Most missionaries do not really listen. They want to do what they have planned and will do their own plan regardless of what we North Africans say or think of the appropriateness of their ministry strategy. Far too often Western missionaries look for North Africans whom they can fund to do church planting for them. This corrupts good people and makes them seek money from missionaries. Some come to develop an attitude of unhealthy dependence on missionaries.

We see expatriates with a big car, a big house, a huge salary, and they are doing nothing in ministry. All of the money inside missions is rotting ministry. We live on one-tenth the salary and are comparatively quite poor. But we are living very richly, and we are generous with what God has provided for us.

Similarly, Faraj, a Christian pastor in the Middle East who was doing ministry among Muslims in his city, had a largely negative view of the work of expatriates. This is how he expressed it:

Expatriates sometimes speak dismissively of locals. They must be able to love and respect the people. Sometimes Western expatriates come across as arrogant—"We know how to do it here." They need to serve humbly with a learning attitude, helping and supporting local ministries as they are able. At the same time, I have known some expatriates who do not take any initiative at all, and they become a burden on the local churches.

Some BMBs clearly had ambivalence in how they felt about the expatriates they had known. As can be expected from our discussion of money in chapter thirteen, and from Cyprian's account given in this chapter, the issue of contrasting lifestyles can be hugely sensitive. Halima, whom we met in chapter fourteen, is a good example of mixed experiences with expatriates. I met and talked with her in the home of an expatriate colleague with whom she clearly had a good and supportive friendship. She also spoke with great warmth and appreciation for an expatriate couple who had hosted a regular BMB discipleship group until they had left the country a year or two earlier. Yet Halima was critical of the lifestyle and lack of generosity of missionaries:

It costs a lot of money to bring missionaries to our country, and it is very difficult for us to watch them live lives of luxury here. Foreigners can't really understand us since our lives and our daily realities are so different from theirs. Yet, we all need each other. BMBs, local Christians and expatriates all need each other. If an expatriate family can afford to get away out of the city for a short break two weekends a month, it would be great if they would share their resources and send some of us out of the city once a month and go themselves only once a month. We really need such breaks ourselves too. Expatriates need to learn to use their wealth effectively to serve those who need their encouragement.

The perspectives of local believers Faraj, Cyprian and Halima are sobering. They shine a spotlight on the often negative impact of expatriate workers on ministry in Muslim contexts. John, a Middle Easterner raised in the West, found he was able to have good relationships with BMBs. But he remarked that most expatriates have a lot going against them when they arrive. In a culture that elevates the place of status and honor, the automatic expectations that locals have of foreigners can foul relationships from the beginning. Ian believes that fluency in the local language is vital if expatriates have any hope of surmounting the built-in obstacle of local expectations of foreigners.

In light of such pervasive obstacles to effective communication and ministry on the part of expatriates, many believe that the ideal expatriate role is to serve under local Christian leaders and help them accomplish their ministry objectives. Rather than coming in as outsiders confident that they know what needs to be done and how to do it, it would be wiser to come in and seek to learn, setting aside all previous beliefs about the shape of ministry, and submit oneself to serve locally. As noted above, this perspective was expressed most strongly in the Middle East and in Europe, where the number of local Christians vastly outnumbers missionaries.

At its best, when an expatriate embraces the value of the local church and works closely with it, he or she can have a significant ministry in collaboration with local Christians. A former colleague, whom I will call Mark, modeled this strategy well. Over the sixteen years he and his family spent in a large Middle Eastern city, they become closely connected to the leaders of a vibrant evangelical church in the city. With an excellent gift for languages, he became almost native-like in his fluency in Arabic. As he worked closely with a number of people from the church he also developed a ministry of encouraging and discipling BMBs, most of whom had come to Christ through the church. By the time he left the country he had become a deeply trusted and highly respected ministry partner.

Recently, about a decade after leaving that city, he moved to another large city in a neighboring country and has been able to move into a place of service to an evangelical seminary that is serving BMBs across the region. His commitment to working in submission to local Christians on behalf of BMBs has earned him a position of great trust and influence among both BMBs and local Arab Christians. Has he himself directly planted a church of BMBs? No. But numerous BMBs are thriving today in several Middle Eastern countries because of the way he helped build bridges between them and Christian Arab leaders in the region. Putting one's own agenda aside and serving the agendas of local Christians can go a long way to helping fulfill the greater vision that God has given.

Sobering Lessons from History

However, before moving on to our conclusion, I believe it is helpful to describe and reflect on a sobering lesson from mission history. In Kurdistan, for more than three centuries, missionaries deliberately put themselves under the leadership of local minority churches, serving those churches as asked by their leaders, in a region with a strong Muslim majority, and utterly failed to see any churches planted among the Muslim majority. Robert Blincoe wrote a carefully researched history of mission work among the Kurds from 1668 to 1990. He carefully documents the three-hundred-year effort by Western missionary societies to renew and strengthen the Christian communities in the region, with the hope that they would reach out to their surrounding Muslim neighbors (Blincoe 1998). The primary lesson that he draws from the historical study is of the abject and total failure of the three-hundred-year mission strategy of seeking to renew the minority church in the region in order to reach the Kurdish Muslim majority. In terms of the objective of reaching the Kurds with the gospel, the result was tragic. In 1835 the Christian minority was about 40 percent of the population. By 1990 it had shrunk to less than 5 percent (Blincoe 1998, xiv).[2] By the end of the twentieth century, the vast majority of Christians in the region were either killed or emigrated to the Christian West, and they never did reach out to the Muslim Kurdish majority. This is a rather sobering history lesson when one is faced with the mission strategy being strongly advocated by some in the Middle East today, that all expatriates must devote themselves to serving the interests and needs of the local Christian community, when this church is often not at all interested in bringing Christ to the Muslim majority around them.

Blincoe's central argument, reinforced by his historical case study, is that there are too many cultural barriers to overcome for some Middle Eastern Christians to reach out to Muslims. It is humanly difficult for Christians, who come from a despised and inferior ethnic group in the country, to reach out to the Muslim majority. Such cross-cultural outreach is more easily undertaken by people from outside the region. Blincoe quotes an illustrative parable given by Kenneth Bailey in which he envisages Japanese Christians trying to reach non-Christian America with the gospel (Blincoe 1998, 191-92). The Japanese establish a church among the Navajo Indians, then pull back and ask the Navajo to reach the rest of America. The Navajo respond by saying that they cannot reach their traditional enemies (the Sioux), or an inferior ethnic group (the Eskimos) or those who have oppressed them for centuries (the white Americans). This parable illumines the cultural dynamics that undermine efforts to see the Arab church reach out to the Muslim majority.[3] At the same time, this is not the whole story. God is in the business of transforming human hearts, and there is no reason why, as in the parable,

---

[2]These percentages are approximations based on a careful reading of the table in his preface.

[3]I have reproduced Blincoe's telling of Bailey's full parable in appendix E. It is a helpful illustration of the challenges faced in so many Muslim communities in the Middle East, as well as in many other regions of the Muslim world. Understanding these dynamics gives us greater cause for rejoicing whenever we see Christians and churches that have lived under the oppression of Muslim majorities turning and in faith and love reaching out with Christ's love to their traditional oppressors and enemies.

God could not turn the hearts of the Navajo and given them a powerful passion to reach the Sioux, the Eskimos and their former oppressors, the whites, with the gospel.

In Pakistan, India and Bangladesh, which together have more Muslims than the entire Arab world, similar cultural barriers have long prevented the effective spread of the gospel among Muslims. Phil Parshall's passion for contextualization comes out of this context, in which Muslims in majority-Muslim communities despise the Christian minorities as idolatrous and inferior peoples. It is humanly difficult for a typical Pakistani Muslim, for example, to consider joining a group from this despised underclass. These huge cultural issues have to be faced. They cannot be ignored or glossed over, as Livingstone saw when he visited Pakistan:

> I was walking the streets of Karachi with a well-educated . . . Muslim, who as a friend of colleagues, had a good understanding of the gospel and its implications. As a group of street sweepers (who were Christians of Hindu background) passed us, he wrinkled his nose and demanded of me how I could ask him to join those people! He could relate better to us, as westerners, than he could to poor Punjabi Christians in his own city who were citizens of his country. (1993, 155)

However, much caution must be exercised before using the failures in the Kurdish situation as a justification for avoiding strategic partnership with evangelicals and other local Christians who are part of minorities living in Muslim countries today. There were many reasons for the failure of the mission to the Kurds that do not parallel situations in many Muslim-majority countries today. Significant among those reasons was the fact that the mission effort was targeted at the traditional historic churches: the Armenians, Assyrians and the Chaldeans, as well as the Catholics. Throughout the centuries, the leaders and members of those church communities consistently and strongly opposed all efforts to reach out to the Muslim Kurds. The remnants of these ancient churches still strongly oppose any mission to the Muslim Kurds, and they despise the Kurds as almost subhuman (Blincoe 1998, 194-95). It is not surprising that the small Protestant churches that were sometimes started when some of these traditional Christians converted to a living Protestant faith carried with them most of the same prejudices and attitudes against their Muslim Kurdish neighbors as they had before their conversion. Today in the Middle East God is at work among many Arab Protestants and is calling increasing numbers of them to love and minister to their Muslim neighbors. The tragedy of the failure of the mission to the Kurds through the historical Christian communities is great, but I caution against us using it as an excuse for bypassing the churches and godly men and women in the Middle East, and elsewhere in the Muslim world, whom today God is touching and giving missionary vision in unprecedented ways.

CALLING, SUCCESS AND FAITHFULNESS

As you have read this discussion of roles that expatriates fulfill in ministry to Muslims, I expect many different kinds of thoughts have been going through your minds. Why do we expatriates leave our home cultures and invest years in language and cultural learning in order to try to bring Christ to those who have not before known him? Why do we invest countless hours in building relationships with people whom we struggle to understand and relate to? Why do we work faithfully discipling and mentoring our new brothers and sisters with the hope and dream of seeing them strong in Christ and able and willing to disciple others and lead churches and help transform their communities for Christ's sake? Is it all worthwhile?

Early in our career, while learning languages in France before we had moved to North Africa, Jeanie and I had a good visit with a single female colleague who had decided to return to the United States after having spent twenty years living and serving in several difficult situations in Algeria. She did not believe that her ministry had accomplished much, and she had reconciled herself to the conviction that the main reason that God had called her to North Africa was for her own sanctification and growth toward maturity. She was going back home with a sense of having poured out her life for two decades to little avail, other than the profound life lessons with God that she could not have learned any other way. Her vulnerable sharing of her struggle to find meaning in her years in North Africa disturbed me deeply. Her experience jarred with my own sense of having been clearly called to live and serve in North Africa.

Writing twenty-eight years after that conversation and sixteen years after our own decade in North Africa, my understanding of the meaning of our time in North Africa is not significantly different from that of our friend who opened her heart to us nearly thirty years ago. There was some encouraging fruit in the lives of North Africans whom I helped disciple, many of whom still continue on as faithful disciples. Yet, how much did God accomplish through us? How much did we learn? I do not know how much I learned about God's ways in my life during our years there, yet I believe that God had good purposes in taking us there and giving us that life-transforming decade of ministry. In the sixteen years since we left, our lives have been deeply shaped by our years in North Africa.

Pondering the meaning of expatriate roles in discipling in Muslim lands can be done at the level of strategy and fruitfulness. Such reflection can also be entered into at a much deeper, sometimes painful and far more personal level. The wide varieties of roles that we have in ministry reflect differences in our calling, our varied gifting and personal journeys and the tremendous variety in the contexts in which we live and work. We are all called to be responsive to the leading of the Spirit and obedient to our Lord, whether our primary role is doing pioneer church planting, facilitating others in church planting or serving the leaders in the local church and helping equip them for their ministries.

In the final section of *Ministry to Women: Longing to Call Them Sisters*, Elizabeth Learner (pseudonym?) shared her attempt to answer the question "Why am I here?" As a fitting conclusion to this examination of roles for expatriate disciplers, I am giving Learner the last word as she explains why she serves in ministry in a Muslim land.

> When I was asked to speak on the subject of "Why am I here?" I wanted to scream "*I don't know!*" However, I suspected, and my husband agreed, that there was divine purpose in this assignment. Because I had the responsibility of presenting an answer in integrity, I was forced to struggle to think through the subject.
>
> So, why am I here?

My culture tells me to be happy, comfortable, fulfilled and successful. I am not happy, I am not comfortable. I am not fulfilled or successful. I am an American. "Go home, ugly American!" Even Christian brothers and sisters imply this. That hurts.

Why am I here?

My apartment is small. I sweat in the summer. I am cold in the winter. My children have no yard to play in. City life is aggressive. Sometimes the other children are mean to mine, steal from them, and hurt them.

Why am I here?

I struggle with the language. The deep things of my heart still don't flow easily. I am handicapped. How can a handicapped person aid the church in its growth?

Why am I here?

I have come to care about my neighbors. They have become a part of my life. Their struggles are impossible. There is only One who has authority over the impossible. Why can't they see him? Why can't they submit? Why do they not fall down in repentance and recognize Jesus' Lordship? Why do my words seem powerless?

Why am I here?

I am not in control. I have not mastered discerning where to invest my limited energy. . . . In so many ways—ways too personal to share here—I am not adequate for the task before me. . . .

So why am I here? Or rather—Why are we here—both you and I?

We are here because these women were faithful to trust God despite the cost, and God's will was done. We are here because we are challenged by the example of present-day sisters with that same faithfulness.

We are here because closeness to the holy God is an exquisite banquet that we cannot keep to ourselves. We will not eat and let others starve.

We are here by the authority of the Holy Spirit. We are here by God's grace. . . .

We are here because being Jesus Christ's disciple is worth utter, total failure in all the ways that we presently understand success.

That is why I am here. (Learner 2000, 238-41)

Conclusion

Helping Believers and Churches Thrive in Muslim Communities

*After this I looked, and behold, a great multitude that no one could
number, from every nation, from all tribes and peoples and languages,
standing before the throne and before the Lamb, clothed in white robes,
with palm branches in their hands, and crying out with a
loud voice, "Salvation belongs to our God who sits
on the throne, and to the Lamb!"*

*And he [one of the elders] said to me, "These are the ones coming out of
the great tribulation. They have washed their robes and made
them white in the blood of the Lamb.*

*"Therefore they are before the throne of God,
and serve him day and night in his temple;
and he who sits on the throne will shelter them with his presence.
They shall hunger no more, neither thirst anymore;
the sun shall not strike them, nor any scorching heat.
For the Lamb in the midst of the throne will be their shepherd,
and he will guide them to springs of living water,
and God will wipe away every tear from their eyes."*

Revelation 7:9-10, 14b-17

*Converts out of Islam are keenly aware of their positions in the
middle of a geopolitical debate. They are sensitive to being objec-
tified and want to be treated like normal people. At the same time,*

they may want to be treated as special, unique for the particular challenges that confront them as converts. Ultimately, their identity as believers in Christ is something they share equally with all Christians around the world, regardless of the label given. They are not a phenomenon and, without dismissing the very real and difficult challenges they face, it is important to also recall that difficulties are a part of life and putting people on a platform of admiration for their hard lives, objectifies them as much as does dismissal as the "other."

KATHRYN KRAFT, *SEARCHING FOR HEAVEN IN THE REAL WORLD*

R ALPH WINTER GAVE EVANGELICALS a new way of seeing the unevangelized as consisting of unreached people groups (UPGs) during the July 1974 International Congress on World Evangelization (ICOWE) in Lausanne, called and led by evangelist Billy Graham. Following the ICOWE there was a strong unleashing of new energy and vision to complete the task of reaching every unreached people group around the globe, with special attention given to the Muslim UPGs. This positive energy continues to this day and drives much of the recruiting for frontier missions globally. Currently there is a global network of ministries to Muslims that is together tackling ways of engaging every Muslim UPG by 2025. There has been much good come of this still-growing emphasis on reaching UPGs, and it has ignited a new movement for frontier mission work in the decades since the ICOWE. However, I have increasingly been concerned that one unfortunate and unintended consequence of this emphasis on "getting the job done in our generation" has been increasing levels of superficiality in many of our missionary endeavors.

TOWARD A DEEPER DISCIPLESHIP THAT CAN SUSTAIN CHURCHES THROUGH THE GENERATIONS

After God called me to minister to Muslims about forty years ago, I set out to become a church planter among Muslims. In my years of preparation, I had as my ambition to help plant one, or were God to extraordinarily anoint my ministry, two or three house churches among Muslims. In each case, my vision was that, once the church was planted, I would then work to train the leaders so that the church could become strong and deep and able to last for generations in hostile Muslim environments. Now, many people begin their ministry with the ambition of helping launch church planting movements.

The longer I live as a Christian, and the more experience I have in local churches, here in the West and across many regions of the Muslim world, the more I am struck by how slowly God often works. True transformation of a person into deeper and more authentic Christ-likeness often takes decades, indeed, a lifetime. As the passion for launching rapidly reproducing movements of churches increasingly influences evangelical missions among Muslims, I find myself concerned. Does our desire to see hundreds of churches planted ignore the ways that God often works in the hearts of men and women, in which he takes his time and works patiently with us over a lifetime, and in communities, over generations? Do we think that we can somehow speed up the process of discipleship and spiritual transformation so that it happens "overnight"? How healthy is our desire for expansion through rapid multiplication in Muslim lands? The experience of many who have served among Muslims suggests that when Muslims come to love their new Lord, it often takes years of discipling before they reach the maturity needed to be pastors and leaders in local BMB churches.

These are disturbing questions. Have we gotten sidetracked somehow from a biblical vision for church planting? Has some of our evangelical missiology over the past forty years become superficial? What is our vision for these unreached people once they are engaged? Are we hoping to see a few dozen house churches planted among them, or a movement of rapidly multiplying home fellowships? Or do we have a vision for a multigenerational church that gains in size, depth and maturity through the decades, so that it develops its own pastoral training institutions that can continue to equip pastors and church leaders for ongoing generations of fruitfulness among Muslim peoples? Should not our vision for discipleship and the church go deeper than the pragmatic and seemingly speed-obsessed vision that sometimes appears to shape our contemporary expectations and planning?

My vision for what it takes to have the kind of discipleship that leads to enduring, strong, healthy churches continues to change and, I hope, deepen. Eugene Peterson's poignant, grace-filled autobiographical reflection on what it means to be a pastor, entitled *The Pastor: A Memoir* (2011), was both encouraging and sobering. Peterson spent nearly thirty years pastoring one church. This book has had a profound impact on my vision of the church and of the work of church planting and pastoring. In the book, Peterson tells the story of his journey into understanding the pastoral calling and the nature of the local church.

Peterson shared how a group of local pastors had gradually been forged into what they called their "Company" of pastors, who were journeying together into deeper understanding of the pastoral vocation through many years of weekly meetings for prayer, study and discussion. At one point he talks about the allure of the church growth movement and how it pulled one pastor in their Company away from a local church. This account of the concerns that Peterson and his Company of pastors had with the church growth movement at that time parallel concerns that I have about CPMs and insider movements, with their "promise" of amazingly rapid multiplication and fruitfulness.

Peterson tells about his pastor friend, Phillip, who had been invited to leave his church to go pastor a much larger city church. Peterson met with Phillip to try to warn him that he was being enamored more with American values than kingdom principles. Philip was not really listening to Peterson's concerns, so after his lunch with Philip, Peterson wrote him a letter. In the letter he explained his concern that Philip was being drawn down a dangerous path as he was being enticed to seek greater influence in a bigger church:

I certainly understand the appeal [of greater influence] *and feel it myself frequently. But I am also suspicious of the appeal and believe that gratifying it is destructive both to the gospel and the pastoral vocation. It is the kind of thing America specializes in. . . . It is also the kind of thing for which we have ample documentation through twenty centuries now, of debilitating both congregation and pastor. In general terms it is the devil's temptation to Jesus to throw himself from the pinnacle of the temple. Every time the church's leaders depersonalize, even a little, the worshipping/loving community, the gospel is weakened. . . .*

The only way the Christian life is brought to maturity is through intimacy, renunciation, and personal deepening. And the pastor is in a key position to nurture such maturity. It is true that these things can take place in the context of large congregations, but only by strenuously going against the grain. Largeness is an impediment, not a help. . . . Your present congregation is close to ideal in size to employ your pastoral vocation for forming Christian maturity. . . . Can we talk about this? I would welcome a continuing conversation.

That was the end of it. We never did have the conversation. He accepted the call to the big church, and then another, and then another. I would get occasional reports on him from friends. All the reports seemed to document that size was turning out to be a false transcendence in his life.

Meanwhile, the momentum of what was being termed *church growth* was gathering. All of us in the Company agreed that it was misnamed. It was more like church cancer—growth that was a deadly illness, the explosion of runaway cells that attack the health and equilibrium of the body. A year or so later, another of our Company left us. We hadn't realized the rapid spread of the lust for size that was spreading through the American church and was now penetrating our own Company. . . . The two pastors who had left us for what they thought were greener pastures had been a disappointing reminder of the increasing degradation of pastoral vocation, seeping into congregations all over the country like a massive oil spill. (Peterson 2011, 157-59, italics in the original)

There are clear connections in terms of influence and philosophy between the church growth movement and the UPG movement that arose at about the same time, as well as, more recently, insider movements and church planting movements. All are seeking ways to increase vastly the number of people coming to Christ, or joining churches, as quickly as possible. Echoing Peterson in his letter to Philip, I too feel the attraction and the allure of greater kingdom impact. Who would not want to find a way to multiply his impact and find ways of sweeping dozens, if not hundreds and thousands of Muslims, into faith in Christ? Yet, increasingly I find myself questioning the allure of this temptation to have a greater impact for Christ.

So many who labored faithfully among North Africans in my parents' generation and in my own generation poured our lives into those who came to Christ. The kind of discipleship envisioned in this book involves persevering effort over long periods of time. It involves a deep commitment to building community. It involves a commitment to deep-level healing and transformation at God's pace, over time, in both individuals and communities. Are those of us being enamored with the promise of multiplying churches planted among Muslims giving into temptation? Is the hope of changing our methods of evangelism to produce astonishing results a yielding to the temptation of the temple pinnacle, as Peterson called the temptation of the church growth movement of his day? Do we desire to see a movement that will grow and last? Do we need to choose between speed and maturity? Can movements that grow quickly and spread rapidly settle and become strong regional churches? I sincerely hope that our longing for significant rapid growth is a result of God giving us great faith. I hope that it is not a giving into temptation.

Recently I talked with a retired missionary to Haiti about a Haitian saying, "It takes thirty years to grow a tree, but it takes one hundred years to grow a man." He had puzzled over the meaning of this saying for a long time but eventually came to see that in the church in Haiti, which was slowly being made strong through the furnace of suffering and the oppression of voodooism, it was not until the third generation in a Christian family that the influences of voodooism and the darkness of the culture were significantly eradicated. He was seeing that it was often only the grandchildren of first-generation believers who were able to live strong and vibrant Christian lives free of the oppressive shadow of their former religion. He observed that it takes something like a hundred years to grow a Christian person and a strong Christian church in such spiritually oppressive environments. If we desire to see BMBs and BMB communities established as living pyramids rooted in Muslims societies that can transform those societies through the generations, then we must be prepared to foster, over the long haul, the kinds of intimacy, renunciation, personal deepening and authentic community that Peterson mentioned above, that can transform former Muslims into a Christlikeness that will affect their families and communities into the third and fourth generations and beyond.

COMMUNITIES OF DISCIPLES ENDURING FAITHFULLY THROUGH TRIBULATIONS

As we envision the vast regions of the Muslim world and ponder the apparent strength and dominance of Islam over the minds and hearts of hundreds of millions of people across the globe, it is sobering to consider the relative weakness of the Christian church in many of these Muslim lands. Will the convert church in nations like Tajikistan, Pakistan, Afghanistan, Yemen, Lebanon and Libya be larger and stronger fifty years from now than it is today? What reasons might we have to hope that the unbelievably tiny BMB church emerging among Muslim peoples in such nations will ever become large enough to have lasting impact on their communities? If what has been happening in Syria, in Sudan and in northern Nigeria over the past few years, with the targeting killing and persecution of Christians by Islamists, turns out to be typical for other parts of the Muslim world, then even more Christians living among Muslims will be called to walk faithfully along the road of suffering and martyrdom laid out for us in the New Testament.

The text from Revelation that heads this chapter speaks powerfully to me of Christ's call to faithfulness for all kinds of Christians living in Muslim lands. John's vision of the martyrs standing before the throne of God speaks powerfully of the circumstances of many BMBs who struggle toward maturity in Christ in the midst of great tribulations. The great throng dressed in white robes (Rev 7) were those who had come through great tribulations. As Islamist movements, following the example of Muhammad and the first four "rightly-guided" Caliphs, continue their efforts to set up various forms of Islamic caliphates in many regions of the world, there will undoubtedly be an increase in the tribulations that Christians in these regions will have to endure. The book of Revelation was written to encourage first-century Christians living through just such severe tribulations. In Revelation 7, John is told by one of the elders from those seated around the throne of the Lamb that those who are martyred in their faithfulness to the Lamb will one day be standing before the throne glorying in the salvation that God gave them through the Lamb. There is great comfort promised for those who stand faithful even to death—God will wipe away every tear from their eyes!

Listen to Glenn Penner, advocate for the suffering church, as he elucidates the way that believers in the apostle John's day were given grace to endure when persecution threatened to overwhelm:

> In this final book of the Bible, Jesus is revealed as the One who is in the midst of the churches, as One who is in control of history and who will soon bring history to its conclusion. . . . The Christian in Revelation is called to witness for Christ, even to the point of death, in the midst of compromising Christianity and a hostile world, knowing that his reward is coming. Revelation helps us to see that there is always hope. Defeat may seem imminent to those in the midst of persecution; the disciple needs to be reminded that so is victory. . . . The victory is the vindication of the church . . . redeemed, triumphant in heaven, secure forever with the Lamb who has won the victory for himself and the church through his death and his conquest over it. . . .
>
> By refusing to deny their allegiance to him and acknowledge the idolatrous claims of the world order ([Rev] 13:15; 14:9) enduring even unto death, the martyrs share in Christ's victory over it and in his triumph over all the powers of evil ([Rev] 12:11). God has determined to save the world by the foolishness of the cross of Christ and by the foolishness of the crosses of his children whom he has chosen and called for his very purpose. He will be consistent in using this unique method until he achieves his final goal. God will thus bring the nations to himself by the

sacrifice of this obedient Son followed by the sacrifices of his other obedient sons and daughters. (Penner 2012, 74-75)

Things are not as they seem. The victories being achieved by militant Muslims and the governments and armies aligned with them in opposition to Christ and his church are not winning the ultimate victory. That victory along belongs to Christ's disciples who are given the grace to remain faithful in obedience to him in the face of opposition and persecution.

Will regions that are now dominated by Islam one day become regions in which the fragrance of Christ comes to have widespread influence? God alone knows. Today, in Iran, the peculiar Islamic ideology propelling the country's leaders to oppress, imprison and torture Christians with little restraint is also being used by God to draw more and more people to the Lord of the oppressed and abused. There are more Iranians coming to Christ today, both within Iran and in their global Iranian diaspora, than at any time in the history of Persia since the rise of Islam. The historical outcome of these spiritual battles for the direction of nations is in God's hands, but we know who is at work in and through faithful believers living through horrific tribulations.

THE PRIVILEGE AND CHALLENGE OF RELATIONAL COMMUNAL DISCIPLING OF BMBs

It has been one of the great privileges and joys of my life to have been able to walk alongside a handful of young men as they grew to maturity in their Muslim communities. It was astonishing at times to witness the incredible speed at which they picked up central elements of their new faith. More than one new believer demonstrated a profound hunger to read, obey, study and obey the Word of God in ways that I have seldom seen paralleled among non-Muslim-background believers. When I think of all the men and women whom God has called out of Islam that I have been privileged to know and meet as a part of the research for this book, my heart overflows with gratitude to God for the testimony of their lives and witness.

Yet, far too often, many such precious brothers and sisters struggle in profound ways that often have much to do with the failure of Christians to truly reach out to them, love them and welcome them fully into the body of Christ. A BMB friend, who is from the Middle East but now lives in the United States, said that in both the Middle East and the West BMBs often feel that they are "homeless people wandering the streets of Christendom." They experience loneliness and struggle to be noticed and cared for. They wander from church to church, attending for a while, trying to reach out to others, but eventually giving up and moving on because they found no hospitality, no warm embrace, no open homes or open hearts.

In this book we have taken a journey exploring the contours of discipleship and the kinds of processes that, when in place, could greatly strengthen these brothers and sisters and see them press on to maturity in their faith in Christ. I expect that everyone reading this book longs to see far more of the Muslims who encounter Jesus grow to full maturity in Christ and in the church. We all desire to see more BMBs have someone, within a loving Christian community, who will walk alongside them in their journey, through many tribulations and trials, to a place of maturity and great fruitfulness and joy in their lives in Christ. It is my hope that the discipleship processes portrayed in the Living Pyramid Model of relational communal discipling of BMBs will prove a valuable resource for our multidimensional call to disciple those who are coming to Christ in this unprecedented season of harvest among Muslims to persevere through to maturity and enduring presence.

Figure c.1. The Living Pyramid Model of relational communal BMB discipling

We are called to stand with our brothers and sisters in Christ, to nurture Christ in them and to teach them to live in communion with Christ so that they can draw on the resources of the Holy Spirit as they press on in obedience to the One how has bought them with his blood. It is my hope that having read this book, you who are non-BMB disciplers will be freshly inspired and newly empowered to become more effective disciplers of those who have come from Muhammad to Christ. I also hope and dream that you, the BMBs who read this book, will be inspired to grow in your faith, along with the many thousands who have come out of Islam before you, and press on to maturity so that you will experience the powerful, transforming grace of the Spirit through your entire lives, even when you are called to undergo unremitting tribulations.

As we all learn to disciple better, more BMBs living faithfully for Christ in Muslim communities around the world will grow in strength and perseverance. As we seek, by the guidance and anointing of the Spirit, to raise up individual and community living pyramids that will endure strong in the midst of often hostile Muslim communities, my prayer is that much glory will go to God as transformed individuals and communities of believers live to his glory for generations within Muslim communities globally.

Appendix A

THE DEMOGRAPHICS AND DESIGN OF THE RESEARCH CONDUCTED IN THE ARAB WORLD IN 2007 ON BMB DISCIPLESHIP

B Y THE GRACE OF GOD AND with the help of many colleagues and friends across the Arab world, I was able to conduct seventy-five face-to-face interviews with experienced disciplers during two trips into the Arab world in the spring of 2007. There is no doubt that sitting and talking with people face-to-face is the most culturally appropriate way to do research in the Arab world. The interviews typically took two to three hours. I did not record the interviews but rather took extensive hand-written notes during each conversation.

THE SELECTION OF THE QUESTIONS

The content of the questions that I asked during the interviews was determined through a process of reflection and discussion with several friends who had extensive experience in discipling BMBs. Naturally, my own experience discipling BMBs in North Africa helped me identify some of the significant problems and topics to investigate. In addition, the selection and shaping of the questions I asked was an outcome of the reading and reflection I had carried out on the nature and processes of discipleship in the New Testament, in literature on the major church traditions throughout history up until the end of the twentieth century and by those writing on BMB discipleship. In order to keep my investigation to a reasonable size, I chose a few key issues. The final selection of topics, done through reflection and consultation with my advisors, resulted in twelve questions that I asked each person after I had begun by gathering important information about that person's background and experience as a disciple. We explored topics dealing with the nature of discipleship and the spiritual growth process, the challenges of living for Christ in collective cultures and the nature of the challenges to discipleship resulting from the religious, ideological, social and cultural specificities of their contexts; we finished with a discussion of six challenges that I have found to be the almost universal experience of disciplers and BMBs. The questions asked are in appendix B.

THE SELECTION OF THOSE INTERVIEWED

The selection of whom to interview was done through a rather fluid process of following up on the recommendations and introductions made by friends and colleagues working across the Arab world. I communicated in advance the purpose of my research and the kinds of people I hoped to interview. I was impressed with the quality and extent of experience discipling BMBs that most of the people whom I interviewed brought to the interview. In each country I visited, I was led to interview people who were among the most experienced disciplers in the region. In one case, a well-known BMB discipler whom I had hoped to interview had his flight out of the country providentially delayed by about five hours so that I could interview him while he waited. I was able to interview a significant variety of people from diverse backgrounds, with varied perspectives and experiences (see details below). The analysis of their answers to my questions is the source of most of the insights about discipling found in the second half of this book.

My interview process was straightforward. I prepared an interview template, which had the questions written out, and I took detailed, handwritten notes during the interview. A typical interview yielded eight to twelve pages of handwritten notes, though some were much longer. I always began by getting extensive information about personal, ethnic and spiritual background, and the extent and nature of their experience as disciplers. Although sometimes I chose to omit some of the questions due to shortness of time or because the interviewee lacked experience to speak to a particular topic, I usually managed to ask all of the questions.

DEMOGRAPHIC ANALYSIS OF THE INTERVIEWEES

In early 2007 I interviewed seventy-five men and women during visits to Egypt, Jordan, Lebanon,[1] England, Morocco and France. These people had been discipling believers from Muslim backgrounds (BMBs) for an average of eleven years, and they discipled an average of forty-four BMBs each. Collectively, they have been involved in discipling more than thirty-two hundred BMBs! Thirty-six interviewees had more than ten years of experience, and a further twenty-six had more than three years of experience. They also had a remarkably high level of education, with 97 percent having college education or higher. Even though I was a

Table A.1. Age, Experience and Education of Interviewees[a]

Experience Discipling BMBs			Years Discipling BMBs	
Approximate number of BMBs now being discipled	745		0 – 3 years	13
Average number of BMBs now discipling	10		4 – 10 years	26
Estimated total number of BMBs discipled by all	3,290		11 – 20 years	30
Average number of BMBs discipled by each person	44		More than 20	6
Total years of discipleship experience	839			
Average experience per interviewee	11			
Age of Interviewees			**Education Level**	
Age 21 – 30	3	Age 51 – 60	17	High school or less	2
Age 31 – 40	28	Age 61 or more	1	College degree	41
Age 41 – 50	26			Advanced degree	26
				Doctorate degree	6

[a]These numbers are based on the estimates given by the interviewees of the number of BMBs that they are currently discipling and have ever been involved discipling. They are not considered objective numbers.

---

[1]While attending a conference in Thailand I also had opportunity to interview a number of disciplers working in various Arab countries.

man traveling alone, I was able to interview twenty-five women, twenty-one of whom were married.[2] Of the fifty men interviewed, forty-five were married. Further, I interviewed thirty-four Arab-world nationals (45 percent), of whom twenty-three were from a Muslim background (31 percent) and eleven from a Christian background (15 percent). Thirty-eight (51 percent) of the seventy-five interviewees were Westerners. North America workers made up the majority of the Westerner interviewees, and Middle Easterners made up the majority of non-Westerner interviewees. Sixty-one (81 percent) of the interviews were conducted in English, and I interviewed seven people in French and seven in Arabic through interpreters.

Table A.2. Some Demographics of the Interviewees

Regional Nationality[a]		Country of Primary Ministry		Agency Affiliation		Gender and Marital Status	
American	19	Egypt	10	AWM	27	**Men**	50
Canadian	5	Lebanon	10	OM	5	Married	45
European	12	Jordan	9	PMI	4	Single	5
Australian, New Zealander	2	Sudan	1	Other like agencies	9	**Women**	25
Total Westerners	**38**	**Middle East**	**30**			Married	21
Middle Eastern	24	Morocco	23	Church agencies	6	Single	4
North African	10	Algeria	4			**Interview Language**	
Asian	1	Tunisia	3	No agency	24	English	61
African	1	**North Africa**	**30**			French	7
Latin American	1	**Europe**	**10**			Arabic	7
Non-Westerners	**37**	**Arabian Peninsula**	**5**				

[a] Those with dual nationality, for example, Algerian-French or American-Canadian, are counted according to their nationality of birth for the purposes of this table.

One other observation to note is that twenty-seven interviewees (36 percent) were members of my mission; a further twenty-four (32 percent) were members of thirteen other agencies. The remaining twenty-four (32 percent) belonged to no mission agency but rather worked and ministered on their own or in association with various local churches or ministries.

---

[2] The majority of these women were interviewed together with their husbands.

COLLATING AND ANALYZING THE NOTES FROM
THE INTERVIEWS

The analysis of the information recorded in more than five hundred pages of handwritten notes was made possible using a database created with the indispensable assistance of my sister-in-law Miriam Little. I systematically worked through the answers to each question, categorizing the responses and entering them into the database. I was able to ask questions of this collected and categorized data in order to obtain helpfully nuanced understanding. The responses to my questions could also be correlated to disciplers' backgrounds and experience as disciplers. Whenever I needed further clarification, the original notes were consulted.

THE NATURE AND LIMITATIONS OF THE
RESEARCH AND ANALYSIS

Talking with these seventy-five brothers and sisters has greatly enhanced my understanding of discipleship in Arab-world contexts. The second half of this book contains my analysis and interpretation of the experience and insights of these experienced disciplers. It provides research-based understanding of the nature of BMB discipleship and how some of the most serious challenges are being effectively met in Muslim contexts across the Arab world.

A significant interpretative tool that I used in much of my analysis merits explanation. The interviewees were normally asked open-ended questions, and I did my best to avoid hinting at the answers I was looking for, even though I often asked follow-through questions seeking to get the interviewee to elaborate and flesh out their comments and give examples. In doing the analysis, I compared the answers given by different people to each question. For example, when I asked for a short definition of discipling, the interviewees gave a variety of responses. I recorded twelve versions of these definitions in the database. During the interviews, most people gave only one or two definitions of discipleship. Yet, if I had asked them whether they would agree with some of the definitions offered by others, I expect that most would have agreed that they are indeed also valid. This may appear, to some readers, to lessen the significance of the comparisons I make between various similar and divergent answers. Nevertheless, in the analysis I assign considerable significance to the actual answers given and to the fact that other answers were not given. Further, I correlate their answers to interviewees' experience, religious background, gender, and so on. I also attach substantial significance to how often a given response does or does not occur in the data.

It is appropriate to ask whether my assigning significance to slightly nuanced variations in answers to open-ended questions is valid. Although I try not to attach more significance to subtle nuances than the data appear to support, I believe that this weighing of comparative responses provides valuable insight. No attempt has been made to ascertain if my correlations are statistically valid.[3] All of the significance that I give to observed correlations must be treated as at best educated guesses based on my analysis of interviewees' experience and reflection. Yet, I do believe that it is meaningful to observe, for example, that expatriate disciplers tended to give one type of answer to a question, whereas BMB disciplers consistently gave a different kind of response.[4] Ultimately, the reader will have to judge whether the significance I assign to variations in interviewees' responses fits with their own experience as disciplers, and therefore whether or not they are meaningful or valuable for their ministry.

---

[3]Attempting to conduct such statistical analysis in the hopes of increasing the validity of observed outcomes takes one in a direction with which I am uncomfortable. Just because many people say something is true does not make it true. In this research, any outcome that the reader believes to be of value has that value because it rings true to the experience of the reader. Spiritual discernment is not something that can be statistically verified.

[4]One of my research advisors suggested to me that it would be of helpful for me to be able to get the kind of data to enable me to make comparisons between such perspectives as that of BMB disciplers in comparison with that of expatriate disciplers. I have attempted to tease out as much comparison on such points as the interview data permit.

Appendix B

Questions Asked During the Interviews

AFTER THE INTERVIEWEES SHARED THEIR FAITH journey (especially BMBs) or how they came to be discipling BMBs, I asked the following questions. I often varied wording as needed for clarity, elaborating as needed.

1. What would you give as a quick definition of discipling? What is it?

2. How does a believer grow? What is the process that makes growth happen?

3. How do you disciple individuals in a collective culture? Explore individual versus community.

4. What is the BMB's ideal identity in family and community?

5. What have you seen to be the biggest obstacles to seeing people grow to maturity?

6. How do you disciple BMBs through persecution and opposition?

7. Have you had experience with demonic manifestations? If so, what advice do you have?

8. What are the challenges and opportunities that come through the nature of BMB families?

9. Let's explore some of the challenges of handling foreign money and foreign support.

10. What is your integration goal for BMBs? Forming BMB groups? Having them join churches of believers from Christian backgrounds? Other?

11. What is the ideal role(s) for an expatriate worker(s)?

12. How do you deal with oral learners? What is the role of literacy in your discipleship?

13. Anything else? Is there some key thing I have overlooked? Any other comment you want to make?

SUPPLEMENTARY TABLES
GIVING FURTHER INFORMATION

**Table A.3. Understanding of the Discipleship Process
Compared with Reference to Experience Discipling***

Key Factors for Growth	Total	BMBs Discipled			Years Discipling BMBs**		
		20 +	4 – 20	0 – 3	11 +	4 – 10	0 – 3
1. Committed to and in church group, loved by BMBs	61	77%	86%	83%	81%	89%	69%
2. Has a trusted discipler who models and mentors	45	66%	57%	50%	69%	54%	46%
3. Values, reads, studies and applies the Word personally	36	46%	57%	33%	47%	54%	38%
4. Learns how to pray personally and daily	27	34%	39%	33%	31%	39%	46%
5. Receives targeted teaching, in ethics and doctrine	23	26%	36%	33%	28%	27%	46%
6. Reaches out, witnesses and disciples others	22	31%	32%	17%	31%	35%	15%
7. Develops personal walk with God in prayer, Word	20	23%	25%	42%	28%	23%	31%
8. Committed to grow and obey Christ at all costs	18	23%	21%	33%	22%	35%	8%
9. Must understand and use spiritual gifts in service	16	23%	14%	33%	31%	15%	8%
10. Confesses sin, has right relationships, reconciles	15	23%	18%	17%	28%	19%	0%
11. Embraces opposition and hardship as part of growth	14	17%	21%	17%	19%	23%	8%
12. Knows that God is love; Christ gave his life!	10	14%	11%	17%	19%	4%	15%

*The percentages given in this table relate to the percentage who gave a particular answer in a particular experience category. For example, in line 10, a fifth of the thirty-six most experienced disciplers gave this response, and nearly 30 percent of those with four to ten years of experience, whereas none of the least experienced disciplers suggested this element.

**Of the seventy-five interviewees, thirteen had three or less years of experience, twenty-six had from four to ten years and thirty-six had eleven or more years.

Table A.4. Obstacles to Growth Mentioned by Disciplers

Obstacles to Growth	Total	Five Types of Obstacles	Islamic versus Christian	Core Social Collective	Gender	
					M /50	F /25
1. Pressures from Muslim family, family control, especially while single	35	F & C	Islamic	Social	23	12
2. Muslim community's hostility, rejection and/or expulsion	29	F & C	Islamic	Social	18	11
3. Vulnerability due to youthfulness, low social status, weak economic position	28	Soc	Islamic	Social	20	8
4. Fear of all kinds: fear of problems, suffering, persecution & oppression	24	Psych	Islamic	Core	17	7
5. Lack of trust between and among BMBs, BMB groups and lack of commitment to one group	22	Spir	Christian	Social	16	6
6. Challenges for BMB families: child rearing, education, provision, marriage	19	F & C	Islamic	Collective	12	7
7. Spiritual nature of Christian faith: about Holy Spirit, prayer, faith, rather than religious acts	14	Spir	Christian	Core	9	5
8. BMB lack of confidence, inherited complexes, emotional pain, victimization	13	Psych	Islamic	Core	7	6
9. The Satanic hold of Islam, demonic and occult bondages, hate, anger, lust	12	Spir	Islamic	Core	7	5
10. Lack of acceptance of BMBs by non-BMB Christians and their churches and communities	11	Soc	Christian	Social	8	3
11. The love of money; BMBs need to learn to give wholeheartedly	10	Soc	Islamic	Core	6	4
12. Living in a police state where change of religion is not officially/legally possible	10	F & C	Islamic	Collective	9	1
13. The discipler's ineffectiveness, poor response and wrong motives	9	Spir	Christian	Social	8	1
14. Illiteracy and/or low levels of literacy; discipleship needs to adapt to oral learners	9	Soc	Islamic	Social	3	6
15. Poor ethics (shame) and lack of integrity; BMBs must learn new ethics before a holy God	9	Islam	Islamic	Core	5	4
16. Learned Muslim ideology, doctrine, traditions, requiring extensive re-education	9	Islam	Islamic	Core	9	0
17. God is distant and unknowable; difficult to bring God close to BMBs	8	Islam	Islamic	Core	5	3

Obstacles to Growth	Total	Five Types of Obstacles	Islamic versus Christian	Core Social Collective	Gender	
					M /50	F /25
18. Men especially struggle with sexual issues and lust	8	Spir	Islamic	Core	6	2
19. Lack of close relationship with God and the body	6	Spir	Christian	Core	6	0
20. Lack of vision for growth and ministry	6	Spir	Christian	Core	3	3
21. The failure of BMBs to be in the Word regularly, depending on God in faith	6	Spir	Christian	Core	4	2
22. Dependence on foreigners and their resources impedes growth	6	Soc	Christian	Social	5	1
23. Small numbers of BMBs and their sense of being vulnerable	5	Soc	Christian	Social	4	1
24. Limited access to resources, books, CDs to help BMBs grow	5	Spir	Christian	Social	3	2
25. Missionaries: problems with motivation of BMBs; what can they get out of foreigners	4	Spir	Christian	Social	2	2
26. The struggle with one's identity: Am I a Muslim, a Christian, a Muslim Christian?	4	F&C	Islamic	Core	2	2
27. Passive attitude to life, especially women; they don't feel able to make any decisions about their lives	4	Psych	Islamic	Core	4	0
28. Lack of fellowship; being alone	3	Spir	Christian	Social	1	2
29. Christian leaders abusing BMBs to build their own self-esteem and reputation	3	Spir	Christian	Social	3	0
30. Busyness through work; not enough time to be together for worship and teaching	3	Spir	Christian	Social	2	1
31. Need to learn to forgive; this hinders growth	3	Soc	Christian	Core	2	1
32. The Jewish-Israel issue; some BMBs are stopped in their growth over this	2	Spir	Islamic	Collective	2	0
33. Religiosity of Shiite community and value of obedience to community leaders	2	Spir	Islamic	Collective	1	1
34. Immature BMB church group leaders creating tension and conflict among BMBs	2	Spir	Christian	Social	1	1
35. Finding a place for BMBs to meet when one is not married and living with Muslim family	2	Soc	Islamic	Social	2	0

Obstacles to Growth	Total	Five Types of Obstacles	Islamic versus Christian	Core Social Collective	Gender	
					M /50	F /25
36. Willingness to compromise; not willing to pay the full price for following Christ	2	Soc	Islamic	Core	2	0
37. Lack of access by discipler to BMBs; very difficult to spend time with each other	2	Soc	Islamic	Social	2	0
38. Being overwhelmed with many ministry opportunities; not good to expose BMBs to too much too quickly	2	Isl	Christian	Social	0	2
39. Struggle to submit to leadership because they have had no good models of authority	1	Soc	Islamic	Social	1	0
40. Loyalty to a political party over Christ	1	Soc	Islamic	Collective	1	0
41. Negative impact of international politics: "Islam versus the West"	1	Isl	Islamic	Collective	1	0
Totals	**354**				**242**	**112**

Key: F&C - Family and Community, **Isl** - Islamic Ideology, **Soc** - Sociopolitical, **Psych** - Psychological, **Spir** - Spiritual

Appendix D

Navigating Between Two Identities

W HEN A PERSON ACCEPTS THE LORD, he is immediately put in a place of tension. On one side is his new Christian faith, and on the other side are his old religion, family, and community. Usually the convert comes to Christ through the witness and teaching of another believer, and as he grows in the Lord, the tension begins to build. Who should the convert relate to? How can a convert from a religion such as Islam or Buddhism relate his new faith to the family and community in which he lives?

Tragically many converts decide that they cannot reconcile the two. The obvious quick solution to the issue is to develop two faces. With one face they welcome Christianity, meeting with other Christians, praying, reading the Bible, and studying together. This is where their heart is. With the other face, they live and relate to their family and community. They have mothers, brothers, sisters and perhaps spouses and children. This is also where their heart is, and so the tension builds. Soon one of five things will happen.

First, the convert may abandon his new faith and go back to what is familiar to him. This may be because of persecution or pressure, but often it is because he feels he cannot exist in a two-faced situation. As long as he has two faces there is always the strong temptation to abandon the Christian face and assume the old one.

On the other hand, the convert may completely identify with the Christian face and reject his old one. This was often encouraged in the past, as believers took on new names, and identified completely with a Christian community. In the most extreme cases these converts emigrated to the West, or to another country, where they could abandon their old face, and live solely with their Christian face. By doing this, they sacrificed their family and community and their ability to witness to them. In recent years, some of these converts have started to rebuild contact with their family and community, but in most cases this is a very difficult road to take and it is a long time before they are accepted again.

Another situation that may develop is where the new believers live as if they still followed the old ways, with the knowledge that they have received Christ. In many cases they become secret believers, often filled with fear that they will be discovered. One man I know lives in constant fear of his teenage son who comes home from school full of anger and bitterness at the Christians and Jews who, he considers, are the source of the world's problems.

Other converts are so distraught with the two faces that they eventually become mentally unstable. I know of one such man living in my city. He wanders the streets in ridiculous clothing, recognized by all as crazy. In another case, I know of an Arab convert who claims he is not an Arab, but a Westerner. He calls himself by a different name, refuses to recognize his family, and claims he is a citizen of a Western country. His mental condition has slowly deteriorated over the years.

The fifth possibility is that through the work of the Holy Spirit, and often with the help of a discipler, the convert can learn to unite the two faces, discovering freedom in Christ. He no longer hides behind two faces, but now lives with one face, living freely as a follower of Jesus in his family setting. This, I believe, should be the chief and primary aim of a discipler (excerpted from Muller 2006, 108-9).

Appendix E

WHAT ABOUT WITNESSING
AMONG THE SIOUX?

L ET US IMAGINE THAT AMERICA was not Christian and Japan was. The Japanese then come to the United States and establish a church among the Navajo Indians. After one hundred years it is perceived that the Japanese have too much control over the destiny of the Navajo church. The Japanese church leaders then say to the Navajo church leaders, "We are dissolving our Japanese organization in America and turning everything over to you—we will do nothing within the fifty states except at your specific request and under your direct authority."

After a period of time the following dialogue occurs:

"What about witness and service to the Sioux?" ask the Japanese.

"The Sioux are our traditional enemies," comes the answer.

"Well then, we can start work in white America?" say the Japanese.

"White America?" the Navajos reply. "White Americans took our land, killed our grandfathers and shamelessly broke the treaties they made with us. White America is not on our agenda."

"Very well," continue the Japanese, "perhaps we can do something for the Eskimos."

"Eskimos," counter the Navajos, "are also native Americans. But our people look on them as inferiors. Our people will not be able to understand why resources available for the Navajos are being spent on the Eskimos."

The deeper question then must be put to the Japanese. Is it fair to the Navajo church leaders to place on them the burden of providing the vision for witness and ministry for all of America? Vision for all Navajos, yes! But the Navajos also have a constituency that they must take with them. They also live in an ambiguous world and realistically only a certain range of possibilities is open to them. Is it right to say to the Navajo church council, "We the Japanese will not work with the Eskimos unless you, the Navajo church council, decide that teaching Eskimo children is more important than teaching Navajo children"?

Would we want a similar burden placed upon us? (Bailey 1989, 10)

Works Cited

Abou El Fadl, Khaled M. 2005. *The Great Theft: Wrestling Islam from the Extremists*. San Francisco: HarperSanFrancisco.

Adeney, Miriam. 2001. "Rajah Sulayman Was No Water Buffalo: Gospel, Anthropology and Islam." In *No Other Gods Before Me? Evangelicals and the Challenge of World Religions*, edited by John G. Stackhouse Jr., 65-83. Grand Rapids: Baker Academic.

———. 2002. *Daughters of Islam: Building Bridges with Muslim Women*. Downers Grove, IL: InterVarsity Press.

Ali, Ayaan Hirsi. 2007. *Infidel*. New York: Free Press.

———. 2010. *Nomad: From Islam to America, a Personal Journey Through the Clash of Civilizations*. London: Simon and Schuster.

Anderson, Neil T. 2000. *The Bondage Breaker: Overcoming Negative Thoughts, Irrational Feelings and Habitual Sins*. Eugene, OR: Harvest House.

———. 2004. *The Steps to Freedom in Christ: A Step-by-Step Guide to Help You*. 3rd ed. Ventura, CA: Regal Books.

———. 2013. *Victory Over the Darkness: Realizing the Power of Your Identity in Christ*. 3rd ed. Ventura, CA: Regal Books.

Andrews, Alan, ed. 2010. *The Kingdom Life: A Practical Theology of Discipleship and Spiritual Formation*. Colorado Springs: NavPress.

Augustine. (397) 1984. *The Rule of Saint Augustine: Masculine and Feminine Versions*. Translated by Raymond Canning. London: Darton, Longman & Todd. Citations are from the Darton, Longman & Todd edition.

Bailey, Kenneth. 1989. *A Tale of Three Cities*. Pasadena, CA: Presbyterian Center for Mission Studies.

Barnett, Paul. 1999. *Jesus and the Rise of Early Christianity: A History of New Testament Times*. Downers Grove, IL: InterVarsity Press.

Benedict. (530) 1998. *The Rule of St. Benedict in English.* Edited and translated by Timothy Fry. New York: Vintage Books.

Biblical Missiology. 2012a. "Lost in Translation: Keep 'Father' and 'Son' in the Bible." http://www.change.org/petitions/lost-in-translation-keep-father-son-in-the-bible. Accessed November 19, 2012.

———. 2012b. "Fact Check: Biblical Missiology's Response to Wycliffe's Comments on 'Lost in Translation.'" http://biblicalmissiology.org/wp-content/uploads/2012/01/LostInTranslation-FactCheck.pdf. Accessed November 19, 2012.

Blincoe, Robert. 1998. *Ethnic Realities and the Church: Lessons from Kurdistan, a History of Mission Work 1668–1990.* Pasadena, CA: Presbyterian Center for Mission Studies.

Boa, Kenneth. 2001. *Conformed to His Image: Biblical and Practical Approaches to Spiritual Formation.* Grand Rapids: Zondervan.

Bockmuehl, Markus. 1998. *The Epistle to the Philippians.* Black's New Testament Commentaries. Edited by Henry Chadwick. Peabody, MA: Hendrickson.

Bonhoeffer, Dietrich. (1937) 1963. *The Cost of Discipleship.* 2nd ed. New York: Collier. Original edition, Munich: R. H. Fuller. Citations here are from the Collier edition.

Bonk, Jonathan J. 1991. *Missions and Money: Affluence as a Western Missionary Problem.* Maryknoll, NY: Orbis Books.

Boyd, Gregory, A. 1997. *God at War: The Bible and Spiritual Conflict.* Downers Grove, IL: IVP Academic.

———. 2001. *Satan and the Problem of Evil: Constructing a Trinitarian Warfare Theodicy.* Downers Grove, IL: InterVarsity Press.

Brown, Rick. 2007. "Brother Jacob and Master Isaac: How One Insider Movement Began." *International Journal of Frontier Missiology* 24 (1): 41-42.

Bruce, F. F. 1988. *The Book of the Acts.* Rev. ed. The New International Commentary on the New Testament. Edited by F. F. Bruce. Grand Rapids: Eerdmans.

Bufford, Robert. 1988. *Counseling and the Demonic.* Dallas: Word.

Caner, Ergun Mehmet, and Emir Fethi Caner. 2002. *Unveiling Islam: An Insider's Look at Muslim Life and Beliefs.* Grand Rapids: Kregel.

Chan, Simon. 1998. *Spiritual Theology: A Systematic Study of the Christian Life.* Downers Grove, IL: InterVarsity Press.

Chandler, Paul-Gordon. 2007. *Pilgrims of Christ on the Muslim Road: Exploring a New Path Between Two Faiths.* Chicago: Cowley Publications.

Coleman, Robert E. 1963. *The Master Plan of Evangelism.* Grand Rapids: Revell.

———. (1987) 1998. *The Master Plan of Discipleship*. Grand Rapids: Revell, Spire. Original edition, Grand Rapids: Revell.

Coppedge, Allan. 1989. *The Biblical Principles of Discipleship*. Grand Rapids: Francis Asbury Press.

Corwin, Gary. 2007a. "A Humble Appeal to C5/Insider Movement Muslim Ministry Advocates to Consider Ten Questions, with responses from Brother Yusuf, Rick Brown, Kevin Higgins, Rebecca Lewis and John Travis." *International Journal of Frontier Missiology* 24 (1): 5-20.

———. 2007b. "A Response to My Respondents." *International Journal of Frontier Missiology* 24 (2): 53-55.

Cunningham, Scott. 1997. *"Through Many Tribulations": The Theology of Persecution in Luke-Acts*. Journal for the Study of the New Testament Supplement Series 142. Sheffield: Sheffield Academic Press.

Daniels, Gene. 2005. *Searching for the Indigenous Church*. Pasadena, CA: William Carey Library.

Dau, Isaiah M. 2010. "Facing Human Suffering." In *Suffering, Persecution and Martyrdom: Theological Reflections*, edited by Christof Sauer and Richard Howell, 107-58. Johannesburg: AcadSA Publishing.

———. 2012. "The Problem of Evil and Suffering: A Comparative Look at African and Western Views." In *Sorrow and Blood: Christian Mission in Contexts of Suffering, Persecution and Martyrdom*. Edited by William D. Taylor, Antonia van der Meer and Reg Reimer, 113-30. Pasadena, CA: William Carey Library.

Demarest, Bruce. 2001. *Satisfy Your Soul: Restoring the Heart of Christian Spirituality*. Colorado Springs: NavPress.

De Neui, Paul H., ed. 2012. *Complexities of Money and Missions in Asia*. Pasadena, CA: William Carey Library.

De Waal, Esther. (1984) 2001. *Seeking God: The Way of St. Benedict*. Collegeville, MN: Liturgical Press.

DeSilva, David A. 2004. *An Introduction to the New Testament: Contexts, Methods and Ministry Formation*. Downers Grove, IL: InterVarsity Press.

Duran, Abraham, Michael Schuler and Moses Sy. 2008. "Expatriates Empowering Indigenous Leaders." In *From Seed to Fruit: Global Trends, Fruitful Practices and Emerging Issues Among Muslims*, edited by J. Dudley Woodberry, 355-65. Pasadena, CA: William Carey Library.

Eims, Leroy. 1978. *The Lost Art of Disciple Making*. Grand Rapids: Zondervan.

Evans, Wendell P. 1985. *Church Planting in the Arab-Muslim World*. Marseille: N.p.

Finney, Charles Grandison. (1835) 1948. *Instructions for Young Converts*. Lisburn, Northern Ireland: Revival Publishing Co. Citations refer to the 1948 edition.

Ford, Leighton. 2008. *The Attentive Life: Discerning God's Presence in All Things*. Downers Grove, IL: IVP Books.

Foster, Richard J. 1978. *Celebration of Discipline: The Path to Spiritual Growth*. San Francisco: Harper & Row.

———. 1985. *Money, Sex and Power: The Spiritual Disciplines of Poverty, Chastity and Obedience*. London: Hodder & Stoughton.

———. 1992. *Prayer: Finding the Heart's True Home*. San Francisco: HarperSan-Francisco.

———. 1998. *Streams of Living Water: Celebrating the Great Traditions of Christian Faith*. San Francisco: HarperSanFrancisco.

———. 2011. *Sanctuary of the Soul: Journey into Meditative Prayer*. Downers Grove, IL: InterVarsity Press.

Fuller, Paula. 2010. "Participating in God's Mission." In *The Kingdom Life: A Practical Theology of Discipleship and Spiritual Formation*, edited by Alan Andrews, 195-221. Colorado Springs: NavPress.

Gabriel, Mark A. 2002. *Islam and Terrorism: What the Quran Really Teaches About Christianity, Violence and the Goals of the Islamic Jihad*. Lake Mary, FL: Charisma House.

———. 2003. *Islam and the Jews: The Unfinished Battle*. Lake Mary, FL: Charisma House.

Garrison, David. 2004. *Church Planting Movements: How God Is Redeeming a Lost World*. Midlothian, VA: WIGTake Resources.

———. 2014. *A Wind in the House of Islam: How God Is Drawing Muslims Around the World to Faith in Jesus Christ*. Monument, CO: WIGTake Resources.

Gaudeul, Jean-Marie. 1999. *Called from Islam to Christ: Why Muslims Become Christians*. Crowborough, UK: Monarch Books.

———. 2006. "Learning from God's Ways." In *From the Straight Path to the Narrow Way: Journeys of Faith*, edited by David H. Greenlee, P. I. Barnabas, Evelyne Reisacher, Farida Saidi and J. Dudley Woodberry, 81-92. Waynesboro, GA: Authentic Media.

George, Ron. 2000. *Issues and Insights into Church Planting in the Muslim World*. UK: Win Press.

Genesee, The Abbey of the. 2012. Daily Liturgical Schedule. http://www.genesee-abbey.org/liturgy/daily-liturgical-schedule. Accessed August 13, 2012.

Gilliland, Dean S. 1998. "Context Is Critical in 'Islampur' Case." *Evangelical Missions Quarterly* 34 (4): 415-17.

———. 2000. "Modeling the Incarnation for Muslim People: A Response to Sam Schlorff." *Missiology: An International Review* 27 (3): 329-38.

Gorman, Michael J. 2001. *Cruciformity: Paul's Narrative Spirituality of the Cross.* Grand Rapids: Eerdmans.

Green, Michael. 1981. *I Believe in Satan's Downfall.* Grand Rapids: Eerdmans.

Green, Tim. 2013a. "Conversion in the Light of Identity Theories." In *Longing for Community: Church, Ummah or Somewhere in Between?*, edited by David Greenlee, 41-51. Pasadena, CA: William Carey Library.

———. 2013b. "Identity Choices at the Border Zone." In *Longing for Community: Church, Ummah or Somewhere in Between?*, edited by David Greenlee, 53-66. Pasadena, CA: William Carey Library.

———. 2014. "Issues of Identity for Christians of a Muslim Background in Pakistan." PhD dissertation submitted 2014. London University, United Kingdom.

Greenlee, David H. 2007. *One Cross, One Way, Many Journeys: Thinking Again About Conversion.* Atlanta: Authentic Publishing.

———, ed. 2013. *Longing for Community: Church, Ummah or Somewhere in Between?* Pasadena, CA: William Carey Library.

Greenlee, David H., P. I. Barnabas, Evelyne Reisacher, Farida Saidi and J. Dudley Woodberry, eds. 2006. *From the Straight Path to the Narrow Way: Journeys of Faith.* Waynesboro, GA: Authentic Media.

Greeson, Kevin. 2004. *Camel Training Manual: The Secret of the Camel Is Out. Muslims Are Coming to Faith in 'Isa.* Arkadelphia, AR: WIGTake Resources.

———. 2007. *The Camel: How Muslims Are Coming to Faith in Christ.* Arkadelphia, AR: WIGTake Resources.

Guthrie, D., J. A. Moyer, A. M. Stibbs and D. J. Wiseman, eds. 1970. *The New Bible Commentary, Revised.* Grand Rapids: Eerdmans.

Hadidian, Allen. 1979. *Successful Discipling.* Chicago: Moody Press.

Haines, John. 1998. *Good News for Muslims: Tools for Proclaiming Jesus to Your Neighbor.* Philadelphia: Middle East Resources.

Hansen, Collin. 2011. "Wycliffe, SIL Issue Guidelines on Translating 'Son of God' Among Muslims." Posted October 13, 2011. www.christianitytoday.com/ct/2011/octoberweb-only/son-of-god-tanslation-guidelines.html.

———. 2012. "The Problem 'Son': Debate Continues Over Translating 'Son of God' for Muslims: Wycliffe Challenged by Assemblies of God." Posted April

3, 2012. www.christianitytoday.com/ct/april/problem-son/html.

Hawatmeh, Abdalla, and Roland Muller. 2003. *The Man from Gadara*. Self-published.

Hawthorne, Gerald F. 1983. *Philippians*. Vol. 43 of Word Biblical Commentary, edited by David A. Hubbard, Glenn W. Barker and Ralph P. Martin. Waco, TX: Word.

Hendriksen, William. 1962. *Exposition of Philippians*. New Testament Commentary. Grand Rapids: Baker Book House.

Hierotheos (Vlachos), Metropolitan of Nafpaktos. 1996. *Orthodox Spirituality: A Brief Introduction*. Levadia, Greece: Birth of the Theotokos Monastery.

Higgins, Kevin. 2007. "Acts 15 and Insider Movements Among Muslims: Questions, Process and Conclusions." *International Journal of Frontier Missiology* 24 (1): 29-40.

———. 2012. "Asking the Right Questions: A Response to Jonathan McNeil." *Evangelical Missions Quarterly* 48 (1): 96-101.

Hoefer, Herb. 2009. "Muslim-Friendly Christian Worship." *Evangelical Missions Quarterly* 45 (1): 48-53.

Holt, Bradley P. 1993. *Thirsty for God: A Brief History of Christian Spirituality*. Minneapolis: Augsburg.

Hull, Bill. 2006. *The Complete Book of Discipleship: On Being and Making Followers of Christ*. Colorado Springs: NavPress.

———. 2010. "Spiritual Transformation from the Inside Out." In *The Kingdom Life: A Practical Theology of Discipleship and Spiritual Formation*, edited by Alan Andrews, 107-38. Colorado Springs: NavPress.

Hyatt, Erik. 2009. "Christian Witness in Muslim Settings." *Evangelical Missions Quarterly* 45 (1): 84-92.

Irwin, Nate. 2011. "Muslim Churches? Another Perspective on C5." *Evangelical Missions Quarterly* 47 (3): 328-34.

Jabbour, Nabeel T. 2007. *Unshackled and Growing: Muslims and Christians on the Journey to Freedom*. Colorado Springs: DawsonMedia.

Kraft, Charles H. (1992) 2011. *Defeating Dark Angels: Breaking Demonic Oppressions in the Believer's Life*. Ventura, CA: Regal Books.

———. (1993) 2004. *Deep Wounds, Deep Healing: Discovering the Vital Link Between Spiritual Warfare and Inner Healing*. Ventura, CA: Regal Books.

———. 1997. *I Give You Authority: Practicing the Authority Jesus Gives Us*. Bloomington, MN: Chosen Books.

———. 2002. "Contemporary Trends in the Treatment of Spiritual Conflict." In

Deliver Us from Evil: An Uneasy Frontier in Christian Mission, edited by A. Scott Moreau, Tokunboh Adeyemo, David G. Burnett, Bryant L. Myers and Hwa Yung, 177-202. Monrovia, CA: MARC.

Kraft, Kathryn Ann. 2007. "Community and Identity Among Arabs of a Muslim Background Who Choose to Follow a Christian Faith." PhD diss., University of Bristol.

———. 2012. *Searching for Heaven in the Real World: A Sociological Discussion of Conversion in the Arab World*. Oxford: Regnum Books.

Lane, Timothy S., and Paul David Tripp. 2006. *How People Change*. Greensboro, NC: New Growth Press.

Learner, Elizabeth. 2000. "Why Am I Here?" In *Ministry to Muslim Women: Longing to Call Them Sisters*, edited by Fran Love and Jeleta Eckheart, 237-41. Pasadena, CA: William Carey Library.

Lederleitner, Mary T. 2010. *Cross-Cultural Partnerships: Navigating the Complexities of Money and Mission*. Downers Grove, IL: IVP Books.

Leonard, John S. 2006. "Oasis: An Ethnography of a Muslim Convert Group in France." PhD diss., Trinity International University.

Lim, David S. 2012. "Effective Partnerships for Church-Multiplication and Insider Movements." In *Complexities of Money and Missions in Asia*, edited by Paul H. de Neui, 121-39. Pasadena, CA: William Carey Library.

Little, Don. 2005. "Discipling Believers from Muslim Backgrounds: A Literature Review." Major paper, Gordon-Conwell Theological Seminary.

———. 2009. "Effective Insider Discipling: Helping Arab-World Believers from Muslim Backgrounds Persevere and Thrive in Community." DMin thesis, Gordon-Conwell Theological Seminary.

Livingstone, Greg. 1993. *Planting Churches in Muslim Cities: A Team Approach*. Grand Rapids: Baker Book House.

Love, Rick. 2000. *Muslims, Magic and the Kingdom of God: Church Planting Among Folk Muslims*. Pasadena, CA: William Carey Library.

Manji, Irshad. 2005. *The Trouble with Islam Today: A Wake-Up Call for Honesty and Change*. Rev. ed. Toronto: Vintage Canada.

Maranz, David. 2001. *African Friends and Money Matters*. Dallas: SIL International.

Marsh, Charles. 1980. *The Challenge of Islam*. London: Ark Publishing.

Marshall, I. Howard. 1978. *The Gospel of Luke: A Commentary on the Greek Text*. The New International Greek Testament Commentary. Edited by I. Howard Marshall and W. Ward Gasque. 13 vols. Grand Rapids: Eerdmans.

Marshall, I. Howard, Stephen Travis and Ian Paul. 2002. *A Guide to the Letters and Revelation*. Vol. 2 of *Exploring the New Testament*, edited by David Wenham and Steve Walton. Downers Grove, IL: InterVarsity Press.

Massey, Joshua. 2004a. "Part 1: Living Like Jesus, a Torah-Observant Jew: Delighting in God's Law for Incarnational Witness to Muslims." *International Journal of Frontier Missions* 21 (1): 13-22.

———. 2004b. "Part II: Living Like Jesus, a Torah-Observant Jew: Delighting in God's Law for Incarnational Witness to Muslims." *International Journal of Frontier Missions* 21 (2): 55-71.

———. 2004c. "Misunderstanding C5: His Ways Are Not Our Orthodoxy." *Evangelical Missions Quarterly* 40 (3): 296-304.

McCurry, Don M., ed. 1979. *The Gospel and Islam*. Monrovia, CA: MARC.

———. 2001. *Healing the Broken Family of Abraham: New Life for Muslims*. Colorado Springs: Ministries to Muslims.

McGrath, Alister E. 1991. *Roots That Refresh: A Celebration of Reformation Spirituality*. London: Hodder & Stoughton.

———. 1999. *Christian Spirituality: An Introduction*. Oxford: Blackwell.

McNeil, Jonathan. 2012. "A Muslim-Born Pastor's Response to a 2009 Insider's Conference." *Evangelical Missions Quarterly* 48 (1): 90-95.

Mether, Thomas. 1998. "Hesychasm: Orthodox Spirituality Compared and Contrasted with Other Religious Traditions." Greek Orthodox Archdiocese of America. www.esicasmo.it/HESYCHASM/Hesychasm22.htm. Accessed August 8, 2012.

Meydan, J. R. and Ramsay Harris. 2008. "Are We Nourishing or Choking Young Plants with Funds?" In *From Seed to Fruit: Global Trends, Fruitful Practices and Emerging Issues among Muslims*, edited by J. Dudley Woodberry, 247-63. Pasadena, CA: William Carey Library.

Moreau, A. Scott. 2002. "A Survey of North American Spiritual Warfare Thinking." In *Deliver Us from Evil: An Uneasy Frontier in Christian Mission*, edited by A. Scott Moreau, Tokunboh Adeyemo, David G. Burnett, Bryant L. Myers and Hwa Yung, 117-26. Monrovia, CA: MARC.

Moreau, A. Scott, Tokunboh Adeyemo, David G. Burnett, Bryant L. Myers and Hwa Yung, eds. 2002. *Deliver Us from Evil: An Uneasy Frontier in Christian Mission*. Monrovia, CA: MARC.

Muller, Dietrich. 1975. "μαθητής (mathētēs or Disciple)." In *The New International Dictionary of New Testament Theology*, vol. 1, edited by Colin Brown, 483-90. 4 vols. Grand Rapids: Zondervan.

Muller, Roland. 2006. *The Messenger, the Message and the Community: Three Critical Issues for the Cross-Cultural Church-Planter*. CanBooks, printed by author.

Mursell, Gordon, ed. 2001. *The Story of Christian Spirituality: Two Thousand Years, from East to West*. Minneapolis: Fortress.

Nickel, Gordon D. 1999. *Peaceable Witness Among Muslims*. Waterloo, ON: Herald Press.

O'Brien, P. T. 1991. *The Epistle to the Philippians: A Commentary on the Greek Text*. The New International Greek Testament Commentary. Edited by I. Howard Marshall and W. Ward Gasque. Grand Rapids: Eerdmans.

Packer, J. I. (1984) 2005. *Keep in Step with the Spirit: Finding Fullness in Our Walk with God*. Grand Rapids: Baker Books

———. 1990. *A Quest for Godliness: The Puritan Vision of the Christian Life*. Wheaton, IL: Crossway.

———. 1992. "Richard Baxter on Heaven, Hope and Holiness." In *Alive to God: Studies in Spirituality*, edited by J. I. Packer and Loren Wilkinson, 161-75. Downers Grove, IL: InterVarsity Press.

Parshall, Phil. 1980. *New Paths in Muslim Evangelism: Evangelical Approaches to Contextualization*. Grand Rapids: Baker Book House.

———. 1985. *Beyond the Mosque: Christians Within Muslim Communities*. Grand Rapids: Baker Book House.

———. 1994a. *Inside the Community: Understanding Muslims Through Their Traditions*. Grand Rapids: Baker Book House.

———. 1994b. *The Cross and the Crescent: Understanding the Muslim Heart and Mind*. Waynesboro, GA: Gabriel Publishing.

———. 2003. *Muslim Evangelism: Contemporary Approaches to Contextualization*. Waynesboro, GA: Gabriel Publishing.

———. 2004. "Lifting the Fatwa." *Evangelical Missions Quarterly* 40 (3): 288-93.

Parshall, Phil, and Julie Parshall. 2002. *Lifting the Veil: The World of Muslim Women*. Waynesboro, GA: Gabriel Publishing.

Penn-Lewis, Jessie. (1912) 1973. *War on the Saints*. 9th ed. Unabridged reprint of the 1912 edition. New York: Thomas E. Lowe. Citations refer to the Lowe edition.

Penner, Glenn. 2004. *In the Shadow of the Cross: A Biblical Theology of Persecution and Discipleship*. Bartlesville, ON: Living Sacrifice Books.

———. 2012. "A Biblical Theology of Persecution and Discipleship." In *Sorrow and Blood: Christian Mission in Contexts of Suffering, Persecution and Mar-*

tyrdom, edited by William D. Taylor, Antonia van der Meer and Reg Reimer, 71-76. Pasadena, CA: William Carey Library.

Peterson, Eugene H. 2011. *The Pastor: A Memoir*. New York: HarperOne.

Petersen, Jim. 1993. *Lifestyle Discipleship: The Challenge of Following Jesus in Today's World*. Colorado Springs: NavPress.

Pietzsch, Horst B. 2004. *Welcome Home: Caring for Converts from Islam*. Cape Town: Life Challenge Africa.

Piper, John. (1986) 2011. *Desiring God: Meditations of a Christian Hedonist*. Revised and expanded edition. Sisters, OR: Multnomah.

———. 2004. *When I Don't Desire God: How to Fight for Joy*. Wheaton, IL: Crossway.

Pocock, Michael, Gailyn van Rheenen and Douglas McConnell. 2005. *The Changing Face of World Missions: Engaging Contemporary Issues and Trends*. Grand Rapids: Baker Academic.

Pryce-Jones, David. 1989. *The Closed Circle: An Interpretation of the Arabs*. New York: Harper & Row.

Richards, E. Randolph, and Brandon J. O'Brien. 2012. *Misreading Scripture with Western Eyes: Removing Cultural Blinders to Better Understand the Bible*. Downers Grove, IL: InterVarsity Press.

Ripken, Nik. 2004. *Servants in the Crucible: Findings from a Global Study on Persecution and the Implications for Sending Agencies and Sending Churches*. Unpublished manuscript.

———. 2008. "Recapturing the Role of Suffering." In *From Seed to Fruit: Global Trends, Fruitful Practices and Emerging Issues Among Muslims*, edited by J. Dudley Woodberry, 355-65. Pasadena, CA: William Carey Library.

Ripken, Nik, and Gregg Lewis. 2013. *The Insanity of God: A True Story of Faith Resurrected*. Nashville: B&H Publishing Group.

Rumford, Douglas J. 1996. *SoulShaping: Taking Care of Your Spiritual Life*. Wheaton, IL: Tyndale House.

S., Mostafa. 2008. "A Middle Eastern BMB Responds to Chandler's Book." *SEEDBED: Practitioners in Conversation* 22 (1): 30.

Salmas, Peter G. 1998. Studies in the Faith/The Orthodox Faith and Tradition/ Orthodox Worship. Belmont, CA: Greek Orthodox Church of the Holy Cross. http://www.goholycross.org/studies/studies_worship.html. Accessed April 2, 2014.

Sanders, E. P. 1977. *Paul and Palestinian Judaism: A Comparison of Patterns of Religion*. Philadelphia: Fortress.

———. 1983. *Paul, the Law and the Jewish People*. Philadelphia: Fortress.

Schlorff, Sam., ed. 1981. *Discipleship in Islamic Society*. Marseille: North Africa Mission.

———. 2006. *Missiological Models in Ministry to Muslims*. Upper Darby, PA: Middle East Resources.

Schreiner, Thomas R. 2008. *New Testament Theology: Magnifying God in Christ*. Grand Rapids: Baker Academic.

Schwartz, Glenn J. 2007. *When Charity Destroys Dignity: Overcoming Unhealthy Dependency in the Christian Movement*. Lancaster, PA: World Mission Associates.

Scobie, Charles H. H. 2005. "A Canonical Approach to Interpreting Luke: The Journey Motif as a Hermeneutical Key." In *Reading Luke: Interpretation, Reflection, Formation*, edited by Craig G. Bartholomew, Joel B. Green and Anthony C. Thiselton, 327-49. Grand Rapids: Zondervan.

Scougal, Henry. (1677) 1946. *The Life of God in the Soul of Man*. Minneapolis: Dimension Books. Citations refer to the 1946 edition.

SEEDBED: Practitioners in Conversation. Vol. 22 (1), The Identity of Christ's Pilgrims in the Muslim World. Parts 1 and 2, 5-31.

Shaw, Karen. 2008. "Affective Barriers and Bridges to the Communication of the Gospel with Special Attention to Religious Affectivity Among Arab Beiruti Sunni Muslim Women." DMin thesis, Gordon-Conwell Theological Seminary.

SIL (Summer Institute of Linguistics). 2012. "SIL Responds to False Accusations. Is It True That SIL Supports Removing 'Son of God' and 'God the Father' in Scripture Translations? No." Posted January 2012. http://www.sil.org/about /news/sil-responds-false-accusations-english-espa%C3%B1ol-portugu%C3 %AAs. Accessed April 8, 2014.

Silva, Moisés. 1992. *Philippians*. Baker Exegetical Commentary on the New Testament. Edited by Moisés Silva. 16 vols. Grand Rapids: Baker Academic.

———. 2001. *Interpreting Galatians: Explorations in Exegetical Method*. 2nd ed. Grand Rapids: Baker Academic.

Sinclair, Daniel. 2006. *A Vision for the Possible: Pioneer Church Planting in Teams*. Waynesboro, GA: Authentic Media.

Siromahov, Rossen Dimitrov, Bishop Photti of Triaditza, Bulgaria. 2012. "Orthodox Spirituality: A Living Tradition." Orthodox Christian Information Center. http://orthodoxinfo.com/praxis/orthspir.pdf. Accessed August 8, 2014.

Smith, B. Linda. 2000. "The Sword of Christ: Muslim Women Make a Costly Commitment." In *Ministry to Muslim Women: Longing to Call Them Sisters*, edited by Fran Love and Jeleta Eckheart, 123-37. Pasadena, CA: William Carey Library.

Smith, David. 2006. "Conclusion: Looking Ahead." In *From the Straight Path to the Narrow Way: Journeys of Faith*, edited by David H. Greenlee, P. I. Barnabas, Evelyne Reisacher, Farida Saidi and J. Dudley Woodberry, 285-304. Waynesboro, GA: Authentic Media.

Smith, Gordon T. 1989. *Essential Spirituality*. Nashville: Thomas Nelson.

———. 2010. *Transforming Conversion: Rethinking the Language and Contours of Christian Initiation*. Grand Rapids: Baker Academic.

Solomon, S., and E. Alamaqdisi. 2006. *The Mosque Exposed*. Charlottesville, VA: ANM Press.

Sookhdeo, Patrick. 2007. *Global Jihad: The Future in the Face of Militant Islam*. McLean, VA: Isaac Publishing.

St. Benedict Ealing Abbey. 2012. "The Rule of St. Benedict" and "Monastic Life." The Monastery. http://www.ealingabbey.org.uk/index.htm. Accessed August 13, 2014.

Steele, Francis Rue. 1981. *Not in Vain: The Story of North Africa Mission*. Pasadena, CA: William Carey Library.

Steinhaus, Steven. 2014. "Reforming Baptism: A Call to Return to the Normal New Testament Way of Committing to Jesus." *SEEDBED: Practitioners in Conversation* 28 (1): 28-42.

Stevens, J. Paul. 2001. *Seven Days of Faith—Every Day Alive with God*. Colorado Springs: NavPress.

Stevens, J. Paul, and Michael Green. 2003. *Living the Story: Biblical Spirituality for Everyday Christians*. Grand Rapids: Eerdmans.

Stevens, J. Paul, and Charles Ringma. 2003. *Down-to-Earth Spirituality: Encountering God in the Ordinary, Boring Stuff of Life*. Downers Grove, IL: IVP Books.

Strähler, Reinhold. 2010. *Coming to Faith in Christ: Understanding Conversion*. Nairobi: SIM—Life Challenge Assistance.

Tahira. 2008–2011. "A Sunni Woman's Heart." Parts 1–7. Published consecutively in *SEEDBED: Practitioners in Conversation*, vols. 22(1)–25 (1).

Taylor, William D., Antonia van der Meer and Reg Reimer, eds. 2012. *Sorrow and Blood: Christian Mission in Contexts of Suffering, Persecution and Martyrdom*. Pasadena, CA: William Carey Library.

Tennent, Timothy C. 2006. "Followers of Jesus (Isa) in Islamic Mosques: A Closer Examination of C-5 'High Spectrum' Contextualization." *International Journal of Frontier Missions* 23 (3): 101-15.

———. 2007. "Ecclesiology: Followers of Jesus in Islamic Mosques." In *Theology in the Context of World Christianity: How the Global Church Is Influencing the Way We Think About and Discuss Theology*, 193-220. Grand Rapids: Zondervan.

Thornton, Martin. (1959) 1988. *Christian Proficiency*. Cambridge, MA: Cowley Publications. Original edition, New York: Morehouse-Gorham.

———. (1963) 1986. *English Spirituality: An Outline of Ascetical Theology According to the English Pastoral Tradition*. Cambridge, MA: Cowley Publications. Original edition, London: SPCK.

———. 1989. *The Heart of the Parish: A Theology of the Remnant*. Cambridge, MA: Cowley Publications.

Thrall, Bill, and Bruce McNicol. 2010. "Communities of Grace." In *The Kingdom Life: A Practical Theology of Discipleship and Spiritual Formation*, edited by Alan Andrews, 61-83. Colorado Springs: NavPress.

Tieszen, Charles L. 2008. *Re-Examining Religious Persecution: Constructing a Theological Framework for Understanding Persecution*. Johannesburg: AcadSA Publishing.

Travis, John. 1998a. "The C1 to C6 Spectrum." *Evangelical Missions Quarterly* 34 (4): 407-8.

———. 1998b. "Must All Muslims Leave 'Islam' to Follow Jesus?" *Evangelical Missions Quarterly* 34 (4): 411-15.

Travis, John, Phil Parshall, Herbert Hoefer and Rebecca Lewis. 2006. "Four Responses to Tennent." *International Journal of Frontier Missions* 23 (3): 124-26.

Trousdale, Jerry. 2012. *Miraculous Movements: How Hundreds of Thousands of Muslims Are Falling in Love with Jesus*. Nashville: Thomas Nelson.

Van Bavel, Tarsicius. 1984. Introduction and Commentary. In Augustine, *The Rule of Saint Augustine*, 3-8, 39-120. London: Darton, Longman & Todd.

Vander Werff, Lyle L. 1977. *Christian Mission to Muslims: The Record: Anglican and Reformed Approaches in India and the Near East, 1800–1938*. Pasadena, CA: William Carey Library.

Warraq, Ibn. 1995. *Why I Am Not a Muslim*. Amherst, NY: Prometheus Books.

———, ed. 2003. *Leaving Islam: Apostates Speak Out*. Amherst, NY: Prometheus Books.

Waterman, L. D. 2008. "Contextualization: A Few Basic Questions." *Evangelical Missions Quarterly* 44 (2): 166-73.

Wenham, David. 2005. "The Purpose of Luke-Acts: Israel's Story in the Context of the Roman Empire." In *Reading Luke: Interpretation, Reflection, Formation*, edited by Craig G. Bartholomew, Joel B. Green and Anthony C. Thiselton, 79-103. Grand Rapids: Zondervan.

Wenham, David, and Steve Walton. 2001. *A Guide to the Gospels and Acts*. Vol. 1 of *Exploring the New Testament*, edited by David Wenham and Steve Walton. Downers Grove, IL: InterVarsity Press.

Whitney, Donald S. 1991. *Spiritual Disciplines for the Christian Life*. Colorado Springs: NavPress.

Wilhoit, James C. 2008. *Spiritual Formation as If the Church Mattered: Growing in Christ Through Community*. Grand Rapids: Baker Academic.

Willard, Dallas. 1984. *In Search of Guidance: Developing a Conversational Relationship with God*. Ventura, CA: Regal Books. Expanded and republished in 1993 as *Hearing God: Developing a Conversational Relationship with God*, it was again updated in 2012 by Willard and published by IVP Books.

———. 1988. *The Spirit of the Disciplines: Understanding How God Changes Lives*. San Francisco: HarperSanFrancisco.

———. 1998. *The Divine Conspiracy: Rediscovering Our Hidden Life in God*. San Francisco: HarperSanFrancisco.

———. 2002. *Renovation of the Heart: Putting on the Character of Christ*. Colorado Springs: NavPress.

———. 2006. *The Great Omission: Reclaiming Jesus's Essential Teachings on Discipleship*. San Francisco: HarperSanFrancisco.

———. 2009. *Knowing Christ Today: Why We Can Trust Spiritual Knowledge*. New York: HarperOne.

———. 2010. "The Gospel of the Kingdom and Spiritual Formation." In *The Kingdom Life: A Practical Theology of Discipleship and Spiritual Formation*, edited by Alan Andrews, 29-59. Colorado Springs: NavPress.

———. 2014. *Living in Christ's Presence: Final Words on Heaven and the Kingdom of God*. Downers Grove, IL: IVP Books.

Wilson, J. Christy. 1952. *Apostle to Islam: A Biography of Samuel M. Zwemer*. Grand Rapids: Baker Book House.

Witherington, Ben, III. 1998a. *The Acts of the Apostles: A Socio-Rhetorical Commentary*. Grand Rapids: Eerdmans.

———. 1998b. *Grace in Galatia: A Commentary of Paul's Letter to the Galatians*. Grand Rapids: Eerdmans.

————. 2004. *The New Testament Story*. Grand Rapids: Eerdmans.

Woodberry, J. Dudley. 2006. "A Global Perspective on Muslims Coming to Faith in Christ." In *From the Straight Path to the Narrow Way: Journeys of Faith*, edited by David H. Greenlee, P. I. Barnabas, Evelyne Reisacher, Farida Saidi and J. Dudley Woodberry, 11-22. Waynesboro, GA: Authentic Media.

————, ed. 2008. *From Seed to Fruit: Global Trends, Fruitful Practices and Emerging Issues Among Muslims*. Pasadena, CA: William Carey Library.

Woodberry, J. Dudley, Russell G. Shubin and G. Marks. 2007. "Why Muslims Follow Jesus." *Christianity Today* 51 (10), 80-85.

Woods, Richard. 1989. *Christian Spirituality: God's Presence Through the Ages*. Allen, TX: Thomas More Publishing.

Woods, Scott. 2003. "A Biblical Look at C5 Muslim Evangelism." *Evangelical Missions Quarterly* 39 (2): 188-95.

Wright, N. T. 1997. *What Saint Paul Really Said: Was Paul of Tarsus the Real Founder of Christianity?* Grand Rapids: Eerdmans.

————. 2005. *Paul in Fresh Perspective*. Minneapolis: Fortress.

————. 2008. *Surprised by Hope: Rethinking Heaven, the Resurrection and the Mission of the Church*. New York: HarperOne.

————. 2012. *How God Became King: The Forgotten Story of the Gospels*. New York: HarperOne.

————. 2013. *Paul and the Faithfulness of God*. Minneapolis: Fortress.

Wright, Tom. 2004. *Luke for Everyone*. London: Society for Promoting Christian Knowledge.

Author Index

Benedict, 103-5
Blincoe, Robert, 115, 295-97
Boa, Kenneth, 78-79, 98
Bonk, Jonathan, 248
Boyd, Gregory, 93, 229, 232-33
Bufford, Robert, 237-38
Chandler, Paul-Gordon, 119, 192
Coleman, Robert E., 75-78
Coppedge, Allan, 75-78
Corwin, Gary, 113, 118
Cunningham, Scott, 212-14
Daniels, Gene, 115, 130, 272
Dau, Isaiah M., 209, 214
De Neui, Paul H., 248
De Waal, Esther, 104
DeSilva, David A., 43, 49, 52, 60
Duran, Abraham, 291
Eims, Leroy, 75-78
Evans, Wendell P., 263, 272
Finney, Charles Grandison, 82-83
Foster, Richard, 85, 87, 97
Fuller, Paula, 152, 163
Garrison, David, 17, 115, 130, 208, 217, 266-69
Gaudeul, Jean-Marie, 33
Gilliland, Dean S., 116
Gorman, Michael J., 50-52, 55, 157
Green, Michael, 235, 237, 240, 242-43
Green, Tim, 169, 183-84
Greenlee, David H., 17, 32, 48, 117
Greeson, Kevin, 18, 130-31, 217-18, 269
Hadidian, Allen, 75-78
Haines, John, 145, 239

Hawatmeh, Abdalla, 115
Hierotheos (Vlachos), 99, 101
Higgins, Kevin, 114
Hull, Bill, 75-76, 151-52, 162
Hyatt, Erik, 114
Kraft, Charles H., 231, 238, 240-41
Kraft, Kathryn Ann, 181-82, 189, 199-201, 302
Learner, Elizabeth, 299-300
Lederleitner, Mary T., 248, 261-62
Leonard, John S., 165
Lim, David S., 262
Livingstone, Greg, 115, 130, 272, 283, 297
Love, Rick, 115, 141, 239, 271, 275
Maranz, David, 245, 248
Marsh, Charles, 16, 282-84
Massey, Joshua, 46, 114
McCurry, Don M., 16, 115, 128, 133, 144-45, 225, 228-29
Mether, Thomas, 100-101
Meydan, J. R., 258
Moreau, A. Scott, 230-31
Muller, Roland, 115, 129-30, 141, 181-82, 197-98, 326
Nickel, Gordon D., 216-17
Packer, J. I., 82
Parshall, Phil and Julie, 1, 34, 113-15, 130, 217, 269-70, 297
Penner, Glenn, 213-14, 308-9
Petersen, Jim, 75, 80-84, 152
Peterson, Eugene H., 304-7
Pietzsch, Horst B., 129, 145, 216, 229, 239, 271, 281, 283
Piper, John, 85
Ripken, Nik, 214
Rumford, Douglas J., 86-88

S., Mostafa, 119
Sanders, E. P., 44
Schlorff, Sam, 272
Schreiner, Thomas R., 39
Schwartz, Glenn J., 248-49
Scobie, Charles H. H., 60-61
Shaw, Karen, 176
Sinclair, Daniel, 115, 141
Smith, B. Linda, 215-16, 269-70
Smith, David, 13, 18
Smith, Gordon T., 25, 28-31, 36, 86
Sookhdeo, Patrick, 18, 120-21
St. Benedict Ealing Abbey, 104-5
Steinhaus, Steven, 37
Strähler, Reinhold, 27, 33
Tahira, 176
Taylor, William D., 214
Tennent, Timothy C., 111, 113, 122
Thornton, Martin, 75, 95, 98, 102, 106-8
Thrall, Bill, 151
Tieszen, Charles L., 212, 214
Travis, John, 113, 118
Trousdale, Jerry, 164
Waterman, L. D., 10, 114
Wenham, David, 43, 59, 64
Whitney, Donald S., 86-87
Willard, Dallas, 28, 57, 73, 76, 81, 86-93, 129, 138
Witherington, Ben, III, 43-46, 49, 59
Woodberry, J. Dudley, 17, 33-35
Woods, Scott, 114
Wright, N. T., 44-45, 62, 67

Subject Index

Anglican/Episcopal, 97-99, 105-10

the apostles, 61-62, 67, 72, 98
teachings of, traditions of, 42-43, 69-70

Arab world, 10, 15-16, 167, 170-71, 181-82, 187, 199, 203-8, 218, 221-22, 234, 250-51, 253-54, 259-60, 274, 290, 313-17

Arabian Peninsula, 176, 203-4, 248, 277, 286-87, 292, 316

Augustine and Augustine's rule, St, 36, 102-4, 109-10

baptism, 25, 29-37, 161
in the ancient church, 35-36
in Muslim contexts, 32-37, 142, 161
See also conversion

Benedict, Saint and Benedictine, 102-6, 109, 160

Bible study groups, 26, 32, 58, 76, 88, 96

calling (vocation), 51, 104, 285, 298, 299, 304

Catholic, 32, 33, 85, 97, 101

Christian spirituality, 51, 85, 89, 97, 109

church planter, 202, 284-86, 303

church planting, 17-20, 36, 37, 112, 124-25, 130, 142, 152-53, 207, 228, 256, 258, 272, 281-300, 303-7

collective culture, 20, 192-97, 314, 319

coming out (as a BMB), 17, 197-98

community
Christian community, 20, 30, 32, 58, 68-72, 82, 96-97, 179-83, 203-8, 221, 296, 325-26

monastic, 102-5

Muslim community, 14, 34, 110, 114-15, 120-25, 142, 154-56, 171-76, 179-83, 185, 189, 191-92, 217-19, 249, 274

role of community in discipleship, 54, 66, 72, 94, 129, 156, 191-203, 239, 251-53, 290,

of the Spirit, 61, 71

transformation in community, 55, 59, 72, 82, 92, 96, 109-10, 269, 305, 306-07, 310-11

contemplative prayer, 80, 85, 97, 100, 138

contextualization, 111-25, 154-55, 191-92, 199, 206, 297-98

conversion, 25-37, 117-20
and baptism, 29, 31-32, 37

definition and dimensions of, 30, 35, 124

discipleship to conversion, 20, 130

experience of, 25-29, 117-20, 123-24, 190-203

and identity, 179-203, 218-19, 278

of Muslims, 17, 27, 32-37, 93, 115, 117-20, 122, 133

nature and meaning of, 27-30, 117-20

in the Old and New Testament, 21, 29-32

and repentance, 29-32, 37

sequence of conversion and discipleship, 20-21, 123, 129-30, 179

and understanding of the Gospel, 28-29

vital aspects of, 33, 119, 129

corporate
discipleship, 155, 158, 160
routines, disciplines, 91-92, 105-9, 134-35, 138, 143, 149, 160-61, 163
worship, 30-31, 58, 97, 99, 109, 153, 161, 235

CPMs (church planting movements). *See* movements, CPMs

cruciformity, 51, 54-56, 71, 157

demonic, demons and/or evil spirits, 74, 93-94, 134, 147, 172, 175, 177-80, 186, 225-44, 265, 319, 322

devotional or spiritual practices, 107, 112, 134, 192

disciple
of Christ, 26, 28, 52, 57, 90, 97, 123, 129, 133, 217
use of word in the New Testament, 42-43

discipleship, 13, 15, 17-21, 23, 27, 29, 35, 40, 57, 123-24, 128
biblical foundations, 77-79
contemporary approaches to, 74-79
definitions, goal of, models of, 57, 63, 66-67, 70-71, 76-77, 80, 82, 85, 89-91, 125, 128-33, 145, 151-52, 154-55, 161, 318
demands of, 63-64, 80
in history of the church, 75, 95-110
modernist, 75-85, 92, 140
in the New Testament, 32, 35, 41-43, 75, 77, 155-56
in Luke-Acts, 43, 57-72, 77-78, 134, 157-58, 212
in Paul, 43-56, 134, 155-56, 158

obedience-based, 163-64
  principles of, 78-80, 124,
    159, 234, 272, 303
  process of, 20, 33, 37, 59,
    70, 76, 84-85, 92, 109-10,
    133-43, 165, 170, 228-29,
    310
  stages in, 28, 79, 146-49
  vision for discipling
    BMBs, 71-72, 130, 149,
    165, 271, 304-7
doctrine, 44, 95, 98, 100-101,
  106, 109, 124, 134, 136, 145,
  189, 321-22
  Islamic, 171-87, 189, 241
ecclesiology, 123-24
eschatological age,
  community, promise, 31,
  46-47, 52, 63, 65-67, 71
evangelical(s), 16-17, 41, 75-76,
  81, 85-86, 88, 92-93, 97, 109,
  113, 123, 125, 137
evangelism, 17, 20, 25-27, 34-35,
  80, 130, 165, 213, 215, 217, 266,
  277, 284, 286, 290, 306
extraction, 154-55, 217
faith in Christ, 5, 14-16, 19,
  20-21, 26-27, 31-36, 44-54,
  115, 117, 310
freedom in Christ, 44, 119, 231,
  237-38, 244, 326
Fruitful Practices Conference
  in 2007, 17, 34, 291
fulfillment of the law. See
  Torah, fulfilling the law
Galatia, 44-47, 55
Galatians, 39, 42-50, 55, 155-56
Global South, 16, 132, 136,
  172-73, 193, 262
Gospels, 21, 41-43, 75-77, 84,
  90, 106
Holy Spirit, 84, 99, 172, 178,
  180, 186
  anointing of, 69-70, 134,
    311
  filled with, 31-32, 39-40,
    72, 86, 240
  gift of, 25, 29, 99, 153, 162
  led by, guided by, 108-9,
    115-16, 128, 134-35,
    143-44, 160-61, 199, 210,
    243, 310-11

living by, living according
  to, 36, 40, 43-49, 51, 55, 57,
  71, 82, 99, 134-35, 155-58,
  160, 311, 326
power of, 40, 69-72, 128,
  133-35, 143, 149, 156, 158,
  161, 164, 228
presence of, 97, 149
through the Spirit, 19, 27,
  39, 53-55, 59, 88, 92,
  100-101, 116-17, 128, 156,
  160, 238, 240
wind of, 17, 123, 208
house church(s), 14, 16, 26, 36,
  39, 50, 58, 112, 123, 128, 133,
  142, 152-53, 190, 198, 207, 255,
  275, 272, 288-89, 303
identity
  adhesive identity, 181-82,
    201-2
  in Christ, 32, 54, 111,
    118-19, 147, 154, 157-58,
    169, 185, 189-208, 302
  as a Christian, as a
    believer, 15, 114, 119, 169,
    189-208, 325-26
  in the church, the new
    community, 72, 141-42,
    169, 179-83, 189-208,
    264-65
  core/personal, social and
    collective/corporate, 119,
    141, 157, 160, 169, 181-87,
    192, 198, 265
  development of, 181,
    183-85, 196, 200
  religious identity (as
    Muslims), 118-19, 141-42,
    154, 169-70, 179-83, 185,
    189, 264-65, 325-26
insider movements. See
  movements, insider
  movements
intimacy with God, 89, 137-38,
  159-60, 305, 307, 310
Islam (the religion or faith),
  15-18, 33, 41, 90, 97, 114-15,
  117-24, 137, 142, 147, 170-87,
  189, 192, 197, 208, 216-18, 222,
  228, 232-33, 238, 250, 270, 278,
  280, 301, 307, 309, 311, 322-25
  dark and oppressive

nature of, 120-22
  folk, 112, 228, 239
  religion of works, 44, 48
Islamic contexts. See Muslim,
  contexts
Islamic ideology, doctrine,
  114, 124, 154, 170-87, 216, 238,
  264, 273
Islamic influences, systems,
  structures, 34, 114, 119, 122,
  125, 138, 154, 170-87, 216, 228,
  241, 273, 307
Islamism (radical, political
  Islam), Islamists, 33, 120-21,
  210, 219, 307-9
the Jesus Prayer, 100-101
law of Christ/love, 39, 47-48
Law of Moses. See Torah
Living Pyramid Model, 151-65,
  170, 310
Luke-Acts, 57-72, 155, 157, 212
  journeying in Luke-Acts,
    59-68, 63
  Luke, the author, 30, 61-67,
    69, 71, 134
  purpose in writing,
    themes, 59-61, 68
  the rich man and Lazarus,
    65
  the structure of Luke,
    60-61, 63
  Zacchaeus, 65
marriage, 172-74, 178, 180, 186,
  234, 241, 264, 271, 273-77,
  279, 322
mentoring, 36, 76, 108, 125,
  133, 143-45, 149, 161-62, 275,
  283, 298
Middle East, 16, 116, 144, 177,
  182, 192, 200, 204, 286, 310,
  316
money
  the handling of in
    discipleship, 175, 245-62,
    293
  in Luke, 64-66
Mosaic Law. See Torah
movements, 17-18, 36
  church planting
    movements (CPMs), 18,
    36, 130-31, 163, 207, 217,
    266-67, 291, 303-7

insider movements (IMs),
113-19, 124-25, 304-7
Muslim(s), 5
  coming to Christ, 32-33,
    208, 306, 309, 310
  communities. *See*
    communities, Muslim
  contexts, 15-20, 29, 32-37,
    71-72, 93-94, 102, 113-17,
    123-25, 138-40, 143, 147,
    154-56, 169-87, 214-15,
    233, 249, 258, 294, 317
  family(s), 5, 71-72, 115, 119,
    137, 141-42, 154-55, 164,
    169, 171-203, 218-23,
    263-80
North Africa, 15-16, 18, 20,
  25-26, 35-36, 76, 96, 111-12, 118,
  175, 181-82, 204, 286-87, 316
obstacles to discipleship,
  167-87,
occult, occult practices, 172,
  175, 178, 180, 229, 236,
  239-40, 322
Old Testament, 31, 41, 46, 60-63
oppression (other than
  demonic and spiritual), 121,
  147, 172-73, 179-80, 186, 222,
  296, 322
Orthodox, Eastern, 85,
  97-102, 106, 109-10, 134,
  138, 160
persecution, 26, 35, 50, 58, 124,
  139-40, 147, 169, 172-73,
  178-80, 202-3, 209-23, 250,
  265-66, 268-70, 273, 279,
  307-9, 319, 322, 325

Philippians, 42, 49-56, 59, 133,
  155-57
  main themes of, 49-50
  the role of love in, 50-52,
    55-56
Protestant, 16, 75-76, 109,
  297-98
repentance, 88, 239, 270
  and baptism, 29-32, 35,
    37
  and faith in Christ, 26, 42,
    67, 300
role of the discipler in
  discipling, 79, 143-46,
  281-300, 320, 307
rule (patterned prayer and
  Scripture reading), 99,
  102-4, 106-7, 109, 134-35, 161
sanctification, 44-45, 84, 215
the Scriptures, 40, 75, 80, 93,
  99, 104, 112, 125, 140, 144-45,
  147, 153, 160-63, 213, 221, 229,
  230, 236, 239, 255, 310
sharing the Gospel, witness,
  140, 148, 154, 163-64, 280, 282
spiritual disciplines, 81-94,
  134, 160, 240
spiritual growth process, 50,
  55, 75, 101, 128, 133-43, 153,
  159, 314
spiritual maturity, 5, 18, 28,
  40-42, 45, 53, 71, 77, 79, 83,
  89, 92, 97, 101-2, 110, 123, 129,
  132, 133, 138, 140-42, 146,
  148-49, 153-54, 163-64, 171,
  175, 183, 207, 271, 283, 298,
  303-7, 309-11, 319

spiritual transformation, 23,
  40, 49-50, 53-55, 59, 68,
  74-77, 81-82, 84-85, 88-89,
  91-92, 97-98, 134-35, 137, 139,
  143, 150, 153, 159-61, 165, 167,
  268, 303, 306
stages in spiritual growth, 33,
  77, 89, 127, 146-49
Ten Commandments. *See*
  Torah, the Ten
  Commandments
theology, 232, 262
  biblical, 106, 212
  Christian, 112
  of conversion, 124
  of discipleship, 77-78, 213
  Orthodox, 98, 101, 107
  Paul's, 46, 50
  of persecution, 211-13, 215,
    217, 219-22
  of religion, 123
  spiritual, contemplative,
    85, 95, 99, 106
  of spiritual warfare, 93
  of suffering, 209, 211-12,
    214-15, 222
  Western, 101
Torah
  fulfilling the Law, 47, 55,
    61, 63
  Mosaic Law, 39, 44-46, 53,
    55
  Ten Commandments,
    47-48
  Torah observance, 44-48,
    53, 70
Zwemer, Samuel, 16-17

Scripture Index

Old Testament
Deuteronomy
27:11–28:68, *61*

Psalms
119:1, *47*
119:176, *47*

New Testament
Matthew
4:17, *28, 31*
4:23, *28*
5:14-16, *189*
9:35, *28*
10, *220*
10:34-39, *263, 273*
10:36, *273*
11:18-20, *89*
12:26, *232*

Mark
1:15, *28, 31*

Luke
1:1-4, *59, 60*
1:3-4, *59*
1:5–2:52, *60*
3:1–9:50, *60*
4:16-30, *64*
4:43, *28*
5:32, *31*
6:12-16, *61*
6:17-49, *61*
6:20-49, *61*
6:23, *62*
8:1-21, *62*
9:3-5, *62*
9:18-27, *62*
9:23-25, *57*
9:28-36, *63*
9:51, *63*
9:51–19:44, *60, 61, 63*
9:53, *63*

9:57-62, *63*
10:17-20, *225*
11:19-23, *233*
11:24-26, *227*
12, *65*
12:13-34, *64*
12:22-34, *64*
12:49-53, *64*
13:3, *31*
13:22, *63*
13:33, *63*
14:26-27, *63*
14:33, *64*
15:7, *31*
16:1-9, *64*
16:19-31, *65*
17:11, *63*
18:18-30, *65*
18:31, *63*
19:1-10, *66*
19:11, *63*
19:28, *63*
19:45–23:56, *60*
22:16-18, *66*
22:30, *66*
24, *60*
24:33, *69*
24:44, *67*
24:46-49, *67*

John
1:12-13, *21*
3:3-8, *21*
4:1-42, *125*
7:17, *163*
16, *220*

Acts
1–7, *68*
1:8, *60*
1:14, *68*
1:15, *69*
2:38, *25, 29, 30*

2:42, *69, 95*
2:42-47, *68*
2:44-47, *95*
4:2, *69*
4:18, *69*
4:32-35, *68, 103*
4:33, *69*
4:34, *69*
4:34-35, *69*
5:1-11, *69*
5:12-16, *69*
5:21, *69*
5:25, *69*
5:28, *69*
5:42, *69*
6:1-6, *69*
7, *220*
11:19-30, *70*
13:1-3, *70*
14:22, *187*
15, *44, 70, 125*
15:30-35, *70*
16, *49*
16:10-40, *59*
16:30, *29*
19, *220*
20:6, *59*
20:7-13, *70*

Romans
8:35, *169*
10:9-10, *28*
14:17, *28*

1 Corinthians
2:14-16, *21*
9:19-23, *125*
10:13, *220*

2 Corinthians
4:1-2, *281*
4:5, *281*
5:17, *185*

Galatians
2:16, *44*
2:19-21, *47*
3–5, *47*
3:2-5, *45*
5:2-5, *46*
5:4, *47*
5:5-6, *47*
5:6, *50*
5:13-14, *39*
5:15-25, *48*
6:1-10, *48*
6:13-18, *47*

Ephesians
2:1-10, *21*

Philippians
1:9-10, *50*
1:9-11, *50*
1:27, *51*
1:27-30, *50, 51*
2, *262*
2:1, *51*
2:1-4, *51*
2:1-11, *50, 51*
2:1-16, *261, 262*
2:2, *51*
2:3-4, *52*
2:5-8, *52*
2:6-11, *52*
3–4, *52*
3:1, *52*
3:2, *52, 53*
3:2–4:1, *50, 52*
3:3, *53*
3:4-6, *53*
3:7, *53*
3:7-11, *53*
3:12–4:1, *54*
3:17, *133*
3:20–4:1, *54*
4:12-13, *245*

4:15, *245*
4:19, *245*

Colossians
1:13, *232*
1:21-23, *21*
4:14, *59*

1 Thessalonians
1:9-10, *21*

2:7-12, *127, 144*

1 Timothy
4:7-8, *73*

2 Timothy
2:2, *83*

Hebrews
10:32-36, *209*

1 Peter
1:3-9, *21*
2:4-10, *159*
2:9-10, *111*

2 Peter
1:3, *151*
1:5-8, *151*

3 John
1:2-4, *13*

Revelation
7, *307, 308*
7:9-10, *301*
7:14, *301*
11:15, *232*

Finding the Textbook You Need

The IVP Academic Textbook Selector
is an online tool for instantly finding the IVP books
suitable for over 250 courses across 24 disciplines.

www.ivpress.com/academic/